UNDER THEIR OWN FLAG
A HISTORY OF 47 SQUADRON 1916-46

Published in 2016 by Fighting High Ltd
www.fightinghigh.com

British Library Cataloguing-in-Publication data. A CIP record for this title is available from the British Library.

ISBN – 13: 978-0993212994

Designed and typeset in 24pt Coluna Rounded Condensed and 9/11pt Adobe Minion by TruthStudio Ltd. www.truthstudio.co.uk

Illustrations by Chris Davey
(Aircraft profiles on pages 146-149).

Printed and bound in the UK by Gomer Press.

UNDER THEIR OWN FLAG

A HISTORY OF 47 SQUADRON 1916-46

Owen Clark

Foreword

BY GROUP CAPTAIN MICHAEL NEVILLE CBE

Officer Commanding No. 47 Squadron 2003–2005
47 Squadron Association President

Under Their Own Flag is a fitting title for a book celebrating and recording the history of No. 47 Squadron RAF, as almost from the very beginnings of the Squadron's proud service it has operated in far flung corners of the world, often unsupported, and frequently as the sole representatives of the Royal Air Force and our Nation. The demands, and rightly so, of operational security have, for now, prevented the telling of the Squadron's more recent history. However, I can, without fear of censor, state that the trials and challenges faced and overcome by the courageous men who served with the Squadron from its birth in Yorkshire in 1916 to the cessation of hostilities following the Second World War have been faced in some guise or other many times since.

47 Squadron of today prides itself on its ability 'to get the job done' enabling the wider collective effort to achieve its often strategically important objectives. Through innovation and adaptation it overcomes environmental and operational factors and I was struck with the similarity between the circumstances of today and those of yesteryear when 47 Squadron pilots, whilst attacking enemy aircraft over Hudova, urged their aircraft (restricted to 100 knots) to a previously untried and untested speed of 120 knots. The Squadron armourers and engineers also 'jury rigged' a second Lewis gun to fire obliquely from the front of the aircraft. This spirit of innovation and courage, pressing boundaries, doing all within their gift, and sometimes recognising but challenging rules and regulations, is as present today as it was in the beginning and is no doubt the principal reason for the Squadron receiving seven Battle Honours and a wealth of individual operational awards.

A century of operational activity has not all been smooth flying, for partaking in military operations is inherently a risky business. The Battle Honours help to tell a story of where we have been. The awards list shouts of gallantry and going above and beyond, and the operational losses compel us to remember that what we have asked and continue to ask of the Squadron is not a simple task absent of danger. But that the task is done 'Sans Peur' reinforces the courage, determination and intelligence of our airmen. What our forefathers on 47 Squadron achieved against the odds, which were at times seemingly overwhelming, beggars belief and although they may have marvelled at what the Squadron of today does I can honestly say that it is nothing compared to what was done on a daily basis in the harshest of conditions and in a new operating dimension. On behalf of all serving and surviving members of 47 Squadron we salute you for a job well done under the flag of 47 Squadron – our Flag!

INTRODUCTION

by Owen Clark

47 Squadron is one of the few remaining RAF Squadrons that can trace a heritage of almost constant service since its formation in March 1916. To each task given to it, and place it has been sent, 47 Squadron has risen to the challenge and carried out its duty with professionalism, dedication and bravery, despite the conditions on the ground, or the state of the kit entrusted to it.

The period covered in this book only deals with the first thirty years of the Squadron's existence, but it covers the birth and growth to maturity, not only of the Squadron but also the RAF and airpower. I have tried to tell the story not only of the men of the Squadron and their operations and aircraft, but also to give some idea of the larger picture, why they were there and what was going on around them. These men were on the whole volunteers – all in the case of air crew. They were willing to risk their lives in the interests and defence of their country. Over 150 men died serving and many more were injured or endured incarceration at the hands of the enemy. During my contact with the modern 47 Squadron I have seen that this spirit of honour, duty, modesty, humour and generosity is alive and well. Those who went before can be proud of those who carry on the traditions.

I have tried to be consistent in the spellings of locations, however in Squadron records and written accounts there are a number of different versions for the same location, and some places have changed their names since the Squadron was there. Others were called different names depending on local custom, for example Salonika and Thessalonica, Abyssinia and Ethiopia. I apologise if this is not entirely accurate, but without taking some liberties the book would become a mess of alternative spellings.

During the nearly 20 years I have been working on this project I have had the privilege of meeting some remarkable people who have shared their experiences openly and freely, they have also loaned their log books, diaries, photographs and correspondence. Many are mentioned in the bibliography but many more have made contributions and my gratitude goes to all. There is much more that could be written, and stories that could be told, but space, unfortunately, precludes their inclusion.

I would also like to express my gratitude and thanks to my wife, Sarah, for putting up with my hours of reading and sifting through information, visits to RAF Lyneham and RAF Brize Norton, and taking delivery of numerous parcels containing yet more books. She and my daughters Kate and Rosie proof read the drafts, but any errors are mine alone.

Owen Clark, February 2016

CONTENTS

Armstrong Whitworth
FK Beverley, mid 1916.
FAA

Chapter 1

BORN IN YORKSHIRE

UK, 1916

During the second half of the nineteenth century there was a growing recognition of the value of balloons for artillery spotting and observation of the enemy, and they had been extensively used during the American Civil War of 1860–64 and the Franco-Prussian War of 1870–71. They were limited in their capabilities, being unpowered and susceptible to the vagaries of the wind, but they led to the development of powered airships late in the nineteenth and early twentieth centuries. This increased the possibilities for their military use, and the 'Proof of Concept' of heavier-than-air aeroplanes demonstrated by the Wright brothers in 1903 opened up new opportunities. The British were not oblivious to this and, after it became known the Italians had used aeroplanes against Turkish forces in Tripoli in October 1911, the Committee of Imperial Defence formed a subcommittee in November 1911 to examine the question of military aviation. On 28 February 1912 the subcommittee reported its findings, which recommended that a flying corps be formed and that it consist of a naval wing, a military wing, a Central Flying School and an aircraft factory. The recommendations of the committee were accepted and on 13 April 1912 King George V signed a royal warrant establishing the Royal Flying Corps. A month later, on 13 May, the Air Battalion of the Royal Engineers became the Military Wing of the Royal Flying Corps. The Air Battalion of the Royal Engineers had only been formed in February 1911 from the School of Ballooning (established in 1888).

It comprised two companies: No. 1, with airships, under Captain Edward Maitland, based at Farnborough, Hampshire; and No. 2, with aeroplanes, commanded by Captain John Fulton, based at Larkhill on Salisbury Plain. Pilots were selected from throughout the Army and had to hold a Royal Aero Club certificate gained from a private flying school, there being no military training facility. The £75 charge was reimbursed if the student passed the course.

The Flying Corps' initial allowed strength was 133 officers, and by the end of 1912 it had 12 manned balloons and 36 aeroplanes. The RFC originally came under the responsibility of Brigadier General Henderson, the Director of Military Training, and had separate branches for the Army and the Navy. Major Sykes took charge of the Military Wing and Commander C.R. Samson the Naval Wing. The Royal Navy, however, with different priorities to that of the Army and wishing to retain greater control over its aircraft, formally separated its branch and renamed it the Royal Naval Air Service on 1 July 1914, although a combined Central Flying School was retained.

At the declaration of war in August 1914 the Royal Flying Corps dispatched four of its seven squadrons to France, leaving behind a corps of experienced officers to form new squadrons, and by the end of 1915 it had a theoretical strength of thirty-one squadrons; eighteen of these were in France with a further three overseas (India, Mesopotamia and East Africa). The balance was building up or had been temporarily retained for home defence. Another tranche of five squadrons had formed at the beginning of 1916 and on 1 March Lieutenant Colonel Marindin authorised by letter the creation of service squadrons Nos 37 to 48.

No. 47 Squadron, RFC, was nominally formed at Beverley, Yorkshire, on the racecourse just to the west of the town, on 1 March 1916, as part of this rapid expansion to meet the threat posed by German Zeppelins and the transfer of more squadrons to France to support the forthcoming summer offensive. The initial orders were for 47 Squadron to be developed from 34 Squadron, which had been founded at Castle Bromwich in January 1916 but was now preparing to go to France. Thus new orders were issued on 20 March making 47 Squadron's parent formation 15 Reserve Squadron (RS). The squadron was originally designated for home defence, but was not actually issued with any aircraft it could call its own until 13 April, when four BE2Cs with RAF engines were transferred from 15 RS. Some five days after the squadron's creation an attack by three Zeppelins (L11, L13 and L14) on Hull, unharried by aeroplanes and with largely ineffective anti-aircraft fire, caused eighteen deaths and some £25,000 worth of damage.

In the UK the RFC Home Establishment was not only responsible for training air and ground crews and preparing squadrons to deploy to France, but also for providing squadrons for home defence. The RFC (and the Royal Naval Air Service) initially had limited success against the German raids, largely through the problem of locating the attackers and having aeroplanes of sufficient performance to reach the operating altitude of the German raiders.

With the bulk of the operational squadrons engaged in France, few could be spared for home defence purposes. Therefore, training squadrons were called on to supply home defence aeroplanes and aircrews. Night flying and defence sorties were often flown by instructors in aircraft deemed worn out and sometimes obsolete for front-line service, although the pilots selected as instructors were frequently among the most experienced in the RFC.

The composition of an RFC squadron varied depending on its designated role, although the commanding officer was usually a major (in a largely non-operational role), with the squadron 'flights' (designated A, B, C, etc.) the basic tactical and operational unit, each in the charge of a captain. A 'recording officer' (of captain/lieutenant rank) would act as intelligence officer and adjutant, commanding two or three NCOs and ten other ranks in the administration section of the squadron. Each flight contained on average between six and ten pilots (and a corresponding number of observers, if applicable) with a senior sergeant and thirty-six other ranks (as fitters, riggers, metal-smiths, armourers, etc.). The average squadron also had on strength an equipment officer, armaments officer (each with five other ranks) and a transport officer, in charge of twenty-two other ranks. The squadron transport establishment typically included one car, five light tenders, seven heavy tenders, two repair lorries, eight motorcycles and eight trailers. Thus, a squadron's nominal roll would be 15 to 20 officers and approximately 150 other ranks, although this would vary considerably depending on the squadron's role, location and recent casualties.

The officer appointed to command 47 Squadron was Major F.G. Small. Major Small had been posted from 5 Squadron and was an experienced pilot, having originally gone to France in the first wave of RFC squadrons in August 1914. He took part in probably the first air-to-air combat when he and his observer, Lieutenant L.A. Strange forced down a German two-seater on 22 November 1914. The Avro 504 they were flying was fitted with a Lewis gun for use by the observer, although this may not have been officially sanctioned and was probably against squadron orders. At that stage of the war the sole purpose for aeroplanes was to observe and carry out reconnaissance, and not to go swanning about interfering with the Hun's aeroplanes.

During March, Major Small was joined by Lieutenant N.H. Bottomley (later Air Marshal Sir Norman, Assistant Chief of Air Staff in 1944, one of the many 47 Squadron members to reach senior rank in the RAF) and Lieutenant D.C. Rutter as flying officers. Also arriving were Second Lieutenant H.G.

Corby and Second Lieutenant D.J. MacDonald, the assistant equipment officer, although both these men were posted out on 6 April. During April a number of officers joined the squadron as follows.

Second Lieutenant S.A. Laird Assistant equipment officer	5 April
Second Lieutenant H. Munder Observer under instruction	9 April
Second Lieutenant F. St J Hartley Observer under instruction	18 April
Second Lieutenant G.H.B. Streatfield Pilot under instruction	24 April
Second Lieutenant A. Lowery Pilot under instruction	26 April
Second Lieutenant K.F. Balamin Pilot under instruction	27 April
Second Lieutenant W.H. Smith Assistant equipment officer, photography	7 April

By 26 April the squadron had been formed into three flights, but only A Flight had any aeroplanes, comprising four BE2Cs and a Bristol Scout. The lack of equipment was reflected in their activity, so that in May, the first month where records exist, only six flights amounting to some 4 hours 15 minutes' flying time was achieved. In June this figure increased to some eighty-five flights and over 32 hours' flying time. The squadron's stock of aeroplanes had also increased to include eight BE2Bs and FK3s, four BE2Cs and six Avro 504s.

The Zeppelin was, to the British, the terror weapon of the day; even before the war the threat of the Zeppelin gripped the public imagination. Books like H.G. Wells' *War in the Air*, published in 1907, had put in people's minds the vision of death being delivered from vast unstoppable airships. The Hague Conventions of 1899 and 1907 strove to outlaw bombing from the air, the latter precluding bombing of undefended places. The Germans had been developing airships since 1900, mostly for use by the navy where the potential for a long-range machine – capable of speeds far in excess of warships and with an endurance of over 30 hours and a range of vision from altitude – had significant attractions.

In Britain, the attention was focused on defence, but in 1912 no aeroplanes currently available or on the drawing board could compete with the rate of climb or ceiling of the airships, never mind deal with their onboard machine-gun defences, or find a solution to bring them down. In July 1912, the Committee of Imperial Defence declared: 'It appears probable that, for the immediate present, the surest method of attacking airships would be by a superior force of armed airships.'[1] Britain had no such force and nothing in the planning to build one.

The first Zeppelin raid was carried out on the night of 19/20 January 1915, when two airships attempted to bomb the Humber, but the weather blew them south and the first British town attacked was Great Yarmouth in Norfolk. The airships then meandered around, unsure of their position, and scattered bombs around Norfolk, causing some £7,740 (in 1915 terms) worth of damage, killing four civilians and injuring a further sixteen. The British defences failed to deter the assault. Over the next few months further raids were undertaken by the German army and navy Zeppelins, and on the night of 31 May/1 June, the first attack on London was carried out. For the rest of the year and into 1916 strikes continued. Weather and navigation problems meant that most bombs were dropped on targets of opportunity as the airships roamed over the UK, but the British defences had no real answer, although some airships were damaged by ground fire or lost through accidents and mechanical failure. Navigating the airships at night was problematic; they were vulnerable to winds and difficult to keep on course. One of the reasons why so many raids on the UK started at the Humber was because this was a very large and distinctive landmark on the coast and required only a relatively short sea crossing from the Zeppelin's bases on the other side of the North Sea. The public perception was that nothing could be done, and even some Army recruiting posters were based on the premise that it was better to die in the trenches with a rifle in your hand, than skulk in your bed defenseless against the 'baby killers'. Not quite that unsubtle, but not far off.

Thus in the spring of 1916 the RFC was devoting significant resources to home defence and most, if not all, UK-based squadrons, no matter what their operational status, maintained a couple of aeroplanes on standby for anti-Zeppelin tasks.

Of these the BE2 was the most numerous, designed before the outbreak of war as a scout aeroplane that was stable and easy to fly, and by the middle of 1915 it made up some two-thirds of the RFC's squadrons in France. However, the air war had moved on and with the introduction of the Fokker monoplane in German service equipped with interrupter gear – which allowed the machine gun to fire through the propeller arc – the days of the BE2 were numbered, where its basic attributes, being easy to fly and stable, also meant a lack of manoeuvrability. Further poor defensive armament was to add to their downfall and they soon earned the unfortunate nickname of 'Fokker Fodder'. Attempts were made to withdraw the aircraft, but the lack of a suitable replacement meant they were still being lost in significant numbers some twelve months later.

Nevertheless, despite these disadvantages in front-line service they were put to good employment as a training aeroplane and also night fighter for home defence use, although the lack of speed, poor rate of climb (45 minutes to 10,000 feet), and no early warning system would make any interception of the high-flying Zeppelins difficult indeed. The airship could easily out-climb the BE2 and was well defended with numerous machine guns on what was a very stable gun platform. Even if the pilot managed to get into an advantageous attacking position, he was then faced with the challenge of bringing the Zeppelin down. Fitted with a single 0.303 Lewis gun mounted on top of the wing to fire outside the propeller arc, the pilot could shoot away in the hope that the incendiary ammunition would set alight the hydrogen gas, spectacularly destroying the airship in the air; or, alternatively, trust the hits would cause a sufficiently large tear in the fabric that the loss of gas would force the airship down. However, if the pilot could get above the target he could use Rankin darts. These were a slim dart with an explosive head and four sprung vanes on the rear, the theory being that the dart would pierce the skin of the Zeppelin and the fuse would explode, causing the destruction of the airship. If the explosion didn't work, the vanes would cause a rent adequate enough to bring the airship crashing to earth anyway. But these were early days and it was not until the night of 2/3 September 1916 that Lieutenant W. Leefe-Robinson of 33 Squadron would succeed in bringing one down over Britain. He was cited a hero and awarded the VC for the destruction of a Zeppelin. (Strictly speaking, SL11 was actually a Schutte-Lanz airship and thus, officially, not classified as a Zeppelin, but it was reported in the press as being Zeppelin L21, and the word Zeppelin played better with the press and public.)

Another aeroplane available to the squadron was the Bristol Scout. It was a promising little single-seat aircraft that seems to have been largely ignored by the War Office and the RFC, few being built and even fewer getting on to front-line squadron service, although most squadrons had one or two on charge at sometime during the war. It was on 47 Squadron's books for home defence purposes, and later some would serve with the squadron on the front line in Salonika.

The Avro 504 was a successful, pre-war plane. It had first appeared in 1913 and was among the first RFC machines to have been used in action, but by early 1916 it had been largely relegated to training use. The Avro 504 was so successful as a trainer that it was to remain in this role long after the war, the last ones serving well into the 1930s. The RAF did not declare the final Avro 504Ks obsolete until March 1933.

The Armstrong Whitworth FK3 was to be a long-term friend of the squadron; known as the 'Little Ack', though this only came about once the FK8 'Big Ack' became available later in the war and in Squadron records the FK3 was usually referred to as the AW. It was similar to the BE2 and while in England was used by the squadron for training, but once overseas it was to become the unit's standard reconnaissance and bombing aeroplane for nearly two years.

The squadron's primary task was the training of pilots and observers, the home defence role being secondary. These sorties would be flown by instructors, and after a day of training the young, keen and inexperienced pilots to hone their flying skills and try to avoid killing themselves, the instructor would be on standby to take off to attempt to intercept the regular Zeppelin raids. By July 1916 the RFC Order of Battle had twelve squadrons, including 47 Squadron, allocated to home defence, but it is unlikely that this would have amounted to more than thirty aeroplanes and pilots available at any one time.

No 47 Squadron had 'Zepp strafing' flights initially based at Doncaster and later at Coal Ashton near Sheffield and at Bramham Moor/Tadcaster between Leeds and York. These were under the command of Major J.H. Herring who came from 15 Reserve Squadron.

On the night of 1/2 April 1916, 47 Squadron carried out its first sortie. One of the squadron's BE2Cs (pilot not recorded) was dispatched from Beverley when German navy Zeppelin L17 (KapitanH. Ehrlich) was detected, but little more is known except the flight ended with the crash of the aeroplane following engine failure, although no casualty is recorded or significant damage to the machine. The next mission was on the night of 5/6 April when two aircraft, BE2C 2720 (Lieutenant N.H. Bottomley) and BE2C, serial not known (Major F.G. Small), were ordered to intercept navy Zeppelin L11 (KorvettenkapitanV. Schutze). At 21.05 hours L11 crossed the coast at Hornsea on the Yorkshire coast and headed for Hull where it was greeted by heavy but ineffective AA fire. The airship dropped four bombs and moved back out to sea. The intention was to attack later, approaching on a different course. However, the combination of engine failures and bad weather forced L11 north and it headed for Hartlepool, but it eventually bombed the iron works at Skinningrove, about 15 miles south-west of Hartlepool, at around 02.15. Both 47 Squadron aeroplanes took off at approximately 22.00 hours, but found nothing and returned after 90 minutes or so. Lieutenant Bottomley experienced throttle problems, but was able to land safely with only minor damage to his plane.

On the night of 2/3 May, 47 Squadron was again in action to intercept a major Zeppelin raid. Eight navy Zeppelins and one army machine were sent to attack targets at Rosyth, the Forth Bridge and Manchester, but most of them were forced further south. Two squadron BE2Cs, 2720 (Lieutenant N.H. Bottomley) and 2721 (Lieutenant D.C. Rutter) each loaded with four 16lb bombs, six incendiaries and a box of Ranken darts, were on standby. They waited through driving rain in case a firm threat to Hull developed and eventually took off at about 03.00 hours, but the rain and heavy cloud made their patrol of the Humber looking for stragglers very difficult and they returned to Beverley after 45 minutes without seeing anything. The Zeppelins, scattered by the bad weather, dropped bombs over much of the north-east. L20 ultimately crash-landed in Norway.

After a break from 9 May to 19 June – according to the daily flying returns held in the National Archives[2] when very little flying was recorded – a new batch of keen young pilots and observers arrived. At the time there was no comprehensive curriculum for pilot training. Their instructors would usually be experienced pilots who had returned from France, but again there was no formal training for them either. It seemed that it was assumed that because they had flown for some time and not been killed, they would be proficient at passing their skills on to their pupils. Recruitment for the RFC was on a purely volunteer basis, most of the men coming from Army regiments and looking for adventure or a simple chance of getting out of the trenches. Initially used as observers, which required no knowledge of flying, they could then move on to be trained as pilots, if deemed suitable. The chaotic and disorganised state of pilot training was becoming obvious from the number of men being killed, either during training or very soon after being posted to a front-line squadron, and in May 1916 new training schools were being set up as a stage between going solo and being sent to the front line. But it was not until 1917 that a fully integrated training programme for pilots was established.

The squadron continued to work up during June and July, a training unit by day and home defence by night, but there were to be no more defence sorties. However, it did have delivered to it on the 4 July a BE2C (2661) specifically designated for home defence use. No 47 Squadron's strength, as shown on the daily returns,[3] expanded from 6 officers and 157 men on 1 June to 18 officers and 245 men by 31 July. Daily flying time also increased and was averaging 10 to 15 hours, dependent on weather and aeroplane availability. Many of these flights were of limited duration, just circuits and bumps, but as the student pilots and observers grew in confidence and skill, long air training exercises and cross-country would be undertaken.

In early July orders were received to transfer two flights to 33 Squadron, also based at Beverley, along with many of the squadron officers and mechanics. On 11 July Major Small was posted to the Central Flying School and Captain J.A. Cunningham assumed temporary command until Major C.C. Wigram was appointed as officer commanding (OC) on 11 August.

The names of some of the instructors on the daily returns would become familiar as regular squadron pilots when the unit was posted to Salonika, men such as Captain Gordon and Second Lieutenant Denning, but others would be sent to different squadrons. The task was not without its hazards and at least two aeroplanes are noted as 'wrecked' – FK3 5545 and FK3 5515 – both on 22 July and both being flown solo by pupils, Second Lieutenants Burrell and Hancock respectively, although 5545 appears to have been repaired to flying condition as it is noted further on in the daily logs.

Some of the frustration of the instructors can be seen on the returns. Second Lieutenant Denning spent a morning instructing Second Lieutenant Normington on the art of landing, making numerous touch-and-go attempts, but notes: 'This officer is a very slow learner.'[4]

It would appear that by mid-August, after the appointment of Major Wigram, the squadron's role was changing; the pupils had left to ply their newly acquired skills in different units and the squadron mobilised for posting overseas. As shown in the daily returns, new and apparently qualified pilots and observers were posted to the squadron, and the training moved to prepare the unit for becoming operational. During the next month the squadron was flying longer flights, covering Yorkshire, Lincolnshire and beyond, weather allowing, carrying out photo reconnaissance and bombing practice, artillery cooperation and other tasks that would become its daily duty, until it was deemed to be fully operational.

In September, 20 FK3s fitted with 90hp RAF engines and another without an engine were delivered and crated up for transport by sea to Salonika. The squadron strength would have been in region of 20 officers and 170 NCOs and airmen. No 47 Squadron left Beverley on 5 September to move overseas. It was to return to the UK in September 1946, exactly thirty years later.

Chapter 2

CORPS SQUADRON

Salonika, 1916–1919

When the squadron left for Salonika it was under the command of Major C.C. Wigram, with Lieutenant D.F. Woodford as adjutant. It was divided into three flights, comprising the following officers:

A Flight Major M.A. Black
Second Lieutenant R.E. Buckingham
Second Lieutenant H.R. Hawkins
Second Lieutenant H.J. Gibson
Second Lieutenant D.H. Glasson
Second Lieutenant B.H.M. Jones
Second Lieutenant E. Churcher

B Flight Captain J.W. Gordon
Captain G.M. Croil
Lieutenant L.R. Andrews
Second Lieutenant H.O.S. Pilkerton
Lieutenant L.N. Sutherall
Lieutenant H.W. Durtnall
Lieutenant N.H. Bottomley

C Flight Captain A. Goodfellow
Second Lieutenant C. ff Denning
Second Lieutenant D.E. Nicholle
Second Lieutenant D.J. Taylor
Second Lieutenant A. Ashton
Second Lieutenant W.H. Farrow
Second Lieutenant A. Ball
Lieutenant A.D. Pocock

The squadron left Devonport harbour on the evening of 6 September aboard the transport *Menominee.* The ship sailed via Gibraltar and Malta and arrived in Salonika on the evening of Tuesday 19 September. The next day the men of the squadron marched to a rest camp at Karaissi about 2½ miles north-west of the town and then proceeded to Mikra Bay, 50 miles or so south of the border with Bulgaria. Mikra Bay was the home of 17 Squadron, which had arrived in Salonika from the Middle East in July, and the members of it had had first call on any available accommodation. Thus when 47 Squadron took up residence there was no space for the men and most of the first few days was spent erecting tents where they could, and settling in. Nos 47 and 17 Squadrons were to be the only two RFC squadrons on this front until April 1918, when the creation of the RAF also saw the formation of 150 Squadron by the transfer of the two existing squadrons' Scout flights – as the role of the fighter was referred to in the nomenclature of the time – into the new unit.

The squadron's equipment and aeroplanes began to arrive on 2 October, but there was no lifting gear at the docks and it had to be manhandled off the ship. It was over a week before all the kit and stores had been offloaded and the first of the aircraft assembled so that operations could begin. On 20 October A Flight moved from Mikra Bay to Yanesh, which was some 20 miles north and approximately 15 miles south of the Bulgarian border. (Yanesh is usually referred to as Janes, in the contemporaneous squadron records, the squadron history written by H.A. Jones and contemporary diaries and logbooks, and therefore it will be Janes in this account.) It was joined by the squadron HQ, and B Flight on the 27th. C Flight was sent to Kukush about 5 miles south, arriving there on 30 October. Janes was the squadron's main home over the next two and a half years, but with various flights distributed about the area and detachments further afield as operational requirements demanded. The three flights of the squadron were not to be based together until February 1919, when they all assembled at Amberkoj. The aerodrome at Janes, like most airfields in the area, consisted of little more than a relatively flat and well-drained piece of land with a group of tents and prefabricated hangars, close to a railway station and not far from the headquarters of XII Corps, the squadron's main source of business.

French and British troops had arrived in Salonika in October 1915; their task was to take pressure off the Serbian army to the north, which had fought off two invasions by Austro-Hungarian forces since 1914, but was now exhausted and was unlikely to withstand a third attack. With no suitable landing areas on the Adriatic coast, the Allies chose Salonika. However, Greece was still neutral. King Constantine had led the country well during the two Balkan wars of 1912 and 1913, but these had been costly victories. Furthermore, he was married to the Kaiser's sister and although he wished to keep his country out of the ongoing conflict, his sympathies were with the German cause. He was opposed in this by his prime minister, Eleftherios Venizelos, who favoured the Allies.

The British 10th (Irish) Division under General Sir Bryan Mahon and the French 156th Division commanded by General Maurice Sarrail, were transferred from Gallipoli, but both were lacking a full complement of men and equipment and would take some time to get up to full strength. Unfortunately, on 6 October, the day after the French and British arrived, the Austro-Hungarians attacked Serbia, and were joined by the Bulgarians a week later.

The conditions the British troops found themselves in were, on the whole, atrocious, and bad weather turned camps into quagmires. Stores began to arrive, but the lack of modern dock facilities and ware-housing meant that much was left in the open with insufficient guarding and thus quite a bit disappeared into the local economy. Over the winter four more divisions arrived from France after a long and uncomfortable journey.

The French managed to get three infantry battalions with supporting artillery across the Serbian border by 15 October and were joined by the first British forces on 31 October, by which time the Serbs had been all but defeated. The arrival of winter badly hindered the Allies' ability to defend their positions against the Bulgarians, lack of suitable clothing and disease soon depleted the abilities of the troops further, and in early December the British and French started to withdraw from Serbia.

On 7 December after three days of heavy artillery barrage the Bulgarians launched a

Left to right: Armstrong Whitworth FK3 5504 in the sea, October 1916, Pilot Lieutenant Durtnall and Observer Lieutenant Daw, rescued, aeroplane written off. *FAA*

Armstrong Whitworth FK3 'Wallaby' Lieutenant. D. L. Graham. *FAA*

Armstrong Whitworth FK3s at Janes, winter 1916/17. *Author collection*

full offensive against the British lines, forcing them back. The fighting retreat continued throughout December, and although the British and French forces had not prevented the defeat of the Serbs, it had distracted the Bulgarians sufficiently to allow the remnants of the Serbian army to escape into Albania.

In Salonika an agreement had been reached with the Greek government for the Allies to start building defensive works in Macedonia and for the removal of half the Greek garrison, whose support for the Allied cause was suspect. The local countryside was ideal for a defensive line, with the River Vardar and extensive marshes to the east, a chain of hills and lakes to the north and west, with vast plains north of that line making observation of any advancing army a much better prospect. The new divisions were soon put to work, but the lack of manpower meant that a continuous trench line was not possible and thus defensive positions were built for machine guns with covering artillery behind. The massive wiring of the front line soon gained the area the nickname of the 'Birdcage'.

Work continued throughout the winter and spring of 1916, under the unpredictable local weather, warm and dry for one day, followed by days of heavy rain, snow or gales. Slowly the area was converted into a huge military base with hospitals, stores and ammunition dumps. However, with Greece neutral the enemy powers still had consulates in the city and could report back to their home governments on details of Allied facilities and reinforcements. Thus on 30 December 1915 the French, under a British plan, moved to round up all known spies, and move against the consulates. A month later the French made another bold move and removed Greek troops from a fort and artillery battery at the mouth of the River Vardar, further securing their positions.

Left to right: Armstrong Whitworth FK3 (A1469) with twin Lewis guns. *FAA*

Armstrong Whitworth FK3 5512. *FAA*

The Allied presence continued to expand and the British forces became the British Salonika Force (BSF), under French command, their role being limited to the operations for the defence of the city. The BSF also answered to HQ Mediterranean Expeditionary Force (MEF) based in Cairo. But this was not altogether a happy arrangement as the MEF tended to rank the BSF low down in its priorities. The BSF got its independence in September 1917, but this hardly improved matters when it came to men and equipment; it was still well down the British military pecking order.

In March 1916, with the Bulgarians emplaced along the northern Greek border, General Sarrail advanced out of the 'Birdcage', up the valley of the River Vardar and into the Struma Valley. In April, Mahon was informed that the BSF could advance up to, but not over, the Serbo-Greek border; in May Mahon was replaced by Lieutenant General George Milne.

Things began to move apace. Later in May the Bulgarians advanced down the Rupel Pass; the Greek forces holding the fort there were ordered not to resist and to withdraw. This infuriated the Allies and brought the unsatisfactory relationship with the Greeks to a head. France and Britain moved to blockade Greek ports and threatened to bombard Athens. In response King Constantine cooperated with Allied demands and disbanded the army.

Soon the British had advanced some 30 miles to take up their new defensive positions between the River Vardar and Lake Doiran, a front line that was to change little for the next two years. However, the position was at the bottom of the surrounding mountains and overlooked by the enemy.

By May 1916 there were some 250,000 British, French and Serbian troops in the region, soon to be joined by 16,000 Italian and Russian

soldiers. As all the troops seemed to do was dig, they gained the nickname the 'Gardeners of Salonika'.

In July the Romanians, seeing a potential opportunity, decided to join the Allies and attacked Austro-Hungary, but the adventure ended in disaster. The Romanian army hoped an Allied offensive from the south would keep the Bulgarians from turning all their forces against them. However, such an attack was not planned and the Romanians were decisively defeated in four months.

General Milne realised that to successfully keep back the Bulgarian forces now holding the high ground he would need aeroplanes to fly reconnaissance sorties. The French were the first to send air support, sending six squadrons (escadrilles) of modern aeroplanes, including the excellent Nieuport Scouts, and these squadrons took on the role, but Milne wanted his own RFC units under his command. Thus on 1 July Lieutenant Colonel P.R.C. Groves arrived to make an initial assessment. His report pointed out some issues that would face the squadrons in carrying out their role, not least a lack of appreciation of what could be achieved. Apparently an artillery officer requested some fifty-six hours of flying in one day even before any aeroplanes were available.

No 17 Squadron was the first to arrive from Egypt, in early July 1916, with an advanced detachment following closely in Groves's footsteps. The squadron was based at Mikra Bay some 5 miles outside Salonika. All their kit, including hangars, aeroplanes, spares, tents and so on had to be brought up from the harbor in 3-ton Leyland lorries to a flat grassy area close to the sea. Work immediately commenced on setting up the airfield and an adjacent aircraft park to provide central servicing for the squadrons. Soon after arriving at Mikra Bay 17 Squadron were sent up to the village of Lahana in the hills west of the Struma Valley, which was to become their main base for the rest of the war.

It was into this situation that 47 Squadron arrived to join 17 Squadron. They were joined by 17 Kite Balloon Squadron. Kite balloons were tethered balloons used for observation of enemy positions and reporting fall of shot. They were an important part of the military machine and a frequent target for enemy aeroplanes, which would try and shoot them down. On 30 September they were formed into the 16th (Corps) Wing, RFC, under the overall command of Lieutenant Colonel G.W.P. Dawes, a pre-war RFC pilot. The wing formed part of the RFC's Middle East Brigade, which embraced all the RFC units in the Middle East, Mesopotamia, Salonika, East Africa and Palestine, overall a huge parish and under the command of General W.G.H. Salmond. The aeroplane squadrons' role was that of a corps squadron, providing support for artillery spotting and reconnaissance, but they also were obliged to carry out many other tasks as circumstances demanded. No 47 Squadron's main equipment was the FK3 with a few BE12s and Bristol Scouts, while 17 Squadron had BE2s and BE12s. All these types were considered obsolete for the Western Front and therefore available for service on less important fronts. Enemy air support was supplied by about fifty German machines based at Monastir, Hudova and Xanthe which, on the whole, were of more modern and effective designs, including Halberstadt Scouts. The RFC was starting at an obvious disadvantage. The British policy of giving this front a low priority meant that spares, replacement aeroplanes and resources were slow in coming until early 1918. The strain on keeping the units operational was huge. Fortunately, air fighting was rare, but just keeping enough aircraft available for all the work demanded of the units was a challenge.

As mentioned above, 47 Squadron's equipment comprised the FK3, Bristol Scouts and BE12. The BE12 was a development of the BE2; it was basically a single-seat BE2, with the front observer's cockpit removed and replaced with a large fuel tank and fitted with the more powerful 150hp RAF 4 engine. It also carried a synchronised 0.303 Vickers machine gun. However, as pointed out in *The British Fighter Since 1912* (F.K. Mason, published in 1992), it 'was evolved, for reasons of expediency, from an existing design of barely adequate mediocrity'. Within two months of the aircraft entering service with 19 Squadron on the Western Front in August 1916, it was withdrawn from the fighter role at the personal insistence of Lord Trenchard, the RFC C-in-C. It was then confined to training, home defence and squadrons overseas. In Salonika its good endurance of around 3 hours and useful bomb load of up to 336lb could be put to good use by both 17 and 47 Squadrons

Left to right: BE12 (6557) 'The Kirec Scout'. *FAA*

SE5A (B692) early 1918, with camouflaged FK3 behind. *FAA*

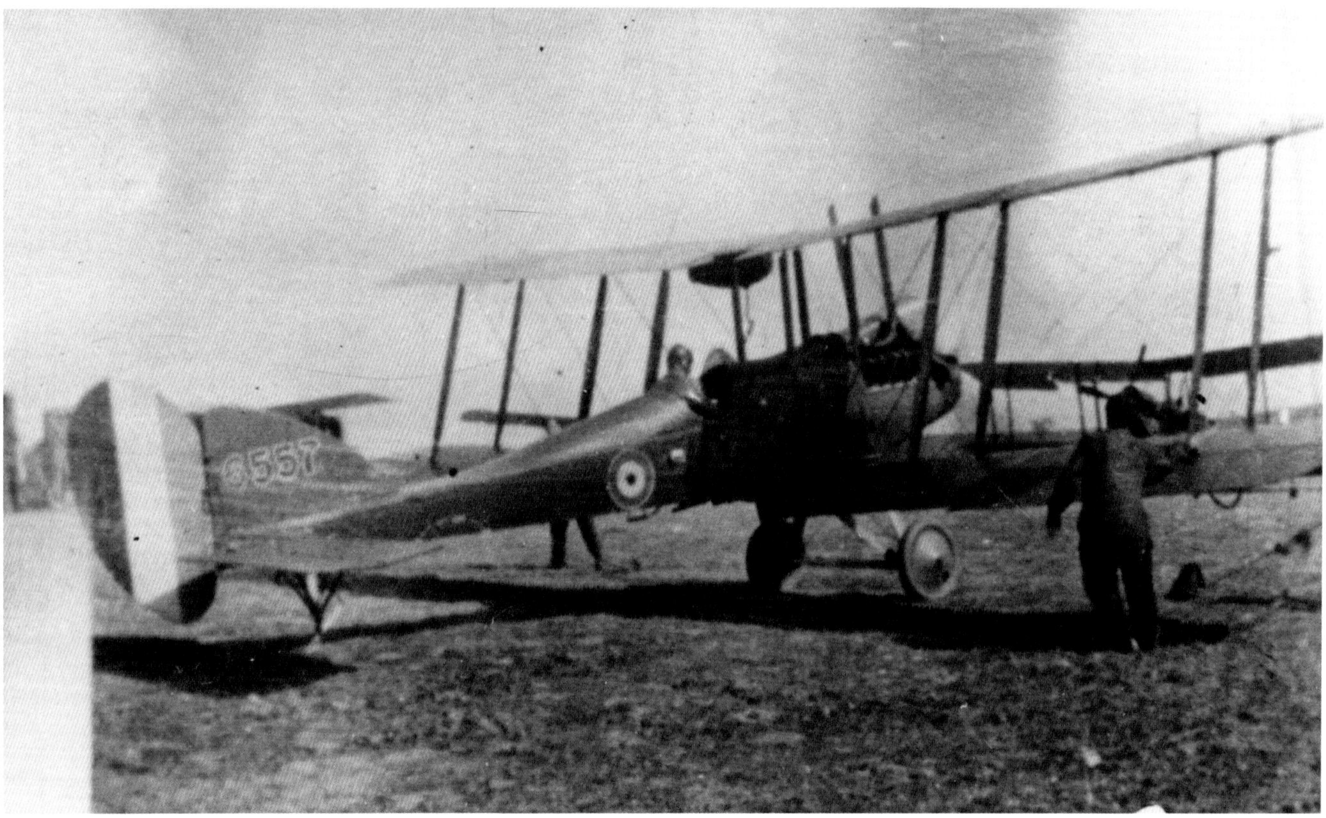

as a long-range bomber/reconnaissance aeroplane and escort fighter.

The Armstrong Whitworth FK3, as previously noted, was a perfectly adequate trainer, but as a corps squadron aeroplane it was not much better then the BE2 or BE12. It had been designed in 1914 as a simpler and slightly improved BE2, and did offer some advantages in respect of rate of climb, ceiling and cockpit layout, but carried a smaller bomb load. It was powered, initially, by the standard RAF 1a 90hp engine. It was rejected for service in France, probably as it did not offer sufficient advantages over the BE2, which was already in use, and was relegated to a training role. Some 500 FK3s were ordered and with no demand at home, and the training role being fulfilled by other types, there were enough surplus FK3s to fit out 47 Squadron. The men were already familiar with the aeroplane and the squadron became the only one in the RFC to use the FK3 in front-line service, which it continued to do well into 1918, with at least fifty FK3s passing through squadron hands from March 1916 to July 1918. When flown as a bomber no observer was carried, due to weight restrictions.

The flying characteristics of the front were also very different to those experienced in France and Belgium. Flying over the mountains the crews were subject to sudden rising or falling air pockets caused by colder air from the mountains meeting the warmer air coming up from the coast. This was also responsible for frequent thunderstorms. Winds also played havoc with navigation, as they swept down the valleys causing confusing cross-currents, making the navigators' task of estimating ground speed and course very difficult. In winter the duty was made even more challenging and uncomfortable, with cloud often obscuring the higher parts of the mountains and, of course, very cold temperatures at altitude. Another local meteorological phenomenon was the Vardar wind, which could reach 65mph in winter making flying impossible. The prevailing wind was from the north-north-west, which tended to favour the German attacking aeroplanes, as pursuit into a headwind was difficult, especially when one took into account the appalling rate of climb of the available British aeroplanes.

When 47 Squadron arrived, 16th and 12th Army Corps held the British front from the sea at the Gulf of Orfano to Vardar, with an Italian division separating the two corps. The eastern end was relatively low lying, but plagued by malaria; the western end was on higher ground, but overlooked by Bulgarian forces strongly entrenched on the Grand-Couronne and Pip ridge, making movement difficult to carry out unobserved. To the west French, Serbian, Russian and Italian units held the line. No 47 Squadron carried out its first sortie, a reconnaissance of Dram, an

airfield just behind enemy lines. This was undertaken by Lieutenant Churcher, with Lieutenant Faull acting as his observer. Unfortunately, the engine of the aeroplane seized through lack of oil, losing two cylinders, and the crew were obliged to make a forced landing, which they achieved without injury. The machine came down at Chai Aghizi, just behind the British front line, but within range of Turkish artillery, which opened fire in an attempt to destroy the downed aircraft. The fire was ineffective and no further damage was inflicted, and it was possible to the retrieve the FK3 under cover of darkness. It was taken to Stavros and returned to Salonika on a lighter. The crew made their own way home.

Engine and general serviceability problems were to continue to plague the squadron throughout its time in the region, despite the best efforts of the ground crew. A number of local modifications were tried to alleviate the issues, but reliability would still be responsible for a number of aeroplane and crew losses. On 9 October, Lieutenant Andrews's aeroplane suffered an engine failure at 6,000 feet over Lake Langaza. Andrews was able to make a successful forced landing and the aircraft was recovered by ground crews. On the same day, Lieutenant Durtnall, flying with Lieutenant Daw as a passenger, suffered a similar problem, but he was only at 300 feet and over the sea. He brought the FK3 (5504) down on to the water and he and Daw were soon picked up by French boats. The aeroplane lay half submerged overnight before recovery efforts were attempted, but on being pulled from the sea the FK3's back broke and it fell back in. The wreck was eventually pulled ashore and was of no further use except for spares. It was struck off charge (SOC) on 24 October.

On 1 November Janes had its first visit from the German Air Service when the airfield was bombed, three devices being dropped by an enemy aeroplane from about 9,000 feet, but no damage was done. Captain Goodfellow (C Flight) in a Bristol Scout attempted to intercept the retreating bomber, and eventually caught up with it over the lines near Guevgueli; he shot off half a drum of ammunition at the enemy plane, but the range was too great and no damage was observed, although no doubt Captain Goodfellow felt better for making the squadron's presence known. Two days later Goodfellow had another opportunity when he intercepted a German aircraft that was returning to base, having bombed Salonika, but on this occasion his gun jammed and he was unable to free the blockage. On 12 November, while on an armed reconnaissance, Goodfellow came across what was reported as a Fokker LVG and an Albatros, both of which he attacked, but again without success.

Towards the end of November the squadron was heavily involved in flying reconnaissance and artillery observation in support of British infantry pushing towards Krastali. Low cloud between 2,000 and 3,000 feet kept enemy aeroplanes away, but also meant that 47 Squadron was operating at a height well within range of Bulgarian anti-aircraft fire – 'Archie' as it was commonly referred to in the RFC – and most machines returned from sorties with a few holes. On 27 November Second Lieutenant J.B. Ackroyd and his observer, Second Lieutenant G.C. Wheatly, were lucky to return safely in their badly damaged FK3.

General Salmond visited the squadron on 9 December and stayed for two days, impressing those who met him with his knowledge of their problems, although little was to be done to alleviate them in the immediate future. He was also familiar with a number of the squadron personnel – even two years into the war the RFC was sufficiently small for most officers to have mutual friends and acquaintances.

Throughout December and into January 1917, the squadron continued its efforts, flying regular sorties over the lines on reconnaissance and artillery spotting tasks in deteriorating weather conditions. On 10 December Lieutenant J.R. Wilson and his observer Lieutenant C.B.M. Dale, in cooperation with a French artillery unit, successfully directed accurate fire leading to the destruction of a railway bridge south-east of Guevgueli. Throughout this time there were engagements with German aeroplanes tasked with similar roles and on the 22nd two FK3s flown by Second Lieutenant H.J. Gibson (serial unknown) and Second Lieutenant W.H. Farrow (FK3 5528) with Second Lieutenants A.P. Adams and F.C. Brooks as observers, were carrying out a reconnaissance sortie over Hudova at 10,000 feet when they spotted two German aircraft below them. The British pilots dived, reportedly reaching speeds of 120mph, which as the FK3s published maximum speed was only 100mph or so, must have been disconcerting for the observers, hanging on for dear life in the back, with no parachutes and probably no safety harness, the wind screaming through the wires and the engine straining, all the time trying to bring their Lewis guns to bear on the enemy. Initially the FK3s had no forward-firing machine gun, but 47 Squadron had jury rigged a fitting for a second Lewis gun, which allowed the pilot to fire forward, although without interrupter gear it had to be fitted at an oblique angle to shoot outside the airscrew. This made aiming accurately challenging, and thus on most occasions it was all down to the chap in the back. FK3 6198, which was lost on 15 January 1917, was an aeroplane fitted with two Lewis guns.

Farrow's right wheel struck one of the German aeroplanes that had turned towards him, but despite Adams and Brooks letting fly with a drum of ammunition each, at point-blank range, the German aeroplanes dived away and escaped apparently unharmed from the encounter. Although Farrow claimed the destruction of one of the German aeroplanes, this was unconfirmed. After this abuse – and as has been already noted, the reliability of the FK3 was not of a high standard – Gibson and Farrow thought it prudent to turn for their own lines and home. Soon Farrow's engine began to cut out and the course was changed for the nearest friendly airfield at Snevche. Over Rabrovo they were engaged at long range by two German aeroplanes and later shot at by anti-aircraft guns over Furka, but eventually Farrow was able to make a successful landing, with no further damage to the machine.

Above: BE2C A3070. *FAA* **Below: DH2.** *Author collection*

The next day, on 23 December, victory finally came and the squadron notched up its first air-to-air success when Captain W.D.M. Bell in a BE12, returning from an unsuccessful attack on an observation balloon, spotted a German two-seater of unidentified type. Bell dived and attacked from behind, opening fire at a 50-yard range. The enemy was seen to go into a spin and lost its top wing before crashing into no-man's-land near to Sejdeli. However, on the same day the squadron CO, Major Wigram, was struck down with dysentery and was repatriated home. Captain Gordon took over as temporary CO until Major Frederick Frank Reilly Minchin, MC and bar, arrived from 14 Squadron in Palestine to take over the unit in January. Minchin had been born in India in 1890, the son of Major General Minchin, but in the tradition of the time, was sent back to England to be educated. He entered Sandhurst in 1909 and was commissioned into the Connaught Rangers in 1910. It seems, though, that he was more interested in flying and in February 1913 obtained his Royal Aero Club certificate (No. 419); unfortunately he had failed to inform his CO and was threatened with a court martial. Minchin was allowed to resign his commission and left for Canada. He joined up in 1914 and quickly arranged a transfer from the Canadian infantry to the RFC and was soon sent out to the Middle East.

With the approach of Christmas a new task was added to the squadron's repertoire and an aeroplane was dispatched to fly low over Lake Ardzan to put up ducks for a brigadier general from XII Corps to shoot at. It seems that if not doing useful war work one might as well use aircraft to provide some sport. On Christmas Day 47 Squadron sent an aeroplane to drop Christmas greetings on the German aerodrome at Hudova and pass on condolences for their recent loss to Captain Bell's guns. Thus 1916 came to a quiet end on what, in today's attitudes, would seem a slightly bizarre and quaint note, but the men of the RFC and the German Air Service still thought themselves gentlemen and honourable men, although they would have no hesitation in trying to kill gentlemen of other countries as soon as the opportunity arose.

One of the early sorties of 1917 took place on 5 January, when – in what for the squadron amounted to a maximum effort taking into consideration the availability of aeroplanes and crews – eight FK3s with a mixed load of 20lb and 100lb bombs and an escort of BE12s led by Captain Goodfellow set off to bomb the airfield at Hudova. As a bomber the FK3 dispensed with the observer and therefore its defence. Significant success was reported with one camp set on fire and workshops destroyed. However, Second Lieutenant A.D. Pocock failed to return. Either hit by anti-aircraft fire or suffering from engine problems, he was last seen going down near Guevgueli, although Pocock managed to land safely. Regrettably the aeroplane was destroyed and Pocock was captured and became a POW. This was the squadron's first aircrew loss in action.

Bad weather kept the squadron on the ground for the next week or so, but on the 14th the weather cleared. With cloudless skies the mountains stood out in the sunshine, and with this return of flying weather the squadron was soon back in action. Enemy air activity also increased. During another raid on Hudova a message was dropped on the airfield, requesting information on Pocock's fate and reporting news of German airmen recently captured by French forces. On the 15th Major M.A. Black and Lieutenant S.J.M. White with observers Second Lieutenants A.P. Adams and H.A. Matthews set out on a reconnaissance of Hudova and Petrich. Near Petrich the aeroplanes were intercepted by two German machines of Ja25. White's FK3 (6198) was shot down by Oberleutnant F-K Burchardt, crashing into a pine forest near Smolari. Both men on board were killed. Lieutenant White, aged twenty-seven, formerly of the 1/4th Norfolk Regiment, was from Potter Heigham near Great Yarmouth in Norfolk, and Second Lieutenant Matthews, aged thirty-two, formerly of the 24th Battalion Royal Fusiliers, was a married man from Cottingham in Yorkshire. After being recovered from where they had been buried by the Germans, the bodies of the men were reinterred after the end of hostilities in the Salonika (Lembet Road) military cemetery.

Two days later a message was dropped over Snevche:

The German aviators are very sorry to inform you of the death of the two English Aviators which were killed on the 15th January 10:30 a.m. after a fight with our aeroplanes. The English aviators had been fighting very bravely, but their aeroplane dropped after about 5 minutes fight and killed. They died as heroes and have all our respects. Their bodies will be buried with all military honours.

We are informing you also of your Lieutenant Pocock having been made a prisoner by the troops without being blessed. [French for wounded is 'blesse'.]

We are obliged of your having informed us of the four German aviators which have been made your prisoners.

Revenge for the loss of White and Matthews came quickly, with Lieutenant C. ff Denning sending down an Albatros two-seater out of control over Prastan.

On 17 January while carrying out a spotting sortie for an artillery battery, Second Lieutenant Adams, acting as observer for Second Lieutenant R.E. Buckingham, was about to commence a shoot when he noticed some ground markings indicating the presence of an enemy battery. Using Bulgarian signal codes he was able to persuade the guns to open fire, giving away their exact position, and Adams was able to direct an accurate counter-battery shoot by the 138th Siege Battery. Adams later qualified as a pilot and was posted to 30 Squadron flying RE8s in Mesopotamia.

Lieutenant Denning was credited with a second victory on the 19th. Flying a BE12 while on escort duty he spotted an Albatros two-seater, and although the enemy aeroplane had the advantage of a higher top speed, Denning was able to get in behind his victim, which he damaged, even though early on Denning's gun jammed and he could only fire single shots between manually cocking the gun. The Albatros spiralled down to make a forced landing near Kilindir. Denning followed his prize down, landing beside it, and rushed across to prevent the German airman destroying the aeroplane. The Albatros had a damaged fuselage and the starboard inner rear strut and aileron control had been shot away. Unable to take off again Denning secured his prisoners and his prize and returned to base. In the evening a recovery party was sent out. Arriving after dark at Kilindir Station with a tender, the party worked until 02.00 hours on both aircraft in the pouring rain while under intermittent Bulgarian artillery fire. Lieutenant John Wilson, an observer with the squadron who went out with the recovery team, records in his diary that Denning was able to take off at dawn the next day. The team worked all day on the Albatros and were finally able to remove it by 21.00, stopping overnight with a Royal Artillery unit at Hirosova House, although not without incident, nearly losing a tender over a cliff. The roads were awful because of the constant rain and tenders soon got bogged down. The next day the party started off again for Janes in a general service wagon with a team of six horses. With the Albatros on board they finally made it back to the aerodrome early in the afternoon through sleet and snow. The tender made it back much later with the tailplane. The captured machine was then taken away for further examination.

The weather now turned bitterly cold, with hard frosts, and although the Germans were operating over the front, little flying was done by 47 Squadron because of aeroplane serviceability. Wilson flew as an observer twice on the 22nd but on both occasions was forced to return with engine trouble. The following day two BE12s tried a reconnaissance sortie to Hudova, but had to return because of engine issues. Later in the day Wilson was in the air on a reconnaissance with a BE12 acting as escort. The BE12 returned early – yet more engine trouble – but Wilson and his pilot, Second Lieutenant D.H. Glasson, carried on to complete their allotted task, being in the air for 1 hour 31 minutes. This was to be one of the last flights for some time as the weather got steadily worse, with heavy rain alternating with snow.

The weather in the first part of February remained atrocious, knee deep mud and almost constant freezing rain making everybody's life, whichever side of the lines they were on, a misery. As soon as the weather cleared sufficiently and the airfield dried out enough to allow flying, aeroplanes were up on reconnaissance of the enemy front line. It was decided that there was an opportunity to launch an attack, on the basis that conditions on the Bulgarian side of the line were grim enough for the enemy to be so badly disrupted that easy gains could be made. Nobody seemed to consider the British front line was in a similar state and coordinating an attack would be very difficult. The Devons went over the top, but little progress was made to justify the casualties.

Accidents were an ever present concern, the airfield conditions were poor and on returning from a reconnaissance over the lines on 2 February Second Lieutenant Brufton with Wilson as observer made a poor landing and piled into FK3 6210, but neither aeroplane was badly damaged or crew hurt; however, 6210 does not appear to have been repaired sufficiently to allow operations until the end of April.

The living conditions for all were very inadequate, officers and men living in tents and huts, and not enough hangars for the aeroplanes, which had to spend most of their time outside in the rain and snow, making maintenance a serious issue and leading to a number of machines retuning early from sorties with mechanical problems, but the ground crews made sure that at least a few aircraft were available for operations. Another concern was boredom; there was little to do for entertainment locally and only opportunities to travel to the relative excitement of Salonika on rare occasions. Wilson's diary contains numerous references to taking long walks with fellow officers, although how much fun that was in the prevailing weather conditions is open to conjecture.

On 5 February the weather cleared sufficiently for a number of sorties to be carried out. First off, Wilson went aloft with Major Black to look for targets, but returned after 55 minutes with little to report. In the afternoon Wilson went 'Hun hunting' with Wilkinson for over two hours. They dived on one enemy aeroplane over the salient: 'Had a brief scrap and chased him back to Hudova, saw a Hun chasing an AW with another AW on top of the Hun, Dived down like hell but the Hun went off home very low down. Glasson's AW riddled with bullets but landed OK. We had two bullet holes in our Armstrong.'

Unfortunately the weather closed in again, meaning a planned raid on Hudova was scrubbed, but an artillery captain was taken up for a joy ride instead. Snow returned and again flying was cancelled but the opportunity was taken to bring over artillery officers from the batteries 47 Squadron was working with to improve cooperation. The weather cheered up on the 10th and the snow melted during the day, so patrols were soon sent up covering the 26th Division's front in preparation for an attack that night. French Nieuports were also active in the area and that evening the guns opened fire in support of the attack, which could be heard by 47 Squadron.

On 11 February the squadron launched another maximum effort and dispatched nine aircraft to bomb the airfield at Hudova. The raid was not a success; engine problems forced four of the FK3s to turn back, leaving the remaining four FK3s and the escorting BE12 to carry on. Lieutenant Denning had his work cut out protecting the vulnerable bombers, being involved in three dogfights, but claiming one enemy aeroplane driven down, although this was not confirmed. Major Black leading the force in FK3 6196 was attacked by Leutnant O. Brauneck of Ja25 over the target. His machine was seen to go down in a spinning nose dive and two days later it was confirmed that he had been killed. Major Black had arrived with the squadron in September and was A Flight commander. Formerly of the 5th Dragoon Guards, he is buried in Skopje military cemetery in the present day republic of Macedonia.

The next day brought a further loss when Second Lieutenant A.C. Stopher, flying FK3 6219, failed to return from a sortie. The events surrounding the loss seemed to cause some embarrassment to the squadron. Stopher had left Snevche airfield to fly to Janes, but apparently got lost and landed at the French aerodrome at Gorgop, some 15 miles away. He left the following day and his navigation skills seemed to have failed the young pilot again; he had only just turned nineteen and was new to the squadron. He was seen flying over Janes, but the aeroplane came down behind enemy lines south of Demir Hisar about 30 miles from Janes, and Stopher was captured, spending the rest of the war at the POW camp at Philippopolis. The aeroplane was taken intact and re-branded in Bulgarian markings, in whose colours it continued to give sterling service as a night bomber until at least June 1918, outlasting most of its contemporaries serving with 47 Squadron!

During this time 47 Squadron had been working on ways to improve their FK3s. As well as the early attempts to fix an additional Lewis gun for use by the pilot, an extra camera rail was fitted to the fuselage, allowing the camera to be operated by either the observer or, if flying solo, the pilot. However, the most obvious modification was to the engine. Most of the FK3s built were fitted with the 90hp RAF 1a engine, but some had the more powerful 120hp Beardmore, and it is apparent that some of the 47 Squadron FK3s were thus fitted when first delivered to the squadron. But it is clear from the evidence of photographs and contemporary accounts such as Wilson's diary,and Jones' *Over the Balkans and South Russia* and especially the article by Michael Kelsey in *Cross and Cockade International* (autumn 2013), that some aeroplanes were refitted with the Beardmore engine in the field.

The first of these believed to have been converted locally was FK3 6218. Wilson in his diary has a drawing of the aeroplane dated 7 February, showing a RAF 1a engine, but makes several references to the 'Beardmore AW coming along' and on 13th February as 'nearly finished'. The re-engined FK3 made a somewhat ungainly looking machine with a huge cowling to enclose the engine and various bits, such as a top wing-mounted gravity tank that may have come

Armstrong Whitworth FK3 (6219) captured by Bulgarians, and in their air service. This was Second Lieutenant Stopher's aeroplane, which went missing in February 1917. *FAA*

Vickers Bullets (A5225 in foreground) with BE12/12a s behind from A Flight detached for attacks on Monastir, August 1917. *Authors collection*

Armstrong Whitworth FK8 (B3347), 1918. *FAA*

from a BE12. Certainly the pilot's forward view looks to have been seriously restricted. It was very different from other Beardmore engine FK3s. It would appear that the aeroplane was ready by 14 February, when Wilson refers to the first flight of the Beardmore AW 6218, and continued to be operated by 47 Squadron until the end of June when it was flown to Salonika and the crew returned with a different FK3. It may be that either the promised increase in performance from the more powerful engine was not forthcoming, or just the complications of trying to maintain a non-standard engine was felt to be too much. Other FK3s from earlier production batches were fitted with Beardmore engines on delivery to the squadron, but most were refitted with the RAF engine fairly quickly. For example, FK3 5504 was originally built with a Beardmore engine, but by the time Lieutenant Durtnall ditched in the sea on 19 October it was using an RAF engine.

About the same time some FK3s were beginning to receive the RAF 4a engine, which was rated at 140hp. The new engine provided an improved performance with a rate of climb of 10,000 feet in 21 minutes, with a passenger, and a speed of 100mph at 500 feet. It had a further advantage over the Beardmore aircraft in that the pilot's forward view was not obstructed. In the squadron records these were often referred to as the AW12 (reflecting its 12-cylinder engine), but this was a strictly unofficial designation. However, as has been noted, the squadron records are incomplete and not to be taken as entirely accurate, with a number of frustrating typos adding to the confusion.

Towards the end of February 1917 the air war in the region took an unwelcome turn for the Allies when the Germans transferred Kampfgeschwader 1 (KG.1) to the front. This was an experienced bomber unit and equipped with eighteen modern bomber types, comprising single-engined Halberstadt Scouts, and twin-engined AEG, Rumpler and Friedrichshafen aeroplanes. The twin-engined aeroplanes carried gunners fore and aft, three machine guns, plus bomb loads of 1,000–1,200lb, powered by Mercedes engines of between 220 and 260hp. They were vastly superior to anything the Allies had and especially the RFC could put up in response.

The new bombers first made their presence known with an attack by twenty aeroplanes on 26 February against the French aerodrome at Gorgop, destroying eight and damaging a further four machines on the ground. That afternoon the German bombers turned their attention to 47 Squadron at Janes. The squadron was able to get most of its aircraft off the ground, but due to the German aeroplanes' superior performance they were unable to intercept the formation. The bombing, in material terms, was less devastating, but seven men were killed on the ground and a further nine, including the equipment officer, Lieutenant Howes, wounded.

The bombing campaign continued the next day when a formation of twenty attempted to bomb Salonika, but the formation was broken up by attacks by 17 Squadron and one Halberstadt Scout was forced down. The bombing was scattered but the British base camp at Summer Hill was hit, causing a large number of casualties. No 47 Squadron intercepted the machines on their way back to their own lines and although there were a number of combats, there were no claims made by either side.

There were to be repeated attacks on Allied positions, ammunition and supply dumps and camps. On 14 March a hospital was hit at Dudular near Salonika, although it was unlikely to have been deliberate as the hospital was placed among an area of legitimate targets. That day the RFC responded with an assault by eighteen aeroplanes from 17 and 47 Squadrons – twelve bombers escorted by six BE12s. The force dropped 600lb of bombs and thirty-five 4.5-inch artillery shells, fused to explode on impact, on the aerodrome at Hudova; in the afternoon nine bombers and five escorts attacked Cestovo.

The tit-for-tat raids continued, with the German bombers focusing on the dumps and military camps behind the Allied lines. The Allied forces were concentrated in a

A Flight 47 Squadron, March 1918. *MacEwan via author*

relatively small area between the front lines and the coast and, thus, in today's terminology, it was a 'target-rich environment' and the attacking bombers could hardly fail to find something of interest to drop their bombs on. But it did mean that there were occasions when strictly non-offensive targets were hit, and on 12 March another hospital was struck at Vertekop, where the casualties included two English nurses killed. Again, the RFC attacked Hudova aerodrome, with thirteen bombers and seven escorts. As the formation approached, enemy aircraft took off to intercept, and in the ensuing engagement Second Lieutenant Glasson in FK3 6212 was seen to go down. Glasson survived the crash, but succumbed to his wounds on the same day. The shooting down of Glasson was claimed by Leutnant Hinsen of KG.1. The Germans responded with a raid on Janes in the afternoon and a note was dropped reporting that Glasson had died.

The German bomber squadron was becoming a real concern and a combined 17/47 Squadron fighting flight was formed at Hadzi-Junus, comprising three BE12s of 17 Squadron and one BE12 and two DH2s from 47 Squadron, under the command of Lieutenant F.G. Saunders from 17 Squadron. The RNAS was also called upon to assist and four Sopwith fighters (one and a half strutters) and a Sopwith Triplane were sent on 27 March. Unfortunately the triplane crashed on landing and had to be returned to Mudros for repairs. Before the arrival of the RNAS the composite flight had been in action, and on 18 March two bombing raids were broken up before they could reach their targets and one machine was shot down by Captain Murlis Green of 17 Squadron in a BE12.

New efforts were put in place to improve the effectiveness of the Scouts, with much time being spent training; however, during one combat practice a DH2 of 47 Squadron (Lieutenant E.R. Wilkinson) collided in mid-air with a BE12 of 17 Squadron (Lieutenant J.L. Bamford). The BE12 lost its tailplane and rudder and immediately began to fall earthward out of control. The aeroplane flipped on to its back at 5,000 feet and crashed. Remarkably Bamford was not killed, only suffering from concussion. Wilkinson landed safely, his DH2 collapsing 'like a pack of cards' as it stopped.

In April the British forces on the ground received reinforcements, with the arrival of the 60th London Division, and there were rumours of either a forthcoming Allied offensive or an attack by the Bulgarians. During this time the RFC squadrons were given no rest and continued their personal war against KG.1, bombing their base at Hudova both night and day.

Second Lieutenant Farrow claimed an Albatros near Bogdanci on 5 April, although this is unconfirmed. Farrow was wounded by return fire in the action but was to make it home safely. On the 12 Second Lieutenant L.H. Stowell and Lieutenant J.J. Boyd Harvey were also lucky to get back from a photo-reconnaissance sortie when their FK3 was hit by AA fire over Stojakovo, losing rudder, and most of the elevator effectiveness; the aeroplane fell from 8,000 feet to 3,000 feet before a modicum of control could be regained. Later in April Farrow claimed another enemy aircraft shot down out of control, but he was unable to see it crash due to ground fire and an engine that was giving him trouble.

According to Jones's *Over the Balkans and South Russia*, the RNAS suffered a devastating loss towards the end of May when an accident, as their aeroplanes were being bombed up, caused an explosion in a hangar that killed four ground crew and destroyed ten Sopwiths and eleven Cleget engines, effectively putting the squadron out of action. Elaborate measures were put in place to hide the evidence of the accident, but the RNAS was, for the time being, out of the game in Salonika. Details of this accident have been difficult to confirm.

No 47 Squadron suffered a loss when on 2 May the aeroplane being flown by Second Flight Sub-Lieutenant H.L. Gaskil (RNAS) attached to 47 Squadron, with 47 Squadron's Second Lieutenant J. Watt as observer, broke up in mid-air at 5,000 feet above the aerodrome at Hadzi-Junas and crashed killing both men. It was thought that the aeroplane may have been damaged by AA fire as they returned over the lines from a reconnaissance sortie.

On 10 May a reconnaissance of the bomber aerodrome at Hudova revealed that KG.1 had left, the hangars had been moved and the train usually sitting in the sidings close to the aerodrome had gone. It was eventually found to have transferred to Belgium. Why they had been suddenly withdrawn was not known, but it was later learned that they were being used in operations against London. But for the Allies in Salonika it was of considerable relief. During their brief three-month period of operation in the area the KG.1 had caused much damage and stretched the combined RFC, RNAS and French air force resources.

On the ground the predicted Allied offensive had begun on the night of 24 April. The territory gave a great advantage to the defender who had had over a year to prepare trenches and machine-gun pits; the Bulgarian artillery had these positions zeroed in to provide supporting fire. The Bulgarians held the high ground and attackers were forced to use narrow ravines to advance, all the time being under enemy observation. Reconnaissance by 17 and 47 Squadrons provided some idea of the Bulgarian positions, but many were well camouflaged or protected by strong AA defences, making a completely accurate picture difficult to produce. General Milne, the British commander, was fully aware of the issues his ground forces could expect, and took as careful preparations as he could, but this was a combined operation with the French and other Allied forces, and Milne's choice of timing was compromised. The Bulgarians were also aware of the forthcoming offensive and strengthened their artillery and infantry reserves to meet the attack. The British opened an artillery barrage on known Bulgarian positions several days before the offensive was opened and 47 Squadron were kept busy directing artillery fire.

Just before the attack the intensity of 47 Squadron's operations was increased and a photographic lorry with all the equipment to process the plates from the aeroplane cameras was sent up to Janes to enable the more urgent work to be done quickly. The squadron was involved every day on either photo-reconnaissance sorties or artillery cooperation, directing fire on enemy gun positions. On one occasion an ammunition dump adjacent to the artillery position was hit and destroyed. Unlike on the Western Front the RFC in Salonika had no aircraft suitable for flying contact patrols and giving direct support to the infantry on the ground during an attack. The training was not in place, largely because with only two squadrons available there was simply not the time or resources to devote to the tactic. If the Army high command had paid more attention to this backwater and supplied General Milne with the resources he requested, including additional and more up-to-date aeroplanes, then possibly more could have been done to improve the success of the forthcoming offensive.

Two British divisions were involved: the 26th on the right of the line and 22nd on the left. The 22nd gained all its objectives on the first night and sustained light losses – only one officer and six other ranks killed – and held on despite determined counter-attacks. The 26th was not so lucky, failing to take any of its objectives and suffering 50% casualties (killed, wounded, missing and captured). Effective and heavy artillery barrages from well-emplaced Bulgarian guns caught the British infantry even before they reached their assembly points. Some small bodies of men, the survivors of much larger groups, did make some ground but most were forced back. The 10th Battalion, Devonshire Regiment, in the middle of the 26th Division assault, lost 16 officers and 402 other ranks.

Continued attacks over the next few days, pressed with the utmost determination, still failed to take many of the first-day objectives, and after sustaining further heavy casualties the British were forced back and the offensive was called off.

During the last week of May the squadron received some well-deserved recognition from the commander of XII Corps, with which it had been working closely in the preceding months. He wrote to express 'his great appreciation of the zeal shown by all ranks and the good work performed. … He realizes clearly the strain imposed, not only upon pilots and observers, but also upon other ranks of the Royal Flying Corps in carrying out their duties at high pressure.'

The arrival of summer brought new challenges for the squadron. The Vardar winds that had brought snow and rain during the winter now delivered fine dust, which covered everything, but the coming of the sunshine and hot weather also gave rise to swarms of flies during the day and mosquitoes at night, making everybody's life a misery; the mosquitoes also brought malaria, adding another burden to be borne. The temperatures during the middle of day meant that only absolutely essential work was undertaken and flying was made more difficult with rapid up and down drafts and poor visibility of the ground due to the dust. Snakes were also a concern, but more psychological than dangerous.

The squadron made attempts to make life more comfortable. A tennis court was created, but only enjoyed for a short time before a summer storm swept away the court, rackets and net. Tennis was now off the entertainment agenda. One of the squadron officers, Lieutenant L.P. Sedgwick, had big ideas and commenced building an officers' mess. Unfortunately he came down with a fever before the works could be completed, but on the night of the official opening the band of the 7th Wilts played, white-coated mess corporals were on hand at the bar and a special dinner put on for invited guests. Sadly Lieutenant Sedgwick was still in hospital and unable to attend. The mess was a huge success and pilots and observers returning from operations were highly appreciative of the long cool drinks available.

Some entertainment the men had to arrange for themselves and there is a photograph in the squadron archives, unfortunately not good enough for reproduction, showing an observer officer with a wide grin as he holds between his teeth, by the scruff of its neck, a not very happy looking local cat! What sort of bet the officer lost to take on this challenge one can only hope was worth it. In the spring large numbers of white storks would come to Salonika to breed and the men of 47 Squadron, having an affinity with fellow flyers, would adopt any waifs and strays, feeding them on frogs, which were plentiful and very noisy at night.

During the hot summer months, operations were confined to early morning or late afternoon and evening when the crews could be assured of clear, still air. Throughout June there was plenty of air activity, from both the RFC and the enemy. A new enemy scout squadron (JA 38) was reported to have arrived at Kanatlarci, and many patrols were carried out to shoo away the RFC machines in an effort to conceal ground movements. On 5 June Captain W.D.M. Bell in a BE12 was in combat with a Halberstadt; unfortunately his gun jammed and the German aeroplane broke away, but it was later reported by the French that the aircraft had come down near the village of Mrzenci where it was shelled by French artillery.

The RFC pursued an offensive air policy, flying whenever possible and carrying out the full range of its capabilities – bombing, reconnaissance, artillery cooperation and scouting. Because of the disadvantageous British positions, where observation from the ground was all but impossible, the ability of the RFC to see over the hill was much appreciated. The Germans and Bulgarians had the benefit of being able to watch the British from their positions on the high ground and thus did not conduct much artillery observation. Although the Germans were also very active, little air-to-air combat took place unless one side felt itself at good advantage. June was also a month of unseasonably poor weather with torrential rain and low cloud.

However, when the weather did allow, operations were carried out. On 11 June six 47 Squadron aeroplanes bombed Platanenwald Camp. On the same day an unidentified aeroplane approached the 17 Squadron aerodrome at Orljak and landed; it was flown by a Russian pilot, Staff Captain Smolianinov, who had become disenchanted with the course of the war in Russia and the Revolution and decided to join the RFC, flying a captured German plane to Salonika. He later joined 47 Squadron and flew a number of sorties, both as an observer and pilot, before apparently returning to Russia later in the year.

Raids continued throughout the month and it was noticeable how the Bulgarians increased their AA defences; often 47 Squadron aeroplanes would return with holes that were not part of the original design, but fortunately none were lost and, conversely, the squadron was able to inflict some damage on the enemy. On the 29th a Halberstadt was claimed, but was not confirmed, and on 5 July Lieutenant R.M. Wynne Eyton in a DH2 attacked an Albatros carrying out artillery cooperation and escorted by three Halberstadt Scouts. The Albatros was almost certainly damaged by Wynne Eyton, but he was unable to watch, having to contend with the three Halberstadts, which had belatedly taken up their task of protecting the reconnaissance machine.

During June a new type of aeroplane was added to the squadron's strength with the arrival of the first of four Vickers FB19s, known as 'Bullets'. This machine was a single-engined scout of mediocre performance; six were sent to France for evaluation, but were considered unsuitable; twelve, however, were sent out to the Middle East, four of which ended up with 47 Squadron. The aircraft had a chequered and long-drawn-out development from a private venture by Vickers at the start of the war. It initially showed some promise, and as the ES1 (Experimental Scout 1), fitted with a 100hp Gnome Monosoupape rotary engine, it was demonstrated at Hendon showing its ability to be looped continuously and still gain altitude. Yet when first sent to France, service pilots decried the lack of forward visibility and there were serious issues with the build up of petrol in the cockpit, which caused a number of fires, and the aeroplane was declared too dangerous to fly. In January 1916 the aircraft was renamed ES2, although what changes were made are unclear, and a further six ordered. The machine had an excellent rate of climb and speed in comparison to others in service and was fitted with a synchronised Vickers machine gun on the port side of the fuselage. The aeroplanes were now fitted with 110hp Clerget or Le Rhône engines. The poor pilot visibility was still a major criticism and although fast and manoeuvrable, they found no favour when again sent to France for evaluation.

Out of this came the FB19, very similar to the original ES1, but fitted with the 100hp Gnome Monosoupape engine. It suffered the same cockpit view issues, but in Autumn 1916 it was redesigned with staggered wings, the bottom wing being moved 22 inches aft. This was designated the FB19 Mk II; again trials were undertaken in France and again the machine was rejected. However, the machine was easy to fly and retained its excellent manoeuvrability, climb to 5,000 feet was just under eight minutes and 10,000 feet in less than 15 minutes, but the cockpit ergonomics were awful, with the dashboard being reported as 'too close (0") to the pilot's face'.[5] No use in France or for home defence, they were sent overseas, 47 Squadron getting the first ones. Major Minchin test flew A5226 at the end of June, with Captain Bell flying the first operational sortie with the same aeroplane on 2 July. Over the next month or so they were joined by A5225, 5227 and 5228. There is evidence that Squadron aeroplanes had the Vickers machine gun replaced with three Lewis guns, one mounted on the top wing, and two on the lower wing out-board of the propeller arc, fired by Bowden cables from the cockpit. This would have given formidable firepower, though no air to air victories were recorded whilst serving with the squadron.

On 8 July Second Lieutenant Howard Charles Brufton was killed when, after engaging an enemy machine, his aeroplane (DH2 4764) broke up in mid-air over the airfield and crashed. He had been seen by 24 Anti-Aircraft Section in combat with a Halberstadt, and to break off Brufton's aeroplane was seen to dive very steeply before righting itself and heading back over the lines. Whether the machine was damaged in the fight or from its violent manoeuvre one can only surmise.

During July there was intelligence received that the Bulgarians were preparing for a major offensive as troop concentrations were noted behind their lines. The squadron was called upon to carry out numerous reconnaissance sorties; however, they reported that there were no major enemy movements and thus no attack being prepared. These sorties were undertaken in very poor conditions, with the strong dusty Vardar blowing and frequent thick white fogs, making flying in the mountains more hazardous and navigation difficult because of lack of ground references to be seen. Again the commander of XII Corps was prompted to officially record his thanks for the squadron's work.

A Flight, under the charge of Captain W.D.M. Bell, moved to Kalabac on 30 July. It was a poorer airfield than Hadzi-Junus and close to the mountains, from which, during the winter months, an occasional wolf would come sniffing around. In the summer the chief threat was grass fires, which could move rapidly when the Vardar was blowing; at night they would provide a fascinating sight, as long as they were far enough away not to require action.

The weather in August was hot and sultry, and the squadron was requested, with 17 Squadron, to provide aeroplane assistance to the RNAS at Thasos in bombing the aerodrome and seaplane base at Gereviz. Five aeroplanes were dispatched to Thasos and joined seven from 17 Squadron. The next morning the combined force carried out a bombing raid on the target, with three RNAS aircraft dropping some 1,410lb of bombs. A further attack was carried out in the afternoon, releasing 1,964lb of high-explosives. It was reported later that extensive damage had been done, with a petrol or bomb store destroyed and hangars and buildings being hit. Cooperation with the French also took place during the month, bombing camps and aerodromes. The raids included some Nieuport Scouts obtained by 17 Squadron from the French to fly in escort.

Bombing raids on enemy targets continued throughout August, with strikes on the dump at Topolčani and enemy aerodromes and buildings at Kanatlarci, as well as what was believed to be the enemy headquarters at Prilep. Air-to-air engagements were frequent because of the larger formations being used – which included escorts of French Nieuports

DH 9, Lieutenant MacEwan in observer's cockpit 1918. *MacEwan via author*

Armstrong Whitworth FK8 (B3399) Lieutenant Christie (pilot) and Lieutenant MacEwan (Obs) unhurt, 21 April 1918. *FAA*

and Spads – and the aggressive tactics of the German Air Service. On one occasion a two-seater Roland worked its way into the middle of the formation, where he attacked the raid leader; the rest of the formation, fearful of opening fire in return for the risk of hitting their own aeroplanes, could do little to interfere. Fortunately the Roland dived away without causing anybody major damage, although the RFC crews were forced to admire the man's courage and tenacity. This event was recorded in Jones' book, however it would appear that no two seater Roland C.II served in Macedonia, so this likely to be misidentification in the heat of combat.

During a raid on Prilep on 20 August comprising three FK3s from 47 Squadron, with three escorting 17 Squadron Nieuports (seemingly they may have forgotten to return these to the French, and also Lt. Colonel Dawes' desire for the RFC to have access to up to date fighting machines), the formation was attacked and the Nieuports drawn off in defence, one of them (Lieutenant J.L. Bamford) being shot down and the pilot killed. Of the three 47 Squadron FK3s, two transported bombs and no observer, while the last (A1466) carried an observer acting as rear gunner for the formation. A running fight then ensued between the escorting FK3 and up to four enemy scouts. Both British aircrew (pilot Lieutenant F.H.W. Thomas, a former big-game hunter from Rhodesia and observer Lieutenant H.A. Jones) were hit, but managed to keep the scouts away from the bombers until 17 Squadron returned to give assistance. Thomas was hit in the back and fainted twice on the return trip through loss of blood. Jones had been hit in the stomach, jaw and hand. Through an extreme effort of will Thomas was able to bring the aeroplane home. Badly wounded he was evacuated back to the UK, where he died on 5 January 1918 and is buried at Brookwood cemetery, Surrey. Lieutenant Jones made a full recovery and went on the write the squadron history.

Autumn arrived with the slackening of the heat of summer, but no let-up in activity. Casualties, though not high, regularly removed members of the squadron, which after a year on operations had become a close-knit and highly professional unit. On 5 October five machines set out to bomb the supply dump at Cestovo and were intercepted by three Halberstadts near Lake Doiran. Second Lieutenant G.C. Gardner flying FK3 5508 was wounded in the leg and ended up in hospital. His observer, Second Lieutenant A.S. Clark, was unhurt. It is interesting to note that although this is recorded as a bombing sortie, all the FK3s were carrying a crew of two, which would seem to preclude carrying much of a bomb load.

In a force as small as 47 Squadron, every loss was felt. On 6 October Lieutenant E.R. Wilkinson (FK3 5508) sustained a fatal stomach wound on a low-level attack on artillery batteries at Nicilic. He was hit by ground fire and force-landed near Brest. He died of his injury the following day. Later in the month, on the 16th, one of the squadron aeroplanes, an FK3 (AW12) A1463, while taking off for a raid, stalled at less than 400 feet. The machine hit the ground and the bomb load exploded. The pilot, Second Lieutenant Patrick Colin Hunter, and observer, Lieutenant Armar Somerset Butler, were killed and are buried at Sarigol military cemetery, Kriston. They had only recently joined the squadron.

On 29 October Second Lieutenant J.R.F. Gubbin was flying FK3 1478 with second air mechanic T.H. Bury as a gunner, on an attack on Cestovo dump when their aeroplane was attacked by an estimated eight Albatros and Halberstadt Scout aircraft. Gubbin was hit by a burst of machine-gun fire, almost severing his left arm; he tried to make it back across British lines, but received a further wound in the back and crashed. Captured, he died in hospital some two weeks later. Bury spent the rest of the war as a POW. On the same sortie, Second Lieutenant P.D. Montague, flying BE12 A4040, was shot down by German scout aeroplanes and killed.

The loss of six squadron members in the period of less than two weeks must have been hard to take, but the squadron's resolve was undiminished. There was also the constant trickle of non-fatal losses due to diseases such as malaria and dysentery, which were rife in the region.

The coming of winter and less favourable weather conditions gave an opportunity for the introduction of reinforcements from Egypt and a reorganisation of the squadron flights. A Flight in the escort and scout role returned from Kalabac to Hadzi-Junus for the winter. C Flight was at Kiric to carry out the artillery cooperation work; B Flight and the squadron HQ remained at Janes, leaving B Flight to cover the rest of the tasks. To assist in the efficiency of the work carried out by the squadron, C Flight came directly under the orders of the artillery command of XII Corps and the counter-battery staff officer, Lieutenant Colonel Crawford, and had attached to it an artillery officer by the name of Captain MacDonald.

However, although this close cooperation between C Flight and its customer was welcomed by all, there were still practical issues to be overcome that had remained unresolved since the start of the campaign, namely accurate maps; for example, following the full and frank exchange of views that took place after one shoot in which the gunners brought evidence to show the shots had fallen well off target, 47 Squadron produced photos to prove otherwise. After the area was resurveyed it was shown that Lake Doiran was some 400 yards north-west of its assumed position and this affected the surrounding countryside to a greater or lesser degree. Photographic coverage was improved and 47 Squadron introduced stereoscopic prints, which were such a success that soon the gunners turned their noses up at anything not submitted in this form, and a huge effort was made by the squadron to accurately map the front and rear lines of the enemy.

The winter period also provided some long awaited re-equipment. In November 1917 the squadron finally began to receive modern aeroplanes suitable for front-line service in an active war zone when the first of a few SE5a fighters were delivered. However, they also received some BE2Cs, a much less welcome return to the squadron strength, having been gladly abandoned in England some twelve months before. In spring 1918 the first of the Armstrong Whitworth FK8s arrived, along with Bristol M1C scouts. In the meantime, the FK3s and BE12s soldiered on.

The SE5a was a popular addition; the excellent Spanish-designed 200hp Hispano-Suiza (or British-made equivalent) engine was matched to a suitable airframe to produce a fighter of a performance that could compete with the best of the German aeroplanes available. It was fitted with a synchronised Vickers 0.303 machine gun and a further 0.303 Lewis gun positioned over the wing on a Foster mounting. It had a speed of over 110mph at 10,000 feet. The SE5A was sent to France in the summer of 1917, but initial problems with the engine blighted its early promise somewhat, as well as a number of structural issues that delayed full operational service, but despite this it proved an excellently stable gun platform and was the mount of many aces such as Mannock, Bishop and McCudden. Small numbers were delivered to 47 Squadron – no more than seven – and some of these may have arrived too late for the unit to put them into action before they were transferred to 150 Squadron, which was formed in April 1918 to take on the fighter role in Salonika.

Meanwhile, 47 Squadron continued to carry out its tasks with commendable efficiency, although not without incident. While on a photo-reconnaissance sortie on 14 November, Second Lieutenant E. Brewer, in a BE12 (6531), was hit by AA fire that destroyed many of the instruments and damaged the aeroplane. Brewer put the nose down to head for the Allied lines: 'I rather thought my time had come.' Brewer's 'jolly awkward but vital' seatbelt stopped him from slumping forward on to his joystick. He eventually force-landed behind Allied lines near Caussica and was fortunately rescued. On 21 November 17 and 47 Squadrons raided a divisional head-quarters at Vesnik.

Also on the 21 November, the highest-scoring German Ace on the front, Oberleutnant von Eschwege, was killed when attacking a booby-trapped British observation balloon, and in the local tradition a message was dropped over enemy lines informing them of the pilot's death; the next day the Germans dropped a wreath and flag for placing on his last resting place. Honour was served and now the gentlemen could get back to the task in hand of trying to kill the other side's young gentlemen.

As the year drew to a close there were frequent night raids by both camps and on the night of 28 November four 47 Squadron airmen (Air Mechanics Second Class T. Black, W. Goodman, and J. Thorne and Air Mechanic First Class F.T. Rotsey) were wounded in an attack on the aerodrome at Janes. The same day Lieutenants B.R. Apps and A.S. Clark, flying on a photo-reconnaissance sortie were attacked by two enemy scouts, one of which they claimed shot down. In the afternoon two 47 Squadron aeroplanes – Second Lieutenant J.C. Nelson and Lieutenant A.J. Pick in an FK3 and Second Lieutenant Henwood in a BE12 – flew over the area with the intention of recording the destroyed aeroplane; they were in turn attacked, but were able to shoot down one of the enemy machines, which was seen to crash near Bogdanci, the wreck being photographed later.

Air-to-air combat continued, with a number of inconclusive engagements. Captain R.M. Wynne Eaton and Second Lieutenant W.D. Robertson were wounded on 30 November during a running fight with an enemy aircraft. Second Lieutenant F.D. Travers obtained probably the last BE12 victory while flying A4046 on 19 December. The aeroplane was fitted with three machine guns, one synchronised and two on a mounting on top of the wing to fire outside the propeller arc. His victim was an Albatros DIII, last seen out of control over Lake Doiran. Despite the atrocious weather in December, the squadron carried out sorties whenever required, if at all possible, earning the appreciation of the Royal Artillery Corps commander.

The new year started as the old one finished and the squadron suffered its first loss on 3 January when a FK3 (6206) fitted with an RAF 4a engine, and part of a three-aeroplane formation tasked with photographic reconnaissance, was shot down over Lake Doiran; the crew of Second Lieutenant H.A. Tracey and Lieutenant A. Rowan were captured, and after interrogation and loss of watches, they were sent to the POW camp at Philippopolis.

Far away, preparations were being made for the German cruisers SMS *Goeben* and SMS *Breslau* to break out from Turkish waters into the Dardanelles and then into the Aegean, the aim of the sortie to cause as much damage as possible, before returning to the safety of Constantinople. The ships had been bottled up in the Black Sea since sailing from the Mediterranean at the start of war. They were ostensibly flying under Turkish flags, having being transferred to the Turkish government by Germany, but were still German crewed. Also an opportunity to escape was spotted, as the Russian Black Fleet in the area was not seen as a threat, being riven by revolution and lack of coal. The ships had to navigate their way through the extensive minefields, which had been laid by both sides in the narrow channel, but successfully broke out of the Dardanelles and past the naval defences. However, they were attacked by aeroplanes of the RNAS, although ineffectively, but in their manoeuvring to get better positions, *Breslau* struck a succession of mines and sunk. *Goeben*'s progress had also been impaired by hitting mines and it was decided to abandon the sortie.

As luck would have it, the *Goeben* ran aground in the narrow waters on the afternoon of 20 January and was now a sitting duck. Nos 17 and 47 Squadrons quickly sent reinforcements to the RNAS; the first three 47 Squadron BE12s (Captain W.R.B. McBain and Second Lieutenants P.A. Boss and J.A. Beeney) arrived on 22 January, with three more BE12s (Second Lieutenants Henwood and Dickson and Sergeant Spargo) and one FK3 (Sergeant Dowsett) leaving on the 25th. Dowsett got lost and Spargo forced-landed at Iviron on the Athos peninsula, where he was rescued by monks from a monastery and stayed for a few days in their care until he and the aeroplane could be recovered. Over the next few days many attacks were made on the stranded cruiser, by the RNAS and RFC machines, but without any significant damage being inflicted. Despite 270 sorties and 15 tons of bombs dropped, all the aeroplanes achieved were to provide a bounty of fish for the ship's crew! The bombs available, either 65lb or 112lb, were ineffective against the armoured cruiser and the *Goeben* was towed off and returned to Constantinople under her own steam.

On 29 January Lieutenant Marshall Meredith Wilson was reported killed and Second Lieutenant J.S. Jones wounded when FK3 A1469 crashed; however, it is not believed that this was due to enemy action.

February brought heavy snow, and on the night of the 16th/17th a hangar collapsed under the weight of the snow at Hadzi-Junus. According to H.A. Jones, this resulted in the destruction of two BE12s and a Vickers Bullet (although serials are unknown, and all four Vickers Bullets appear to be on squadron strength later in the year) and damage to another Bullet, an SE5a and one of the Bristol M1C monoplanes, which had only just been added to the unit's tally.

Lieutenant Malcolm MacEwan joined the squadron as an observer in mid-February 1918, and it is very fortunate for posterity that he left behind many mementos of his service with it. He was also with 47 Squadron in Russia in 1919. Born in Scotland in 1894 he served with the artillery until transferring to the RFC. Post-war he trained as a doctor and joined the Territorial Army. During the Second World War he was evacuated from Dunkirk, later joining the paras as CO of 16th Parachute Field Ambulance, RAMC. MacEwan did his first parachute drop at the age of forty-seven and took part in operations in Tunisia, and landed in a glider on D-Day. He finished his service as a colonel, having been awarded the DSO and bar, OBE, DFC and TD – a remarkable military career. During his time with 47 Squadron in Salonika he flew some 120 sorties, carrying out the full range of squadron tasks.

In March there was a change to the squadron OC when Major G.D. Gardner replaced

Armstrong Whitworth FK8 (C8485) at SVETA VRAE, October 1918. *FAA*

Major Minchin. It is curious that Jones, who was serving on the squadron under Minchin, fails to mention the man except to record his arrival and departure. It seems very unlikely that a man of Minchin's character would have remained unnoticed to Jones. The parts of the squadron diary that still exists, records Minchin as having taken part in a number of sorties and tested many of the new types of aeroplane that were sent out to the squadron. Maybe they had a personal tiff and it was Jones's way of getting his own back. After the war Minchin left the RAF to take up various positions in the civil flying world and the development of passenger transport. Sadly he and his fellow crew members went missing during an attempted east to west trans-atlantic flight in August 1927, flying a Fokker VIIA monoplane.

The air wing in Salonika was to undergo an important reorganisation in April 1918, with the formation of the Royal Air Force combining the RFC and RNAS into one all encompassing air arm, but more immediately locally was the formation of 150 Squadron as the area's fighter squadron. This meant that the two existing squadrons could concentrate on the task they had originally been formed to carry out, that of corps squadrons. A Flights of 17 and 47 Squadrons became A and B Flights of 150 Squadron respectively under the command of a 47 Squadron old boy, Captain, now promoted to Major, W.R.B. McBain. C Flight would be formed in May. Many long-standing members of 47 Squadron were posted to the new 150 Squadron, but as a specialist fighting squadron 150 Squadron could concentrate on the task in hand, and by the end of the war they had accounted for nearly forty enemy machines, for the loss of only one of their own behind enemy lines.

With the coming of spring the squadron received a new aircraft, the Armstrong Whitworth FK8, known as the Big Ack to distinguish it from the FK3 Little Ack. The FK8 was, as the nickname implies, a significantly larger aeroplane than the FK3 and was a purpose-built two-seat reconnaissance bomber capable of carrying both an observer and a useful bomb load a reasonable distance. It was also fitted with a forward-firing synchronised machine gun and one or sometimes two 0.303 Lewis guns on a Scarff mounting in the observer's cockpit. It had first entered front-line service

DH9 pilot Lieutenant Page, Obs Lieutenant MacEwan, mid 1918.
MacEwan via author

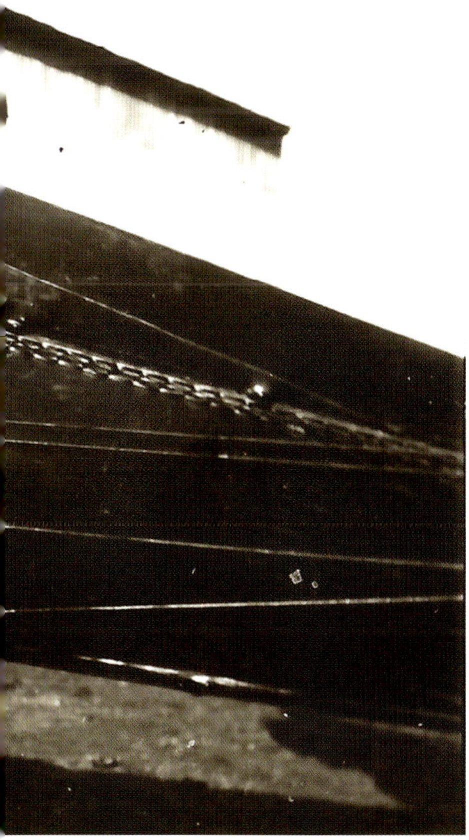

in France in early 1917 and proved to be effective, sturdy and dependable,[6] and popular with its crews. It arrived on 47 Squadron's books in March 1918 and was finally let go in January 1919. Approximately thirteen different aeroplanes were on the squadron's strength at some time, and two were lost, with their crews, to enemy action.

Into the summer the squadron carried on in its role, but now bombing raids tended to be much bigger efforts involving aeroplanes for all three RAF squadrons, usually 17 and 47 Squadrons providing six bombers each and an escort coming from 150 Squadron. Targets remained the same: supply dumps, camps, headquarters and the aerodrome at Hudova. But it was during an artillery shoot observation on 24 June that the squadron lost its first FK8. The aeroplane (C3589), operating on its own over Trapeze De Pobreg and being crewed by Lieutenants D.L. Graham and A.G. Kane, was hit by AA fire and crashed in flames. Both men are buried in Karasouli military cemetery, Greece. Captain C.H. Taylor, carrying out a photo-reconnaissance sortie on 26 July over the Vardar Valley, was also hit by AA fire and wounded, but able to return to the aerodrome. Major Gardner had been invalided back to the UK and on 1 August Major F.A. Bates, MC, took over command.

Major Bates would be responsible for making sure that the squadron was at full preparedness for the tasks to come. It was becoming obvious that by the summer, morale in the Bulgarian army was beginning to falter. On the Western Front the great German offensive of the spring was grinding to a halt, having singularly failed to achieve any of its strategic aims. At home in Bulgaria, as in Germany, the impact of the Allied blockade was giving rise to mumblings of unrest, and parts of the Army were bordering on mutiny.

At the start of June a new Allied commander was appointed – General Franchet d'Espèrey – and he immediately started planning for a major Allied offensive in September in that window of opportunity after the heat of summer and before the rains of autumn.

No. 47 Squadron was also being reorganised, with the re-formation of A Flight under Captain J.R. Milne; it was to be equipped with a new aeroplane, the DH9. The DH9 did not enjoy a good reputation. It was designed as a two-seat day bomber capable of carrying up to 460lb of bombs at around 100mph with an endurance of 4½ hours. It was promised to be an advance over the DH4, but all did not go well and although it saw widespread service and equipped nearly thirty RFC/RAF squadrons, it was not a happy time and in the end production of the DH4 had to be restarted until the DH9A was available, an aeroplane that became a huge success and continued to operate in the RAF for many years. It was a bit like the Avro Manchester to Lancaster story, without having to double the number of engines! And it was the engine that was the problem in the DH9. It was horribly unreliable and suffered from production problems, and did not produce the power promised; thus it was no better than the DH4, an aircraft that was popular with its crews. In front-line service, more DH9s were lost due to accidents and engine failures than enemy action.[7] A Flight was tasked with long-range reconnaissance in support of the Army and during September it flew over 300 hours of sorties, without loss, in contradiction to its reputation elsewhere.

B Flight during August carried out a detailed photo-reconnaissance of areas behind the enemy front lines and created a photographic mosaic map covering nearly 350 square miles of enemy territory between the Vardar and Beles mountains. It also took oblique photos of the Bulgarian front line, all of which was invaluable for planning the imminent attack.

In late August, while carrying out a shoot, the FK8 flown by Lieutenant E.V. Brown with Lieutenant MacEwan as observer was attacked by two enemy machines that dived in turn on the British aeroplane. MacEwan was able to drive them off, one of which was seen to fall away, damaged; the crew then calmly carried on with the shoot.

On 2 September two DH9s pilots – Captain Edwards and Lieutenant Morton with observer Lieutenant MacEwan and an unnamed observer respectively – were carrying out a reconnaissance over Hudova when they were attacked by five enemy scouts. During the ensuing melee one of the enemy machines was seen to go down out of control and fall to pieces in the air. The other scouts were driven off and both DH9s returned safely.

C Flight concentrated on artillery cooperation work, counter-battery shoots and other activities in preparation for the major offensive, which opened on the British right on 14 September. The British troops went into the attack on the morning of the 18th, at 05.08 hours, over much of the ground that had defeated them the year before. The four days beforehand, the Bulgarian front line had been subject to an intensive bombardment, planned using the information that 47 Squadron had supplied. Even so, the advance was going to be challenging, with disease and influenza having reduced some units to half their full strength. The Bulgarians had also had another year to strengthen their defences, with more concrete machine-gun emplacements.

The order for the attack to start was '508 bottles of beer will be sent to you'. The first assaults on 'P' Ridge were thrown back with heavy casualties, and units on their flanks were also forced to withdraw. The next day the battle was resumed and some ground taken, but at a heavy cost in men, killed, wounded and missing. However, the Bulgarians were being pinned down and the advances made by French and Serbian troops to the west forced the Bulgarians to retreat or be cut off. During the attack 47 Squadron was flying numerous sorties, sometimes crews flying three operations a day, carrying out contact patrols and providing close support to the infantry as well as the usual artillery work. A Flight was employed in bombing, machine-gunning and reconnaissance behind the lines. B Flight was undertaking the contact patrols, dropping messages to the advancing infantry, sometimes from below 400 feet. Inevitably from this height the aeroplanes were vulnerable to ground fire and on 18 September the aircraft being flown by Second Lieutenant H.J. Gerhadi with Lieutenant J.A. Brandt as observer was lost, both men being killed. H.A. Jones states that the aeroplane (FK8 C3590) was shot down by ground fire, as do the casualty records held at the National Archives.[8] However, an FK8 was also claimed by Leutnant F. Thiede[9] of Ja38 the next day, which does not match any other loss and may refer to the 47 Squadron machine. The bodies of the two men were recovered from the battlefield and they are buried in Doiran military cemetery.

On 19 September two volunteer pilots were requested, one from 17 Squadron and one from 47 Squadron, to carry out a spy dropping mission behind enemy lines. Lieutenant J. Boyd was the 47 Squadron pilot and he took off in a BE2e from Janes that afternoon with his passenger Lieutenant Lamb from the Royal Scots Fusiliers, and landed north of Strumica. After making sure the officer was well away, Boyd took off again, rejoined his escort and flew back to Janes. The 17 Squadron pilot, Lieutenant Buchanan, was less fortunate. After landing he came under fire from some German soldiers who had seen him come down, and although he was able to get airborne again he finally crashed into a riverbed and was captured, joining the other RAF officers held at Philippopolis.

Back at the front it was obvious by the 21st that the Bulgarians were in full retreat. That day two DH9s of 47 Squadron – flown by Captain J.R. Milne (6236) and Lieutenant A.V. Morton (6217), with Lieutenant J.C.F. Holland and Lieutenant M. MacEwan as observers – took off at 08.30 hours and on landing at 12.00 reported the hangars at Hudova had been removed from the aerodrome, and the supply dump at Demirkapu abandoned. Other dumps were on fire, hospitals dismantled and large numbers of troops were seen moving away from the front line. The next week was one of constant bombing and strafing of the retreating army, which had no air cover or organised AA defences. The soldiers were caught in narrow valleys and passes, which soon became blocked with destroyed transport, dead and dying men and horses. The Kosturino pass – the only escape route available after the collapse of the Vardar line – became a place of untold destruction. In one morning twenty-five aeroplanes from both 17 and 47 Squadrons dropped over 5,000lb of bombs on the pass and then expended all their machine-gun ammunition, flew back to their aerodromes, refuelled, rearmed and attacked again in the afternoon.

As the remnants of the Bulgarian army continued their flight north, those lucky enough to escape the Kosturino pass were caught instead in the Kresna pass, where they had to go through the hell again. On 28 September 47 Squadron logged 57 hours' flying time in sorties to bomb and machine gun the pass and nearby Gjujsevo. The Bulgarian government was desperate to sue for an armistice and an end to the slaughter, and this was finally agreed and came into force in the early hours of 30 September 1918. Sadly, this did not mark the end of the squadron's casualties: Air Mechanic Second Class G. Arden died of his wounds on 4 October, the last of 47 Squadron's thirty wartime deaths. He is buried at Mikra British cemetery at Kalamaria, Greece.

With the imminent coming of peace, 47 Squadron quickly changed roles, setting up a communications and courier service with the DH9s of A Flight to Sofia until road and rail links could be restored some weeks later. However, for the moment there was still a war on, and two FK8s of the squadron with two fighters from 150 Squadron were detached to Gumuldzina to commence operations over Turkey, flying a few reconnaissance sorties until Turkey's surrender on 30 October.

The squadron continued in its communications role during the winter, but it was slowly being run down as men who had been overseas for two years were being returned to the UK for demobilisation. All the aeroplanes, with the exception of the DH9s, were disposed of and in consequence the hours flown declined to a very low level, most crews getting in no more than a couple of hours a month.

Chapter 3

NOW WE ARE HERE

Russia, 1919

On 6 May 1955, Air Vice Marshal Ray Collishaw, CB, DSO and bar, OBE, DSC, DFC, and 47 Squadron OC in 1919–20, wrote a letter from his home in Canada to Squadron Leader D.P. Boulnois, the then OC of 47 Squadron based at Abingdon, describing the squadron's role in south Russia in 1919–20.[10]

Thank you for the copy of Flight commemorating the presentation of 47 Squadron's standard. I thought you might like to know more of the history of 47 Squadron while stationed in South Russia in 1919–20. It was sent from Salonika to South Russia after the war manned by men anxious to be demobilised. Consequently, there was a deplorable reaction and the CAS commissioned me to find fresh personnel to relieve those in Russia. No men could be spared by the RAF and so I sent a personnel letter couched in an adventurous spirit addressed to thousands of demobilised airmen for duty as volunteers and for service exclusively in Russia. The records are inaccurate in one respect: for 47 Squadron moved to Russia with its proper name and remained so until the autumn of 1919 when, as a consequence of political expediency in reaction to criticism in the House, that Britain was taking sides in a foreign civil war, 47 Squadron was renamed 'A' Squadron and an announcement was made in the House that no unit of the RAF was involved and that all those concerned were volunteers.

The history of 47 Squadron in South Russia was unique in many ways as the following summary will indicate:

All the officers and men were personally recruited and conveyed by me to South Russia. They were recruited exclusively for duty in Russia.

a. The flights were not ordinary flights; rather they were flexible formations, the strength of the flight depended on the number of aircraft available, and flights had as many as 50 aircraft, we possessed the aircraft pool war reserve from the Middle East Command. One flight had DH9s one DH9As and one Camel.

c. 47 Squadron provided the sole air co-operation for one million soldiers organised into three armies; because flights were operating 500 miles apart the personnel never saw one another throughout the campaign.

d. The war was confined exclusively to cavalry operations and the fighting extended over an area covering some 2,000 miles. The so-called front was constantly in a state of flux and it frequently advanced or withdrew 50 miles in one day. The flights consequently were accommodated in trains and the operating technique consisted of selecting suitable terrain and then using a railway siding for the RAF train. Squadron work-shops and the base on the Black Sea were nearly 1,000 miles distant

e. 47 Squadron in South Russia achieved historically the following air firsts:

> **a. Put the writing on the wall by sinking 19 out of 23 armed ships which were investing Tsratisna[sic] (later Stalingrad) we used 500 lb light case bombs and employed the near miss technique.**

b. 47 Squadron killed cavalry as a military weapon. We proved beyond doubt that cavalry was out (it was still 'in' then in the British Army). The white army was not defeated in the field but it collapsed because it's rear turned 'Red'.

c. 47 Squadron was the only unit to fight a war without the inspiration of the RAF ensign, we possessed our own flag.

d. 47 Squadron was the only unit to conduct a campaign in the total absence of whisky, but not without Vodka.

f. Due to the home front collapse in our rear and the active hostility of erstwhile supporters the 47 Squadron trains had to fight their way for nearly 1,000 miles back to the Black sea. These trains were handicapped by hundreds of women and children: the dependents of 'White' officers: who swarmed to the English for succour. Hostile armoured trains tried to intervene but were checked by upheaving the tracks behind the trains.

g. Finally 47 Squadron trains entered the Crimea while the 'White' armies withdrew eastward. The military situation in the Crimea was desperate as there were no 'White' troops there. Consequently General Denikin appointed me as temporary governor. Thus on the one hand I tried to organise the Crimea defences and on the other, to keep civilian order. It was some weeks before detachments of the 'White' army arrived in the Crimea.

h. In the spring of 1920 further pressure was placed on the Government in the House to abandon any kind of intervention in the foreign civil war and consequently 47 (or 'A' Squadron) was recalled. Thus we escaped involvement in the final collapse of the Whites in the Crimea.

It may be of interest to recollect that general Denikin's 'White' army had conquered from the Bolsheviks an area of South Russia some 2,000 miles by 1,000 miles. On all sides there was great enthusiasm for the cause of ousting the reds and of the restoration of a conservative government. Alas! There was too much over confidence and reactionary tendencies. The former landowners in Denikin's army pressed him to publicly announce that the replacement regime would restore private property to its rightful owners. General Denikin's momentous pronouncement produced immediate and frightful consequences. In a week, what had been a glorious advance, became a fearful collapse. The home front turned 'Red' and the campaign tottered into disaster.

Yours sincerely
R. Collishaw

P.S. Another first for 47 was air operations with water cooled engines minus anti-freeze at 40 below zero. We did this by padding the radiators and by starting the engines minus oil and water. The latter were added after starting.

Collishaw was born in British Columbia in 1893. On the outbreak of the First World War his first choice had been to join the Royal Navy as he had been working on ships since the age of fifteen, but as he did not get a response for some time, and hearing that the Royal Naval Air Service was looking for volunteers, applied to them instead. He qualified as a pilot in January 1916 and in August was posted to France to join 3 Wing operating Sopwith 1½ Strutters, some as bombers and some as two-seat escort fighters. Collishaw soon opened his score shooting down a German Fokker in October 1916. Over the next two years he claimed a total of sixty victories to become the highest-scoring RNAS pilot. In January 1918 Collishaw took command of 3 Naval Squadron, RNAS, which became No. 203 Squadron on the formation of the RAF.

The context to the political and military situation in Russia when the squadron was dispatched to Novorossiysk, Russia's principal port on the Black Sea in April 1919, is worth some examination. The background to the Russian Revolution and the subsequent break-up of the country into many different factions – some of whom although sharing the same aims were bitterly opposed to each other on ideological grounds – is horribly complicated and thus this is very much a superficial review. The whole thing was not helped by the fact that the Russians were using a different calendar to the rest of Europe until 1 February 1918 when they adopted the New Style (NS) Gregorian calendar, the next day becoming 19 February (NS).

At the beginning of the twentieth century, despite some reforms and the emancipation of the serfs, there was still a large degree of dissatisfaction with the position of tsar as, effectively, an absolute ruler. The government could do nothing without his consent and comprised men that he had appointed; there were no ministers elected by the people. This impatience with the course of reform came to a head in early 1905 and combined the demands of the peasants, factory workers, young educated middle classes and the military. It had started with increased unrest in the factories, which led to a strike in St Petersburg that brought the city to a standstill. When the people marched to the Winter Palace in January 1905 to petition the tsar, the Imperial Guard opened fire and various reports estimated between 200 and 1,000 civilians were killed or injured. Unrest soon spread and in the military the reverses in the Russo-Japanese war and the humiliating defeat of the Imperial Russian Navy expressed itself in mutinies (such as the famous Battleship Potemkin incident in June 1905) and desertion.

The 1905 revolution failed to overthrow the tsar, as the military on the whole remained loyal, and some concessions were made by the tsar with the creation of the Duma, an elected Russian parliament, although this was to have consultative powers only, and did little to calm the situation. Further concessions had to be made, which finally caused the revolution to die out during 1906, but it was only papering over the cracks and over the following years revolutionary discontent continued to fester, expressed in murder and assassination of prominent people and government officials and the execution or internal exile, usually to Siberia, for the revolutionaries.

DH9s, South Russia, 1919.
Author's collection

The start of the First World War went some way in taking people's minds off their dissatisfaction, for the duration at least. An initial poor start was followed by some success in Galicia, where they were able to push the Austrians back, but German reinforcements stabilised the line over the first winter. In 1915 the Russian army were forced into a general retreat, which led to the loss of Russian Poland. The deficiencies in Russian equipment, especially artillery and communications, as well as incompetent leadership, seriously undermined the morale of the army and even the successful Russian offensive back into Galicia in June 1916, did nothing to alleviate the disquiet at home. On 8 March 1917, a shortage of food and fuel led to riots in St Petersburg; on the 12th the soldiers joined with the people. The mob seized the arsenal, distributed weapons, opened the prisons, and invaded the Winter Palace. Three days later, Tsar Nicholas II abdicated and the Provisional Government under Georgy Lvov took temporary control of Russia. In April 1917, Lenin, returned to the country, after being allowed free passage through Germany, accompanied by other exiles, and Trotsky arrived back shortly afterwards. After centuries of autocratic rule, Russia was to undergo a dramatic change, eventually forming a communist government, something the world had never seen before. On the front, the army was largely paralysed and ineffective. Kerensky the Minister of War tried to persuade the army to remain loyal and hold their positions. The war had cost the Russians over 2½ million military dead, 3,749,000 wounded and nearly 3½ million POWs.

Lenin believed that the overthrowing of the tsar would be followed by a provisional revolutionary democratic dictatorship of the proletariat and the peasant, but to his dismay this did not happen, and the Bolsheviks had failed to gain the Petrograd Soviet city

council. Thus Lenin created a national programme that aimed to exploit country-wide difficulties within Russia and the disenchantment with the war, to bring about further revolution. A long-drawn-out social crisis had created the right atmosphere for the Bolsheviks to take control.

Kerensky had succeeded Lvov as leader of the Provisional Government in July 1917 and continued to try and keep its undertakings to the Western powers and keep fighting, but the remains of the Imperial Army started to collapse and units began to fade away from the front line. The October Revolution brought Kerensky's downfall and the Bolsheviks to power on 28 October 1917, when the second All-Russia Congress of Soviets assumed authority. A coalition government, consisting mainly of Left Socialist-Revolutionaries and Bolshevik leaders, had been created; however, Lenin wanted absolute power, and many of his policies were aimed at achieving this, in particular the signing of the Brest-Litovsk peace treaty with Germany in March 1918. This treaty ended Russian participation in the First World War in return for surrendering to Germany 1.3 million square miles and 62 million people, a third of the Russian population. This not only pushed out the remaining Socialist-Revolutionaries within the coalition, who were disgusted over the terms of the treaty, but it also influenced the Allies to do something. The ending of the war on the Eastern Front allowed the Germans to move large numbers of men and equipment to the west and from the Allies' point of view another major concern was the vast stores of arms and equipment held in northern Russia around Murmansk and Archangel. These had been delivered to Russia in the hope of keeping them in the war, but now the priority was to keep them out of the hands of, firstly, the Germans, and then the Bolsheviks. Initially there were not the troops to spare to send to north Russia and it was not until June 1918 that Allied troops could be released.

In the meantime, while the war on the Western Front reached its climax after the failed German offensive in March 1918, there was little the Allies could do about the rise of the Bolsheviks. In Russia itself a civil war had broken out between the Bolsheviks, as they tried to cement their authority, and a disparate grouping of opposition and counter-revolutionary forces, usually lumped together under the heading of the Whites, although this should not be taken to mean they had any sort of centralised leadership or aims. Some groups were looking to gain independence and succeed from Russia, others wanted the return of the old order and the tsar back on the throne. To add to the colourful nature of the participants in the conflict, there was the Green Army fighting in Ukraine and the anarchist Black Army who fought against both the Reds and Whites at different points in the war.

This war would last until 1926, although most of fighting took place between 1918 and 1920, and it cost the lives of up to thirteen million Russians, most from starvation or diseases brought about by the fighting rather than direct military action.

The Russian Civil War can be divided into a number of phases. The initial one lasted from October 1917 to autumn 1918. During this time, the Red Army defeated any forces loyal to Kerensky and the Provisional Government, and used the railways to rapidly spread control. During this 'railway war', trainloads of revolutionaries travelled great distances to root out any centres of opposition. Lenin's new army was made up of the Red Guards formed by factory workers, but it soon became apparent that revolutionary fervour, and the conscription, sometimes under threat, of the rural peasantry, was no substitute for military training, and soon former Imperial officers were being re-employed, but with a party commissar at their side to ensure the Bolshevik ethos was being enforced.

The second phase – and the one that the Western Allies and 47 Squadron had the biggest role to play in – took place from January to November of 1919, when three armies, led by Admiral Kolchak from Siberia in the east, General Yudenich in the north-west and General Denikin from the south, forced the Red Army back and threatened Moscow. This was to be the high point of the Whites' campaign; however, they were unable to support and exploit their advances. Also, for some of their Russian 'allies', they had got what they wanted and simply went home. Red Army counter-attacks turned the tide and they were never to see such success again.

Although Denikin was shown to be the most able of the White Army generals, and despite the assistance given to his forces by Britain, Denikin could not prevail against the military skill of Trotsky and the enthusiasm of the Red Army. He was unable to maintain the advantage that the British and the RAF had helped him gain, and in April 1920 he resigned, handing over military leadership to Baron Pyotr Wrangel.

The final phase saw the last of the White Army holed up in the Crimea under General Wrangel. Of the other White military leaders, Admiral Kolchak had been betrayed to the Reds and shot in February 1920 and Generals Yudenich and Denikin were starting long exiles in France. By late 1920, the Whites' position was untenable and Wrangel organised their evacuation, giving them a stark choice of exile or making their own peace with the communists. The final elements left the Crimea in mid-November and, for the most part, organised large-scale armed resistance in Russia was over.

The West did not want communism to spread; they took Lenin's repeated threats that the Russians would instigate and aid revolution wherever they could in Europe and the wider world very seriously. The Bolshevik revolution had already given impetus to radical movements in most European countries, and disturbances had by now occurred, with uprisings in Germany and instability in other parts of the continent, making the British fears of its unstoppable spread seem justifiable. In addition, the British felt that by defeating the communists, south Russia could form a buffer state, friendly to the UK, and secure the oil fields by the Caspian Sea. General Greenly reported in January 1919:

The need for co-ordination of British Political and Military representation in our zone – in the Caucasus and Cossack territories – is very urgent. The principal aim of the Volunteer Army [the Volunteer Army was the name given to the White forces under General Denikin in south Russia at the time] is to reform a united Russia while separation is the object of the Transcaucasian Republics. To cope with this and prevent local feelings from wrecking the movement of reconstruction it is necessary to leave a British High Commissioner with representation in the Kuban, on the Don, in the Crimea and in Transcaucasia. There are so many economic interests in all these regions that he should have strong consular staffs.[11]

The report stressed the importance of the region as worth preserving, as friendly territory and the potential economic gains to be made. It goes on to point out the advantages of securing the route to India and making sure that Britain was first in before other countries, such as France or Poland, recognised the area's importance. In addition, some British leaders even felt that they had a moral obligation to those Russians who had remained faithful to the Allies during the war.

The British government decided to give military support to General Denikin and the White Army against the Bolsheviks in late 1918. The idea for supporting Denikin stemmed largely from proposals submitted to the War Cabinet by the chief of the Imperial General Staff, General Sir Henry Wilson, in November 1918 when he gave the British government three options: remove all British forces from Russia and establish a protective barrier around Russia and let the civil war run its own course; sanction full military involvement to destroy the Bolsheviks and help establish a regime in Russia that would be friendly to the British; or provide material support to the Bolshevik opposition forces. He had pointed out the importance of south Russia for the British and how supporting the White Army could benefit Britain now the Black Sea access routes were open. The first two options were dismissed as being militarily, politically and financially impractical, and therefore it was proposed to provide material support to the anti-Bolshevik forces.

Britain already had forces in north Russia, but these were struggling to link up with large local forces. In the south there was also a small British presence, with the bulk of the White Russian armies who appeared to be making significant gains against the Bolsheviks, and had secured a well-equipped port on the Black Sea at Novorossiysk, which could be used as a landing point for British-supplied equipment and training missions.

The British operation was to be under the command of Major General Herbert Holman, with an RAF training mission at Taganrog, led by Lieutenant Colonel A.C. 'Sissy' Maund. Maund was born in England, but found himself in Canada at the outbreak of the First World War and immediately enlisted as a private in the Canadian army. He transferred to the RFC in March 1916 and had been posted to north Russia in 1918 before joining the training mission in 1919.

The training mission was tasked with providing RE8s for a flying school for Russian pilots and observers, but as will be seen this had hit serious problems and Colonel Maund requested the deployment of an operational RAF squadron to step into the breach. The overt support offered by the West to the White Army was likely to see it being brought into direct conflict with the Bolsheviks. 47 Squadron – with its long and successful period in the Balkans, experience with army cooperation, reconnaissance and bombing roles – and, due to this area being closest to south Russia, seemed the obvious choice to transfer to south Russia, and on 16 April 1919, personnel of one flight left Salonika for Novorossiysk.[12]

It is clear that foreign intervention had a significant effect on the course of the war. Without help from countries such as Britain and France, the superiority of leadership, weaponry and manpower on behalf of the Reds would have overwhelmed the less cohesive Whites much sooner. This foreign intervention gave the counter-revolutionaries the boost they needed. The White Army commanders, desperately needed Allied support.

At the end of the First World War, 47 Squadron remained in Salonika carrying out communications and survey work while slowly losing air and ground crews as they were demobbed from the RAF. It also ceased to operate the FK8. On 14 February 1919, the squadron moved from its main wartime station of Janes[13] to their new airfield at Amberkoj, some 15 miles south and close to the coast and port.

Stuck in this rather remote part of Europe away from any influence or opportunities back home, it was not in the best of states, and morale was at rather a low ebb when it was called up for a new conflict in 1919. The squadron was under the temporary command of Captain F.W. Hudson; its previous commanding officer, Major F.A. Bates, had been sent to the UK in January 1919.[14] It was as H.A. Jones records: 'At the end of February, the No. 47 were at Amberkoj, sitting, Micawber-like, waiting for something to turn up.'[15]

In April 1919 its wait was ended and orders were received to proceed to southern Russia in support of the White Russian forces under General Denikin,[16] and on 16 April, the first group of eleven officers left for Novorossiysk under the command of Captain H.G. Davis. A second group of five officers who had been transferred from 17 Squadron left on the 20th, with another five from 47 Squadron, led by Captain Hudson, following on the 29th. On 24 April the SS *Warpointer* left Greece with aeroplanes, stores and transport.[17]

47 Squadron was not the only British air unit in south Russia.No.221 Squadron, which had been part of the Royal Naval Air Service in the Aegean during the First World War, flew limited reconnaissance and bombing sorties from Petrovsk in the summer of 1919.[18] Initially, 47 Squadron was totally separate from the RAF training mission. It was tasked with providing direct air support to the White Russian forces and did not have a training role. However, at the very end of the

campaign it did rely on the training mission for support and eventual evacuation.

The RAF training mission provided some 130 RE8 light bombers for the White Russian air force and RAF officers to train them to operate the machines. The RE8 was not popular with the Russian aircrew and often refused to fly them.[19] The RE8, commonly known in the RFC/RAF as the 'Harry Tate', was a two-seat light bomber and reconnaissance aeroplane. It was widely regarded as difficult to fly, and gained a reputation in the Royal Flying Corps for being 'unsafe', which was never entirely dispelled. Although eventually it gave reasonably satisfactory service, it was never an outstanding combat aircraft. The Russians were aware of its reputation and this was not helped by the fact that of the first five RAF instructors to join the training mission, three had not flown for some time and the other two were float-plane pilots. Only one of them had flown the RE8 before and he refused to fly it again. It was not a situation that was likely to inspire confidence in the Russians, whose quality and determination also left something to be desired, and many were pronounced not fit to fly or too undisciplined.[20]

The British also supplied large quantities of arms and equipment for the White forces, including six Mk 5 heavy tanks and six Whippet medium tanks. The British military mission reached 356 officers and 1,102 other ranks,[21] and by 31 December 1919 it had delivered 2,317 tons of guns, 35,540 tons of ammunition and 26,414 tons of ordnance stores.[22] However, General Holman despaired of the Russian supply service, which was highly corrupt and hugely inefficient, with vast amounts of stores going missing, never arriving at the front or simply not being recorded. Douglas MacKinnon, who joined 47 Squadron in July 1919 as an equipment officer after making the journey on his own from England, fortunately left us with a vivid recollection of his time in various letters to 47 Squadron during the 1980s and an unpublished manuscript in the squadron archives. In this he recalls details such as the favoured clothing for the Novorossiysk prostitutes was an adapted Army nurse's

This most interesting group of the officers of No. 47 Squadron, in South Russia, was sent to us by Mr. G. E. Hughes. Front row (left to right).—Doctor Murphy, "Seedy" Broughall, S. M. Kinkead, an unknown Russian, Walter Anderson (recently killed in Surrey), and Doctor Flood. Back row.—Flight-Lieut. Smith, Jock Mitchell, Tommy Thompson (or Thomson), "Gus" Edwards (Canadian), "Sport" Merton, and a Russian interpreter. Photo taken at Ekaterinodar, S. Russia.

uniform. This general chaotic state of affairs was to have an impact on 47 Squadron's operational capabilities through its time in south Russia.

Operationally, 47 Squadron worked alongside the Russian Volunteer Army (sometimes referred to as the Caucasian Army) commanded by General Baron Pyotr Nikolayevich Wrangel in south Russia. Most of those within 47 Squadron at this point had already been overseas for long periods of time and were due for demobilisation. As a result, many were hoping to go home, and were concerned that this may be delayed further by their posting to Russia. Colonel Maund was aware of this issue and had written: 'Considerable difficulties were experienced, owing to the men being war weary and eager to return home for demobilisation and Russia in its condition was hardly a place for discontented men.' That said, many of the 47 Squadron men who were sent to Russia continued to operate in a highly professional manner and coped with the challenges as best they could.

The squadron was also without a permanent OC, Major Bates having returned to the UK in January, and thus a new appointment was required. Major Raymond Collishaw had returned to England from Canada early in 1919 and was planning an attempt at flying the Atlantic. However, all these preparations were put on hold when he was made 47 Squadron's new OC. He was ordered to assemble a replacement unit in London to relieve those in Russia due to be repatriated to the UK, and proceed to the east. Collishaw found a number of volunteer pilots, some of whom had served with him in the RNAS. Many were bored with a peacetime air force and relished the opportunity for new adventures, even if 'one or two pilots managed to mislead me as regards the amount of combat flying they had logged'.[23] Although Collishaw in his letter of 1955 states that all were personally recruited by him, and thus by implication volunteers, this was only partially true. While most of the officers, especially the pilots and observers, came forward of their own volition, many of the other ranks were not given the option and were either 'volunteered' on their behalf or were in south Russia already. Also, the aircrew who carried out the first sorties had come from Salonika and had no choice, albeit almost all returned to the UK soon after Collishaw and his men

47 Squadron members South Russia.
47 Squadron Archives

arrived. Collishaw and his party of 10 officers and 255 other ranks left the UK at the end of May, travelling by train to Brindisi and then by ship, arriving at Novorossiysk on 8 June. Once established the squadron took on a rather naval attitude to squadron life, with rum in the wardroom, airmen referred to as senior ratings, and so on.

47 Squadron had reached Novorossiysk on 24 April 1919 and then moved up to Ekaterinodar, a large aerodrome shared with the Russian Volunteer Air Force, where it first arrived on 4 June, the intervening period being taken up with reassembly of the aeroplanes, sorting out the stores and preparing the first of the squadron trains for the move inland. Ekaterinodar was a major city in south Russia situated on the River Kuban and an important railway junction and industrial base. It was also home to the military college and training schools. Douglas MacKinnon recalls: 'The Tramway system, as all other municipal affairs, were [sic] in a chaotic state: everything, everywhere, shabby and in disrepair. Summer time and the hospitals were crowded … with typhus victims.' The aerodrome was on the outskirts of the city and there were very few facilities, most of the officers and men living under canvas – not too bad in the summer, but when the autumn rains came the whole area soon turned into a mud bath.

The role of the base was to be an area where 47 Squadron could assemble and test aeroplanes and prepare individual flights for detached service when required. Adequate aerodromes within south Russia were practically non-existent; as a result, 47 Squadron and its flights were required to be as mobile and self-sufficient as possible. Trains were set up with quarters, workshops, spares and so on, so that operations could take place where needed in a wide and open country. Doug MacKinnon describes one of the squadron trains:

[Behind the engine] the officer's accommodation consisted of two first-class coaches, a compartment for each officer. These were fairly spacious, offering comfort and, according to the scrounging ability of the occupant, boasted a table, chair and such oddments. Another similar coach formed the day quarters, demolished except for a central partition, thus forming two rooms, one for the wardroom, one for the mess. The feature of the wardroom was the central, almost old baronial style fireplace with large flat mantel on which rested an elegant Russian charcoal fired Samovar with a constant supply of hot water and, alongside, the necessary mugs and a small jar of navy rum as protection from the cold.

Next came another van which had been adapted as a bathroom with pretty good facilities for cloths drying as well as bathing. … Next to the bathroom was a coach for senior ratings and one can imagine they had given thought to their comfort without prompting. Next a coach for other ranks who also knew how to look after them selves. Next came compartments that had been converted into workshops, engine and aircraft maintenance, then a flat car with a couple of valuable lorries. Behind this, vans with spares, then flats with wings, fuselages and all unassembled bits and pieces.

Aeroplanes could fly ahead and find a suitable landing ground close to a railway siding (most of the railways were single track and there were frequent sidings to allow trains to pass), and the squadron could operate from there for a few days before moving on, such was the fluid nature of the campaign and the vast areas that had to be covered. The railways were the most reliable and quickest form of movement in south Russia and both sides relied on them heavily, engagements tending to take place close to the rail heads.

Away from the railways, roads were virtually non-existent and those that could be used were not suitable for movement of large forces. The other strategic communication routes were the rivers, the most important of these were the Volga – which runs nearly 2,300 miles from its source in central Russia to the Caspian Sea – and the Don – which travels 1,200 miles from south of Moscow to the Sea of Azov. In the part of south Russia that 47 Squadron would be working in, the

Volga could be up to a mile wide, and large flotillas of gunboats and barges would operate on them.

The main function for the squadron would be in assisting the White Army in taking the city of Tsaritsyn (renamed Stalingrad in 1925 and Volgagrad in 1961) on the banks of the Volga and the most important city in the region. The Whites under General Krasnov had laid siege to the city in the autumn of 1918 and the Bolsheviks had fallen back towards the river. Reinforcements were requested from Moscow but were denied and in desperation the local chairman of the military committee, a certain Joseph Stalin, recalled – against orders – forces from the Caucasus, who were able to defeat the Whites and push them back, but in June 1919 the White Army had regrouped and been reinforced sufficiently for him to have another go.

On 13 June, Collishaw assumed command of No. 47 Squadron, although it would be some weeks before he was able to get up to Ekaterinodar. At the same time, aircraft and other necessities were arriving in quantity from Britain on the SS *War Foam* and *War Celt*. Over the next few months more aeroplanes reached the area including, it was reported, twenty-one DH9As, although only about fourteen were formally allocated to the squadron in August 1919, and a number of Sopwith Camels and their pilots in September.

For the first six weeks or so in Russia the squadron concentrated on getting men and equipment up from the port to Ekaterinodar, a journey of only about 100 miles, but it could easily take a whole day, or days, depending on the state of the Russian administration and the trains. Once the crated aeroplanes had arrived at the station they had to be transported to the aerodrome where they could be reassembled. This, as will be seen, was not as simple a task as one might expect. Hangars and squadron accommodation had to be erected. While the aeroplanes were being put back together and tested the squadron also had to find and secure the rolling stock and engine to make the train for the flight to operate from. There were plenty of engines available, but many of these were originally oil fired and since the loss of the oil fields at Baku, had limited supplies; many were being converted to coal, which took time and was of variable success.

However, on 10 June the first five DH9s under the command of Captain Davis, comprising C Flight, were sent forward from Ekaterinodar to Velikoknyajaskaya, with the plan to commence operations against the Red Army in Tsaritsyn as soon as possible. But one aeroplane was forced to make a forced-landing in a cornfield due to engine trouble; the crew of Lieutenants E.C. White and J.W. Webb were unhurt and a party was dispatched to recovery them and their machine. This took nearly two days and required some resourceful, persuasive techniques for the squadron equipment officer, Lieutenant Dumas, to achieve. The remaining four aeroplanes now had to wait until the train carrying their ground crews, fuel, supplies and ammunition caught up. The problem was that there was no direct train line from Ekaterinodar towards Tsaritsyn and a long diversion was required before the train was on the right tracks.

Trains were being prepared to go forward, and the job of identifying a suitable landing ground close to a railway became an urgent priority, undertaken by Lieutenants Verity and Thompson. Because of the problems with a damaged bridge, the preferred location at Ramontnaya could not be reached by the train and an alternative rendezvous was chosen close to Gashum, on the Ekaterinodar side of the broken bridge. The train left at 0.400 hours on 11 June and the journey was scheduled to take 12 hours to cover the 55 miles. As noted above, aeroplanes were flown up ahead and the train duly arrived at 18.00 hours. The Russian authorities had promised that the bridge would be repaired the next day, allowing the flight to move forward closer to the front. A message was sent to the Caucasian Army HQ at Kotelnikovo advising that the train would be one of the first across in the morning, but the Army's priorities were food and ration trains.
The next few days saw heavy wind and rain, which delayed the reopening of the bridge and made flying impossible. Further contact with Army HQ elicited a promise that the C Flight train would be over the repaired bridge within two hours of it reopening; however, as the squadron war diary pessimistically states: 'It is impossible to tie the Russian authorities down to anything. They promise everything but rarely carry anything out.'[24] The bridge was not reopened until the afternoon of 15 June, five days after the C Flight train had left Ekaterinodar. It was sixth in line and eventually crossed just after midnight. The train arrived at its final destination of Kotelnikovo, about 70 miles south-west of Tsaritsyn, on 16 June early in the afternoon. Although there was no prepared airfield at the station, there was an area of flat ground close by, but this was dotted with earth humps about 18 inches high; and one of the first DH9s that attempted to land on this surface crashed, breaking its undercarriage, port aileron and tail skid; recovery was not helped by torrential rain that began to fall in the evening. Bad weather continued for the next few days and soon the airfield became waterlogged, but preparations for the first attack continued. A replacement DH9 (F1193) arrived with Lieutenants White and Webb on the 19th. The flight moved further forward on the 20th, arriving at Gniloakaiskaya in the evening, but again an aeroplane was damaged on landing (C6236, flown by Lieutenant G.H. Clavey and Air Mechanic F.J. Smith).

The first sortie with the remaining four serviceable DH9s was attempted on the morning of 22 June, but low cloud forced the aircraft to turn back after only 25 miles. Lieutenant Reynolds crashed on landing, but no harm was reported to the crew. The next day was cloudy with intermittent rain, but the three serviceable DH9s (D2840 with Captain Davis and Lieutenant Mann; F1193 with Lieutenants White and MacEwan; and C6337 with Lieutenants Verity and Thompson) took off at 10.30 hours to bomb Tsaritsyn, loaded with a total of sixteen x 20lb and two x 112lb bombs. They successfully attacked their objective, the south-east railway station, and claimed damage to station buildings, rolling stock and neighbouring houses. After the bomb run the group expended some 1,000 rounds of Small Arms Ammunition (SAA) on barges on the river and nearby cavalry. All the aircraft arrived back safely by 12.10 hours.

Another strike was carried out the following day by the same three DH9s – but with the exception of Captain Davis with different crews – against barges alongside the city's wharf. The flight was now into the swing of things and further raids were executed and included low-level attacks on troop concentrations and road traffic. Serviceability meant that normally only three aeroplanes were available, so often they were flying two sorties a day. No aircraft were damaged and no sign of aerial opposition was encountered. During one attack by three DH9s – piloted by Lieutenants White Verity and Reynolds with observers Lieutenants Thompson MacEwan and Philip – to bomb the stations at Gumrak and Kotlobanski, one 20lb bomb was reported dropped among a group of 200 cavalrymen to (in the words of the squadron war diary) 'good effect'. The intensity of operations continued for the rest of the month. Considering the general state of the aeroplanes – not good, their reputation for reliability very poor, and the primitive conditions the ground crew had to work in – this was a remarkable achievement.

Back at Ekaterinodar, the work on assembling and testing new aeroplanes that arrived

47 Squadron pilots and observers, South Russia, 1919 (Major Collishaw middle row centre).
47 Squadron Archives

almost daily continued apace. Ammunition was procured and stores were built up. Railway carriages were acquired for the B Flight train, but had to be thoroughly disinfected first. The plan called for four trains – one for each flight – and a headquarters train. Two flights would operate DH9s and DH9As and the third Sopwith Camels. On 27 June Lieutenants Verity and Thompson arrived back by air, bringing dispatches for the front, but also alerted the squadron that Lieutenants Watson and Addison, who had left from Ekaterinodar on the 26th, had not arrived at the front. (They finally presented themselves on the 30th, having force-landed, repaired the aeroplane and then made their own way forward.) The same day Colonel Maund appeared to parade all ranks and explain the new conditions of enlistment and pay in the south Russian forces. The diary fails to record if this was good or bad news.

For the men of 47 Squadron in Russia, boredom could be an issue, especially for those serving with the flights out in a railway siding in the middle of the Steppe, a long distance from anything that could even, very broadly, be described as entertainment. Thus one could only fall back on the old staples such as cards or board games. For those back at HQ in Ekaterinodar, the opportunities were much better. The town offered plenty of restaurants, theatres and drinking establishments, varying in quality from the very expensive to downright dangerous. And young men with plenty of roubles in their pocket due to a favourable exchange rate – which, with each revaluation of the currency, got even better – were likely to be on the lookout for a lively establishment where they could meet some interesting new people and imbibe the local alcohol. This could lead to some potentially violent misunderstandings, but in nearly all cases they were diffused by the more sober before coming to blows.

There was also the perennial distraction for the young man a long way from home – the local young ladies. These came in a number of varieties: those who operated on a purely commercial basis; the dispossessed wealthy, often desperate to find any way of getting some security and a chance to escape the Bolsheviks; and just the locals who had no specific agenda. Some tales of these are related in Marion Aten's book, *Last Train Over Rostov Bridge*, but they might have been livened up a bit to make a 'better' story. It is interesting to note that when examining the medical records of the British Training Mission as a whole, of the 736 British service personnel admitted to hospital, 36% were VD cases.

Fresh food was always a challenge and many of the trains had to resort to their own initiative in sourcing suitable supplies, sending out groups of men to barter with local farmers and shopkeepers, no doubt without the benefit of a common language and also a suspicion by the Russians of the continued value or usefulness of the White Russian rouble notes. However, these teams were usually successful and would return leading a group of livestock, from chickens to cows. Fortunately, there was usually somebody among the men with some butchery skills and food was never an issue. Some livestock was kept longer term, such as chickens and geese for eggs. The geese were a source of entertainment, being somewhat feistier than chickens; they were almost kept as pets, fed by hand from scraps off the table and washed down with vodka – as a result they would become aggressive, chasing anybody within reach, much to the amusement of others. Doug MacKinnon even suggested to the squadron in his correspondence during the 1980s that the Russian domestic goose would have been a more suitable mascot than the demoiselle crane that was adopted when they received their official badge in the 1930s.

On 29 June the Red forces were reported to be in full retreat and the Whites moved forward to occupy the abandoned positions. By the end of the month Tsaritsyn had been captured by the Whites, a clear victory for the counter-revolutionaries, made possible by the help given by 47 Squadron and also the tanks that the British had supplied. The tank training crews were not intended to go into action, but in the end the inevitable 'mission creep' meant that the one-armed Major Ewen Cameron Bruce (who had flown on a reconnaissance sortie two days before with 47 Squadron) – commanding one of the Mk V tanks with a British crew – drove into Tsaritsyn on 30 June, routing the Bolsheviks and taking 40,000 prisoners. Bruce was awarded a DSO for his actions and numerous Russian medals.

With the capture of Tsaritsyn, Denikin ordered Wrangel to start the advance on Moscow following the river and railway lines. Wrangel was very much opposed to this, insisting that his men were tired and needed time to replenish and re-equip, but Denikin was insistent; his mantra was 'Moscow by Christmas' and the Volunteer Army and the Don Army on Wrangel's right had already started to push north. Reluctantly Wrangel started to advance forward, initially west to secure the towns on his flanks. At first the Reds were thrown back, but by late July the advance was slowing down in the face of persistent Red Army counter-attacks, both by cavalry on land and gunboats on the Volga as they mobilised the 10th and 11th divisions of the Red Army to counter the threat. The Bolsheviks had also turned to the anarchist Black Army for support, who harried the Whites' extended lines of supply.

To continue to provide air support to Wrangel, C Flight now moved to Beketovka, a Russian aerodrome close to Tsaritsyn. On 10 July 1919, a letter sent by Lieutenant Dumas, an equipment officer with 47 Squadron, shows the hospitable reactions of the Russians to the British presence within the area: 'We collected our kit and wanted to pay but they refused to take any money saying that we had come to Russia to help them and that they were honoured to do something for us.'[25] This friendly attitude appeared to remain throughout the campaign in south Russia.

Targets in early July included the Red Army supply base at Tcherni-Yar, situated downriver on the Volga, and much bombing of river traffic. By mid-July the second squadron train was ready for dispatch and it, with B Flight, was ordered to head towards Kharkov on 15 July, but four days later it was recalled to be sent to relieve C Flight. It left for Beketovka on the 21st and was renamed C Flight; the old C Flight, largely consisting of the original 47 Squadron personnel, was disbanded on its return and most of the men posted home for demobilisation. The new C Flight was under the command of Captain Frogley and was in action by the 23rd July, when two DH9s (D3149 and F1202) bombed Tcherni-Yar. Raids rarely comprised more than three or four aeroplanes, due to the availability – or lack of it – of serviceable machines, and bombing was usually carried out at between 2,000 and 4,000 feet and comprised a mix of 20lb and 112lb bombs, with the observer firing off anything up to 600 rounds of SAA at ground targets, including cavalry, motor transport and troops. Most opposition came from light AA fire, the Red Air Force not being much in evidence.

During mid-July, Collishaw had arrived at Ekaterinodar, taking an early opportunity to observe C Flight's activities at the front. Furthermore, on the 15th, B Flight, equipped with the second-hand Camels under the leadership of Captain S.M. Kinkead, set out with their train from Ekaterinodar to join C Flight at Beketovka.

However, on 25 July the squadron recorded its first aerial victory. Two DH9s (D3147 with Lieutenants Hatchett and Simmons, and D2846 flown by Captain Elliot and Lieutenant Greenslade) left on an early morning bombing raid against barges on the Volga; on the flight back to base they were intercepted by a Red Air Force Nieuport Scout. Hatchett's forward-firing Vickers jammed, but he was able to get the DH9 into a position where the observer, Lieutenant Simmons, was able to bring his Lewis gun to bear and emptied the magazine at the Nieuport, which broke off and went down, being seen to hit the ground. The combat report[26] noted the Nieuport was marked with a large black disc on the rudder and the kill was confirmed by Captain Elliot, who reported the machine had crashed near Kamyshin.

A number of scare stories had emerged concerning the outcome for aircrew who were unfortunate enough to be shot down by the Reds, or crash due to mechanical failure on enemy soil and be captured by the communists. If they were lucky they might be crucified, but otherwise the option was being nailed to a tree by one's genitals and after a while being disembowelled, or some similar imaginative way of being tortured to death, and no doubt if one fell into the hands of those you had just been bombing and strafing, they would have felt fully justified in revenging their late comrades in any way they thought fit.

With these thoughts in mind it is not surprising that aircrews went to great lengths to ensure this fate did not befall themselves or their colleagues. On 29 July three 47 Squadron DH9s took off to attack Red shipping around Tcherni-Yar. Captain Frogley (F1202), with Lieutenant Greenslade as observer, led the formation; the other two aircraft were piloted by Captain Walter Anderson (D2942) and Captain William Elliot (D2846) with their observers Lieutenants Mitchell and Laidlaw respectively. After attacking the vessels, Anderson flew low over the target to get photographs for intelligence purposes. The DH9 was hit by ground fire, and the gravity petrol tank, which sat in the top wing above the pilot, was pierced. Mitchell climbed out of the aeroplane – which was still in flight and within range of the AA fire that had hit it originally – and edged out on to the wing to block the flow of petrol with his thumb, clinging desperately on to the interplane strut. In the meantime, Elliot's aeroplane had also been hit and with no power was gliding down to make an emergency landing. Anderson landed close to Elliot's aeroplane to rescue his colleagues. Mitchell eased back into his cockpit and held off a group of Red cavalry, which had noticed the aircraft land and were charging across the intervening ground. Elliot and Laidlaw squeezed into the observers' cockpit and Mitchell resumed his place on the wing. Somehow Anderson got the severely overloaded machine off the ground and flew the 50 minutes back to Beketovka, all the while with Mitchell with his thumb in the hole in the fuel tank and also getting burned by the hot air from the engine exhaust. To add further to his discomfort in the 100mph airstream, he had become covered in petrol, so any spark from the engine would have been fatal.[27] But all ended well and the four aircrew were flying sorties again the next day.

The demand for air support was unremitting. On 31 July the three remaining DH9s (F1202, D3147 and D2942) of C Flight were in the air for nearly 16 hours in total, carrying out two bombing raids on Achcuba, dropping a total of 1,600lb of bombs on the station and railway sidings. Captain Frogley and his observer Lieutenant Greensalde flew on two of the sorties. During the month the squadron had been airborne for nearly 140 hours in combat, releasing 4,736lb of bombs and expending 8,450 rounds of SAA.

Pressure from the Red Army was so great in mid-August that preparations for the evacuation of the Tsaritsyn by the Whites were complete and the last of General Wrangel's troops were preparing to abandon their positions when a supporting Cossack cavalry division arrived from the south and Wrangel was temporarily able to push the Red forces back. Defences were soon completed to try and hold the city against the predicted attacks. At Ekaterinodar in August much effort was made in rigging and overhauling the DH9s before they were sent to the front and twenty-one aeroplanes were prepared for service. However, it was still the case that the number of serviceable DH9s available at Beketovka averaged four to five.

Fourteen DH9As arrived on the 15th. Most of these had come from 221 Squadron via rail and sea and by the end of the month three were ready for service, but the squadron war diary notes that 'all further work on these machines is practically held up owing to parts and spares either missing or having been stolen in transit. The greatest inconvenience has been caused by this deficiency of essential parts.' This was a familiar story thoughout the British military mission and General Holman despaired at the atrocious treatment of stores and supplies, but to little effect. Yet Major Collishaw did note that the Russian mechanics were 'in some ways, better than our own. They displayed a great deal of ingenuity and initiative and from what would be a pile of scrap could salvage enough parts to assemble a perfectly serviceable machine.' No doubt they expected to receive only half the parts ordered! But Collishaw does go on to say that 'unless they were very closely supervised they could be guilty of grave omissions of routine maintenance that could have disastrous results'. Thus the squadron might be presented with a complete machine, but the risk was that a wing might fall off in flight.

During late August the DH9s flew continually from Beketovka as the White Army pushed back north up the Volga bombing the enemy's rear. During the White Army attack on Tcherni-Yar in the first week of August, C Flight was heavily committed, and in two days the three available DH9s operating from an advanced airfield at Viasovka dropped 181 bombs of various weights and expended 7,800 rounds of small arms ammunition. Shipping was also attacked with bombs and machine-gun fire, often in the face of intense ground fire. On 20 August during a raid on Tcherni-Yar, Lieutenants Cronin and Mercer in DH9 D3147 were involved in an air combat with a Nieuport, which was seen to go down after being hit by Mercer's Lewis gun, but could not be confirmed and was claimed as damaged. Another DH9 was involved in a fight with a Nieuport on the 25th, but no damage was declared. The Nieuport was described as having a red nose and red disc on the rudder, with a black cross on the fuselage.

The squadron suffered its first fatality on 15 August, but not in combat. Captain R.E. Eversden was accidently shot dead by a Russian sentry. Bizarrely he had been seen crawling under the train and, not responding to the sentry's challenge – who had been subjected to intermittent sniper fire during the night – was shot. One Russian aircraft, a Pfalz, was shot down by ground fire and the attacks along the Volga raged on. Tsaritsyn was a vital spot as it controlled movements on the Volga, permitting the transport of supplies and securing the eastern flank of the Donets industrial basin, therefore giving Denikin and his main army the protection to make his push to Moscow, albeit with an over-stretched army lacking in supply and reserves.[28] He never got closer than 200 miles before having to fall back.

During the month the squadron dropped 17,428lb of bombs and expended nearly 20,000 rounds of SAA in over 240 hours of combat flying. But on the 28th it had its first operational casualty, when on a bombing sortie that led to the destruction of a captive observation balloon, Captain McLennon, flying as observer to Captain Anderson in DH9 E8994, was hit by ground fire and died of his wounds.

The squadron was also carrying out numerous armed reconnaissance sorties, reporting on troop movements and location of defensive positions, with the observer taking potshots at any target of opportunity that happened to present itself. Often the DH9s would also carry bombs to be dropped on any suitable target found. On some occasions a senior officer, up to and including General Holman, would be flown over the front line to observe events. Aeroplanes were also constantly flying back and forth between the operational aerodromes and headquarters, and regularly forced landings would be made; sometimes ground crew would have to be sent out to recover the aeroplane, or on some occasions would repair it in situ. Collishaw suggests one instance when a crew who came down had to taxi the DH9 many miles before being recovered, which goes to demonstrate the open nature of the Russian Steppe. In another incident, Captain Elliot after force landing, broke his arm trying to restart an engine by swinging the prop.

In September work continued on assembling the DH9As so that A Flight could move to the front, and on the 19th the Sopwith Camels started to arrive to equip B Flight. Work concentrated on getting the first four ready for the front, which was achieved by the 28th. B Flight was under the command of Captain Samuel 'Kink' Kinkead, a South African who had served with Collishaw in France. By the end of the war Kinkead's score was twenty-three enemy aeroplanes shot down 'out of control', including three shared. He destroyed five, and shared in the destruction of two others. Another was claimed as captured. The Sopwith Camel was the premiere RAF scout by the end of First World War. Small, manoeuvrable and with a good turn of speed, it carried two 0.303 Vickers synchronised machine guns, and two 25lb bombs under each wing, which also made it effective in the ground-attack role. However, in inexperienced hands it could kill the pilot very quickly due to the sensitive rotary engine on take-off. Fortunately Collishaw had chosen his pilots well, and in their hands it was going to be the Bolshevik pilots who were at a serious disadvantage, on the rare occasion they met in air-to-air combat.

'C' Flight attacked boats on the Volga on the 1st of the month, two raids comprising two DH9s each time, and a number of barges were claimed damaged. The flight moved to Gniloaksaiskaya south-west of Tsaritsyn on the 5th. Further attacks on Red barges and gun boats took place over the next week and on the 14th Collishaw made his first visit to the front. On odd occasions the DH9s were intercepted by enemy Nieuport fighters, but no losses were reported, although one was claimed as having been forced to land on the 15th. The Bolshevik forces were increasing pressure on Wrangel's position at Tsaritsyn, by bringing reinforcements and artillery by river, hence the importance of 47 Squadron's sorties against this traffic. Collishaw felt confident enough in the organisation he had left behind at Ekaterinodar to be able to direct operations personally at the front and flew a number of sorties in the DH9. During the month the squadron started to supplement its usual bomb load with 230lb heavy case bombs, which were particularly effective against barges.

As the Bolsheviks continued their advance south they established an aerodrome and seaplane base adjacent to the river at Dubovka. This the squadron attacked on the 17th with two DH9s flown by Lieutenants Cronin and Day, with Lieutenants Mercer and Buckley. This was followed later in the day by a second raid piloted by Captain Anderson and Lieutenant Hatchett, with observers Lieutenants Addison and Simmons, when a barge carrying eight FBA flying boats was hit and Nieuports parked at the aerodrome strafed. Considerable damage was claimed on all targets. In the later half of the month the Whites were able to push the Reds back sufficiently to allow C Flight to return to Beketovka.

At the end of the month, with the arrival of the Camels, it was possible to provide escort protection for the bombers and this soon produced results when on the 30th Kinkead shot down a Red Nieuport into the river while escorting DH9s on a bombing and reconnaissance sortie. The machine was being flown by a pilot called Shchekin; he survived the crash into the water but drowned before being able to reach the shore.

On 12 October Captains Kinkead and Burns-Thomas strafed troops in the Netluban region and, after dropping their bombs, dived down to 10 feet and machine-gunned a large force of Bolshevik cavalry preparing to advance, forcing them to disperse with heavy casualties. Kinkead's machine was hit by rifle fire, although without serious damage.

Collishaw had moved with B Flight and taken part in three patrols, claiming two enemy aircraft at the beginning of September. His tour was cut short, however, due to an attack of typhus and a hospital train quickly evacuated him. Activity continued into early October: bridges were bombed, trains were attacked, and at one point a Bolshevik train received an onslaught by machine-gun fire from Sopwith Camels. Although designed as a fighter, the Camel was an effective ground-attack aeroplane using the twin machine guns to devastating effect, especially against ground units caught in the open. It could also carry four 25lb Cooper bombs under the wings.[29] Convoys from the south were broken up on the Volga. Air combats, though, were now infrequent and it was mainly raids on troops and transport that took up the squadron's time. Back at the base at Ekaterinodar, trains were being fitted for the newly arrived A Flight, under Captain W.L. Slatter. In late September, A Flight was equipped with DH9As and began to make its way to Tsaritsyn.

The rate of operations during the summer and early autumn for 47 Squadron was intense. Sorties, either bombing or reconnaissance, were flown from dawn to dusk, but lack of serviceability and availability of aeroplanes, as well as poor cooperation with White Russian ground forces, meant that much of the effort was strategically ineffective, whatever the local and tactical impacts may have been. Often the mere threat of the presence of aircraft was enough to deter Red forces from aggressive action.[30]

Chapter 4

WE MIGHT AS WELL STAY

Russia, 1919–1920

At the beginning of October two flights of the squadron were operating from Beketovka and the third, A Flight, equipped with DH9As, was just about ready to join them. The DH9A was a huge improvement over the DH9; known as the 'Ninak' it was fitted with either a 360hp Rolls-Royce or 400hp Liberty engine, had a bigger wingspan, was faster, and had better endurance. Its crew layout, armament and bomb load were basically the same, but importantly it was much more reliable. In combat over the Western Front it had suffered far fewer losses than the DH9 and was popular with the crews. For the ten years or so after its introduction into squadron service in June 1918 it was to be the standard RAF single-engined day bomber, and would be with 47 Squadron until January 1928.

Wrangel's troops had by now repulsed the latest Red Army attack and advanced up the Volga to Saratov. It was decided, therefore, that the flight trains would also move up the river, to Kotluban. On 3 October A Flight received orders to proceed to the front at its first opportunity. C Flight continued its attacks on river traffic, and the same day a raid led by Collishaw scored direct hits on a large gunboat and ammunition barge at Tcherni-Yar. The barge exploded and sank, taking the gunboat tied up beside with it. Sorties were being flown throughout daylight hours and if more aeroplanes had been available no doubt the results would have been even more impressive. Nevertheless, the damage that 47 Squadron was inflicting on the Bolsheviks was of great advantage to the Whites. The DH9As of A Flight were soon at the front adding their weight to the strikes and were first engaged in attacking armoured trains, challenging targets as they tended to be well protected with machine guns. The B Flight Camels were reported to have had further success when Captains Kinkead and Thompson shot down two Red Nieuports on the 7th while flying escort to a pair of DH9As; those claims, however, are unconfirmed.

Orders were issued to the squadron at Ekaterinodar to prepare the HQ train for movement towards the front and, after great difficulty in assembling the assorted flat truck and carriages required as well as stores and supplies, it was ready to move out at the end of the month, under the command of one-legged Squadron Leader 'Peg Leg' Gordon, when all the work on the DH9As had been completed.

In the later half of the month the squadron was concentrating its efforts on ground targets, including the bombing and machine-gunning of road traffic, bridges and artillery batteries by all aeroplanes. On the 21st Lieutenant Hatchet, with his observer Lieutenant Simmons, bombed an armoured train with two 112lb and eight 20lb bombs north of Kachalinskaya, bringing it to a halt before strafing the stationary train.

As mentioned, in the second week of October Collishaw was struck down with typhus and had to be evacuated by train back to Ekaterinodar. His condition deteriorated during the journey back and he was taken off the train at a small village on the line, where he was lucky to be cared for by a trained nurse. Collishaw was to all intents and purposes missing for nearly three weeks and when eventually found he had recovered sufficiently to be taken back to a base hospital to recover fully, but in all likelihood if the nurse had not found and looked after him he would not have survived. Collishaw did not return to full duties with the squadron until the end of November, by which time much had changed, and not for the better.

The White forces under a new Red Army counter-attack were forced to fall back and a Red cavalry force, reported to number 5,000 men, broke through a gap in the White lines 40 miles west of Tsaritsyn and threatened to turn the defences. The four Camels of B Flight were called upon to intervene and caught the cavalry out on the open Steppe where they had no cover. First they dive-bombed the horsemen before coming back as low as they dared and opening fire with the twin Vickers. The cavalry scattered but not before many were killed. The Whites claimed to have found 1,600 casualties after the Camels had left and the Red cavalry retreated in chaos. The Camels of B Flight were kept busy harassing the Red Army troops and cavalry, sometimes in cooperation with White cavalry, who would follow the Camels in to finish off the battered remnants of the enemy force, no quarter being given.

Bombing sorties continued throughout the month and on 26 October Colonel Maund went up as an observer on a sortie against river traffic, the same day that Captain Frogley flew General Holman on a three-aeroplane raid against shipping near Budovka, where a number of barges were damaged. The daily stress of flying unreliable aircraft over hostile territory not being enough, one now had a general in the back seat along for the ride.

During the month the squadron dropped

nearly 33,000lb of bombs and expended 14,000 rounds of SAA. There were four squadron fatalities in October: on the 12th Leading Aircraftman Leonard Tait was killed in an accident at Beketovka – details unknown – and on the 24th Captain Basil Keymer and Lieutenant Douglas Thompson became casualties when their bomb load exploded on take-off, killing them instantly. The following day nineteen-year-old Aircraftman Second Class Herbert Adams died in hospital at Ekaterinodar, possibly from typhus. All four are commemorated on the Haidar Pasha memorial in Turkey.

Denikin's army were operating at the extreme end of their supply lines, which were being assaulted by the anarchist Black Army, and with the autumn rains and the approach of winter the offensive was grinding to a halt near Orel, even though they had reached within 250 miles of Moscow, having advanced over 600 miles from Tsaritsyn in three months. The Red Army had grown in strength and with its shorter lines of communication it was able to field two relatively fresh and motivated armies.

The White army was attacked by the Reds at Orel on 20 October and abandoned the city on the 24th, forced to retreat south to avoid encirclement. The Red First Cavalry Army raided Voronezh and took Karsonli, eventually driving a wedge between the Volunteer Army and the Don Army in the west. Kursk fell on 17 November, and by the end of the month the whole of the White Army had lost its cohesion and was in a disorderly retreat. During their advance in the summer Denikin had failed to secure his rear areas, and acts of lawlessness, looting and murder of peasants undermined any support it might have expected or hoped for from the regions 'liberated' from the Bolsheviks. The nature of the warfare, where advances were linked to railway lines and five or so miles either side, left vast areas without a White Army presence, and these could be easily exploited by highly mobile cavalry and guerrilla units. In the UK the government was coming under more pressure to explain why British fighting units were involved in somebody else's civil war. So on 7 October the Cabinet had made the decision to terminate aid to the Whites and the British military mission would be withdrawn from Russia by spring 1920. Churchill was instructed to organise a final packet of British aid.

Reports reaching London were also indicating that the Whites were not going to win militarily and that they were too factionalised to gain the support of the majority of the people, not helped by their tendency to carry out mass executions and loot everything of value in areas they controlled. Though to be fair to General Wrangel he did not tolerate such actions among his troops. The Prime Minister, David Lloyd George, in his speech at the Lord Mayor's Banquet on 8 November admitted that 'Bolshevism could not be suppressed by the sword' and that Britain's debt of honour to the Whites had been paid off. The conclusion was that at some point soon it would be necessary to come to some sort of rapprochement with the Bolsheviks, and this could not be done while British fighting units were still in Russia.

On the 22nd General Holman, the head of the military mission, with Air Commodore A.C. Maund, head of the RAF mission, visited the squadron to announce that it had been decided to remove 47 Squadron from Russia.[31] Both men were highly critical of the decision and concerned that with the removal of the air support that 47 Squadron provided there would be serious political repercussions and issues of morale. The value of the squadron, and the damage it had done to the Bolsheviks, and its effects on the Volunteer Army, were so intense that withdrawing would have the most deplorable outcome. Maund continued to point out that both officers and men were willing to stay on as a unit of the Volunteer Army, and if 47 Squadron was disbanded they would prefer to do this rather than volunteer for the Instructional Mission. The argument was won, many taking the view that 'they had gone to Russia to fight and to fight we wished to remain'. The force consequently remained in south Russia as 47 Squadron of the Russian Volunteer Army.[32] This situation had already been predicted. A telegram dated 1 October from 16 Wing RAF in Constantinople sent to Cairo reads: 'Reference your G.S. 291 29/9/19 Denikin approves Maund therefore proposes to use 47th Squadron as a unit of the volunteer army until end of this year's campaign giving them Russian denomination AAA letter part of your telegram will be answered later AAA. Emphasising the decision further, someone produced the ditty:

We are from 47, 47 are we
We have not lost our identity;
There is no wangle, we are for Wrangel
We are from 47.[33]

Officially 47 Squadron was disbanded at Beketovka on 20 October 1919 to become Nos 11, 12 and 13 Squadrons of the Russian 7th Division,[34] although locally they still referred to themselves as 47 Squadron.

At this time the squadron members were issued with a new badge, the forerunner of the current red, blue and yellow badge still worn by squadron personnel. In his personal recollections, however, Doug MacKinnon insists that the actual colours were red, blue and white, which would appear more logical as they were the colours of the pre-Revolution Russian flag. The Don Cossacks flew a flag of scarlet (representing non-Cossacks), yellow (for Kalmucks) and blue (for Don Cossacks) and it is possible that this was where the badge came from, or maybe there was simply not enough white ribbon to be had locally and yellow was substituted. The original reason for the choice of colours is likely never to be known.

On 28 October, B Flight was ordered to go to the Kharkov front line in order to support the army of General Mae-Mavesky, but it would appear it did not leave Beketovka until 26 November. A Flight was to follow later and C Flight, having been in the front line the longest and also containing most of the original 47 Squadron men who were still in Russia under orders from General Holman, were to be evacuated for home.[35] A new C Flight was formed under Flight Lieutenant Anderson. (Just to add to the confusion, it would appear that squadron personnel were now using RAF ranks, which had been officially adopted in August 1919.)

47 Squadron in front of DH9, South Russia, 1919.
47 Squadron Archives

On 16 November the squadron's HQ train left Ekaterinodar for Beketovka, making the journey in five days. Due to the various movements of the flights – A Flight preparing to go to the Kharkov and C Flight returning to the front – operations were at a lower intensity and during the month only 4,500lb of bombs were dropped and 3,400 rounds of SAA fired. One notable sortie was carried out by Flying Officer Villa and Observer Officer Brockley on the 1st when they were able to persuade their DH9A to carry two 230lb and one 112lb bomb, a total load of over 570lb – somewhat in excess of the aeroplane's published capability, though this load was carried on a number of occasions. On the 10th Flight Lieutenant Kinkead, with Flight Lieutenant Daly and Flying Officer Aten, attacked motor transport on the road to Dekov. During the attack Kinkead's control jammed and the Camel spun on to its back and he was unable to regain control until only 200 feet from the ground.

Troop columns were frequently attacked with bombs and machine-gun fire, the preferred tactic being to drop a 230lb bomb on the front of the column, a 112lb bomb in the middle and the last 230lb bomb at the rear. On the Western Front against well-trained and disciplined German troops this sort of tactic would have been very dangerous, with the raiding aeroplane running a very high risk of being shot down by rifle fire. The Russian soldiers were often too busy desperately seeking cover to return fire. This demonstrated the importance of air power, and with no enemy aeroplanes to interfere the results could be devastating both materially and to the morale of those affected. As one Russian solider was reported to have said: 'You can't surrender to an aeroplane.'

The limited number of aeroplanes available could not hold back the advancing Bolsheviks, despite the efforts by squadron pilots and observers in finding and attacking them, and the magnificent work of the squadron's ground crews in maintaining, refuelling and rearming the machines. Throughout the month the weather deteriorated, with frequent fog and snow, and no flying was capable after the 21st as machines were dismantled to allow the squadron to move. At Ekaterinodar, the re-formed C Flight had passed on its DH9s to the Whites and received a number of RE8s for assembly.

Cold late autumn rains were turning to snow and, as a result, transport was being greatly impeded. Roads and approaches were becoming impossible for cavalry and troop movements, the Volga would soon be frozen, being passable only for sleigh traffic, and the operation of aircraft was going to be very difficult. Clearly a long winter was ahead for 47 Squadron. During the summer months, Tsaritsyn had been the major target for the centre of traffic and supplies; in winter, however, its importance decreased and the Red Army focused its attention on Denikin's forces further west. On 28 October, B Flight was therefore ordered to the Kharkov front. Despite their orders, B Flight never reached Kharkov. It was reported on 3 December that they had only got as far as Kupyansk, 100 miles from Kharkov, and had just two Camels airborne.[36] Chaos on the railways and lack of intelligence reaching the flight on the White Army's positions contributed to the confusion.

While B Flight was journeying further to Kharkov, A Flight was also instructed to go there. Compared to the other flights, A Flight had been at Beketovka aerodrome for a relatively short time, so were fairly well stocked, equipped and able. They were ordered to take a direct route from Tsaritsyn to Goriovka, a junction on the line from Taganrog to Kharkov. In a description written by Doug MacKinnon in the 1980s, he claimed to have encountered A Flight at Debaltsavo, well to the north of Goriovka.[37] During this period it has been suggested that both B and A Flights were caught up in the retreat to Taganrog and Rostov. Collishaw on the other hand, had been at the front at Kharkov on General Holman's train, and presumably crossed the Rostov Bridge before it was destroyed at the end of 1919.

For the movement of the flights it was required that the aeroplanes were dismantled and therefore had to be reassembled once they reached their final destination; this was all very time consuming and reduced the effectiveness of the squadron to almost nil as a result. Over the next three to four months before they were evacuated, few sorties were flown.

A Flight left Beketovka around 1 December to proceed to the area around Kharkov, and according to Collishaw arrived at Peschone to the north-east of Kharkov after around ten days' travel, where it joined B Flight, which had arrived on 5 December, and the squadron headquarters group. Based near Peschone was Z Flight, under the command of Squadron Leader Joe Archer. This flight was formed from the training mission and equipped with RE8s. There had been a plan to use it to bomb Moscow and was moved close enough to carry out such a sortie, although whether the machines had the range to get back again was debatable. Fortunately wiser council intervened and the operation was scrubbed.

There were also a number of units of the White Air Force in the area equipped with DH9s and Camels; unfortunately one of the latter crashed on take-off, killing the pilot, the suspicion being that the Camel's tendency to spin if the engine was not controlled properly being the cause, it's well-known vice catching out an inexperienced pilot. B Flight's Camels were by now in a very poor condition and on 11 December it was sent back to Taganrog, where the RAF mission had set up its headquarters, to refit. However, it was not to fly an operational sortie again in south Russia. By the end of December the area was in chaos and the British were struggling to get trains to be made available because of the lack of engines and/or drivers. The mission finally got away at the beginning of January, taking the B Flight personnel with it, but all heavy equipment, including B Flight's Camels, had to be abandoned. The flight eventually made it to Ekaterinodar and then to Novorossiysk where it again started to re-equip, but events soon overtook it and it was forced to evacuate the area in March 1920.

Pressure from the advancing Bolsheviks meant that there were frequent moves and only a few reconnaissance sorties were flown. Bombs were not carried after an unfortunate incident on the 14th when a DH9A accidently bombed some friendly forces; no casualties were reported, but it was felt that in the confused state of the front it was better to be safe than sorry, unless specific orders were issued. Interestingly, General Holman was flying as the observer in the aeroplane. The weather had turned very cold, with hard frosts, which made the landing grounds suitable for operations. A Flight moved to Popasnaya on the 19th, but only stayed a few days before the situation at the front forced another move. Low cloud and frequent snow, followed by a blizzard on the 22nd meant that no flying could take place. Christmas 1919 was celebrated near Krinichnaya in the traditional fashion, with the officers serving the men. On the following day one of the headquarters railway carriages caught fire, and it was only rapid action that saved most of the train from destruction. Even so, much kit and personal possessions were lost, including some very valuable items of gold and jewellery that had been bought from once-wealthy refugees for a fraction of their pre-Revolution values.

The trains of A Flight, the headquarters and Z Flight continued their slow progress, made slower due to the congestion from other trains and tens of thousands of refugees trying to escape the advancing Bolsheviks. Z Flight became separated from the 47 Squadron trains and continued its own journey by another route. Further difficulties arose from hostile forces operating in areas that would fire at the trains, making the retreat even more dangerous. All this was happening at an average speed of 10mph in mid-winter. The situation continued to deteriorate, and supplies and fuel for the train had to be secured at gunpoint. Lines were ripped up in front of the train, which then had to be repaired. Refugees desperate for escape clambered on to the trains and the squadron took who they could. Soon typhus broke out and many of the refugees, weakened from hunger and poor nutrition, died; with no time to bury them, their bodies were simply left beside the line in the snow.

The squadron trains arrived in Sevastopol around 4 January 1920 after its nightmare journey, an experience that would not be forgotten by anyone who was there. The remnants of the squadron re-established itself at Djankoi once the front had temporarily stabilised in mid-February and according to Collishaw flew a number of reconnaissance and bombing sorties with DH9As, operating as the Crimean Group.

During this time General Denikin was coming under increasing pressure and criticism of his conduct of the war. Cooperation between the British and the Whites was at breaking point, and Wing Commander Maund was so frustrated by his opposite number in the White forces, General Kravtseyvitch, over the state of the Russian Air Service that he felt obliged to resign his command on 23 January 1920. This led to the sacking of Kravtseyvitch. In a message to the War Office in London General Holman stated: 'I wish to place on record my appreciation of the hard work which Wing Commander Maund has done here in South Russia. His devotion to duty and unremitting exertions have been worthy of the highest praise.' Maund was replaced by Squadron Leader Archer.

Despite the continued efforts of A Flight it was becoming obvious to all that the cause was lost and arrangements were being put in place to evacuate the remaining members of the British military mission, Those at Novorossiysk were evacuated in late March. Collishaw writes that the last bombing sortie was carried out on 28 March, when an armoured train and troop and artillery positions were attacked. Collishaw undertook a reconnaissance flight the following day, but on the 30th 47 Squadron was ordered home.

When the time came for the RAF to leave Russia, General Wrangel was commander-in-chief of the White forces. He was re-forming in the Crimea, and recruiting from Ukraine and the west. The main body of the squadron that had been involved in the winter retreat was finally evacuated through the port of Novorossiysk for Constantinople on 27 March 1920. British personnel were struck off strength in south Russia on 31 March, and a few days later a naval vessel arrived at Feodosia to collect any remaining individuals.

Service in Russia had not been without its dangers and casualties. Ten squadron members had died, five from diseases (three from Typhus), two men killed in accidents and three in action. Many other squadron members had been hospitalised at some point from disease.[38] Total British casualties during the campaign amounted to 16 officers and 29 other ranks killed, with another 742 admitted to hospital.[39]

During their time spent in south Russia, 47 Squadron had to deal with a number of problems. When the squadron first turned up, they were faced with worn-out aeroplanes and men who had been expecting to go home. The DH9 was not the best machine for the tasks they had set out to do; it had many engine problems and its reliability was suspect. The RAF was operating over huge areas with poor or non-existent maps, and no landmarks or towns to navigate by. They therefore had to try and follow the railways, which often had Bolshevik armoured trains on them. An almost total lack of cooperation with White Russian ground forces meant that the squadron appeared to operate on an ad hoc basis, with no coordinated structure with local forces. Functioning within an army without structure and a common goal were bound to create problems.

By 1918, the British Army on the Western Front had developed the 'all arms' strategy, where there was full and extremely effective cooperation between aircraft, infantry, tanks and artillery, with each arm being in communication with the others. Support, therefore, could be summoned up to deal with specific local problems in advance. This strategy contributed to the '100 days', when British and Empire troops pushed the Germans back, almost to the German border. This system, however, relied on wireless communications, which appeared to be non-existent in south Russia. There were also often problems with communications between flights, not just on the ground. With the flights being very mobile and operating from trains in remote parts of Russia, communications, sometimes for days, could be easily lost.

Lack of serviceable aeroplanes was also a serious issue. In total the squadron had been issued with 50 DH9 and DH9As, but it was rare for a flight to have more than four aeroplanes serviceable and at the front. Of the Camels, these were usually restricted to four available machines. The squadron's war diary shows how the lack of spares and equipment led to delays in aircraft getting serviced. Furthermore, the operational log book often records raids carried out by single aeroplanes, due to the lack of other serviceable aircraft, which on return is refuelled, rearmed and sent out again with another crew. Thus it was not possible to produce large-scale attacks within south Russia. Few, if any, involved more than four aircraft, and due to the poor reliability of the DH9, pilots would often have to turn back or make forced landings. The almost complete lack of enemy aeroplanes, however, gave the RAF almost unchallenged air superiority and the ability to fly single aircraft without fighter escorts. The Russian air force was still in its infancy during 1919; it consisted of few vintage aeroplanes and poorly trained pilots. Furthermore, petrol was in short supply for the Red Army after they lost the Caucasian oil fields.[40] It is not surprising, therefore, that the Russian skies were dominated by the RAF.

The arrival of Collishaw and his volunteers in late 1919, however, gave a welcome boost to the operation, although the earlier issuing of DH9A and Sopwith Camel aeroplanes would have strengthened the campaign even more. Working conditions within south Russia were bad. Operating from trains and the lack of any permanent airfields, mixed with the plentiful cases of disease, especially typhus,[41] caused morale to be low within Allied camps. Problems persisted for 47 Squadron throughout their time spent in south Russia. Denikin's retreat in late 1919 caused further breakdown of cooperation, with few sorties being flown thereafter. One of the biggest difficulties the squadron had to face was the Russian weather. The DH9 and

DH9As had water-cooled engines, which in a Russian winter were a maintenance nightmare. The Camels on the other hand had an air-cooled rotary engine but, even so, oil, fuel and any other liquids would freeze, and conditions for the crews working in the cockpits were unimaginable. For ground crew trying to maintain the aeroplanes out on the open Steppe without permanent facilities must have tried their ingenuity and commitment to the extreme.

Another complication the squadron had to face was the issue of the White Army itself. Unlike the Red Army, the Whites contained lots of different generals with varying priorities, and soldiers who were serving under them of very diverse capabilities and motivation. The White Army represented a 'spectrum of political factions [with] White monarchist military organisations ... [and] social-democratic Whites',[42] often coming to blows with each other over a number of topics. A disorganised army was a weak army.

In November 1918, Admiral Kolchak had stated: 'I make my main goal the creation of a combat-ready army, victory over the Bolsheviks, and the establishment of law and order'[43]; unfortunately Kolchak's wishes never came to fruition, and by early 1920, the White Army was already in a disastrous position. Despite initial success in areas such as Ukraine, where the Bolsheviks were unpopular, by early 1918 the White Army held no key areas; they had simply been 'built up around the periphery of the European part of Russia'.[44] The White Army consisted of highly disorganised groups who lacked a common strategy and were not cohesive, unlike their Red Army counterparts. Huge distances separated the White forces; they were fighting both in the north and south, and did not have any major strongholds, again unlike the Bolsheviks, who held key areas such as Moscow, a city with excellent railway connections and communications. Furthermore, White supporters often lived in scattered settlements and showed little or no interest in both politics and nationalism. Support of foreign allies was therefore very important. Both Britain and France sent troops to help the White campaign, with Britain supplying the bulk of support, even though 'help was slow in arriving'.[45] Nevertheless, British forces, in particular in south Russia, played a major role within the White forces. Without their help, it is likely that the counter-revolutionaries would have failed much sooner than they did. It was not the foreign support that was lacking or inefficient that ultimately caused the White Army to fail, but the fact that the generals did not use foreign intervention to the best of their ability. They were often half-hearted towards the help they received.

Throughout his time as commander of the British mission in south Russia, General Holman and many of his senior officers despaired at the criminal waste of the supplies sent by Britain; they were either never issued to front-line units, or stolen, or used to bolster certain officers' personal prestige.

In addition, the Red Army was rapidly growing in numbers. Despite the British providing troops and air support for the Whites, the Reds had vastly more military personnel than the Whites were ever able to find. The nature of the war was that units regularly defected to the other side, Red or White depending on their view of the course of the war. It usually required the disposal of officers and/or commissars, but either side seemed happy to take on these soldiers whose loyalty was obviously suspect.

Furthermore, as soon as the White Army began to falter, Britain pulled out their personnel and 'now decided that they would pursue actively their policy of peace negotiations with the Bolsheviks'.[46] It seemed apparent to Britain that the Bolsheviks and the Red Army were a far more superior force; therefore it can be suggested that it made more sense to negotiate with them instead of fight them. The removal of British support was clearly a huge blow for the White Army.

Both the Red and White armies used terror during the civil war; however, the Reds utilised it far more effectively with forces such as the All-Russian Extraordinary Commission, the Cheka, who were used to 'suppress rival political parties'.[47] Furthermore, both the Red and the White armies used propaganda but, like terror, the Reds employed this far more successfully, showing anti-Bolshevik demonic characters and enemies of the Revolution in derogatory ways, supporting the idea that the Reds were the saviors of the Revolution. Moreover, the Whites often underestimated the need for propaganda and the agitation it could cause. The 'political and strategic errors of the leaders who misjudged the psychology of the masses'[48] played a huge role into why the Whites failed. They often exaggerated their early victories and did not successfully secure territories they occupied. The White Army consisted of ex-generals and gentry, many of whom wished to restore autocratic power, something the majority of Russians did not want, whereas the Bolsheviks were a party for the people. When the Whites were eventually defeated in 1920, other counter-revolutionary factions, such as the Socialist –Revolutionary Party, did not possess the necessary infrastructure to directly attack the Reds, resulting in the Bolsheviks being able to implement complete control over the country.

Documenting the squadron's role in south Russia is hampered by a lack of official records beyond late 1919 and being reliant on personal recollections. Collishaw shares his in his book *Air Command*, which is not entirely reliable and needs to be treated with a degree of caution. Doug MacKinnon's account, as sent to 47 Squadron in the 1980s, is of interest; however he was mostly with the HQ base and spent little time at the front. He is also somewhat critical of Collishaw's version. Jones continues the squadron history in his book, but draws a halt when the squadron was officially disbanded in October 1919. Finally, we have *Last Train Over Rostov Bridge*. This was written by Marion Aten in cooperation with a journalist, Arthur Ormond, in 1961, a year before Aten's death. Aten was an American who flew Camels with B Flight in south Russia. Unfortunately, the book is so riddled with errors it makes it very difficult to extract the truth, but it has been used as a statement of record by some of the subsequently published books and articles on the campaign. There is no doubt that Aten was there and wished to record his experiences, but one fancies that Ormond may have used journalistic licence to embellish a story for publication.

Returning to where we started with Collishaw's letter to the 47 Squadron OC in 1955, it is clear that the squadron was not entirely made up of volunteers recruited personally by him, although by the end of the campaign all men there were volunteers. The flights were not up to fifty aircraft; usually five to seven aeroplanes would be serviceable in any flight. The great enthusiasm shown by the local population may have been overstressed, but was certainly the case at some points. Nevertheless, this is not in any way to detract from what the squadron achieved under extremely trying conditions and is a fascinating chapter in the squadron's history and no doubt reflects what Collishaw was looking for in an adventurous spirit.

Establishing claims for enemy aircraft shot down or damaged, is always challenging where records are incomplete or evidence sparse. However, it is possible to give an estimate based on what is known. What is also certain is that a lot of the published information is suspect.

One of the most notable and respected sources for British air-to-air combat claims is *Above the Trenches* by Christopher Shores, Norman Franks and Russell Guest, published by Grub Street in 1990. The book only covers aces, i.e. those with five confirmed victories or more, but a number of the 47 Squadron pilots are included and with them their 'kills' while serving in Russia. This gives a total of thirteen, all in the air, and does not include the four in the squadron war diary credited to DH9 crews, giving a potential total of seventeen air-to-air victories. However, while examining the squadron's war diary and other sources such as combat reports, it would appear to give total claims of eight aeroplanes in the air and six or seven on the ground during 1919. (See the table below.)

There will always be discrepancies, but some of the additional claims look more suspect than others. Marion Aten is credited with five, but three of these are in April and May, before the squadron was operational, and the other two in August, a month before the Camels had reached the front. In his book he claims to have witnessed and taken part in dogfights involving large numbers of Red fighters, but from other evidence (*Aircraft of the Russian Civil War* by Vyacheslav Kondrat'ev and Marat Khayrulin, translated and additional notes by Tom Hillman) it looks unlikely that the Reds had more than three or four combat aeroplanes available in the area at any one time. He also includes in his claims a number of Spads. These aeroplanes, although available to the Reds, were rarely flown because they required good-quality aviation fuel, whereas aircraft such as the Nieuport could be flown on what was available.

It could also be argued that the squadron could have had more victories during the period they were officially not part of the RAF and for which records are not available, but what is clear is that for most of that time the Camels were not in a flyable condition or anywhere near the front line.

None of this is to decry the efforts of the squadron – you can only shoot down what the enemy puts in front of you –and the presence of the Camels, DH9s and DH9As flown by experienced and determined airmen meant that any Red fighter that did happen to stumble across 47 Squadron was as likely as not to quietly slip away before giving any of the RAF men a chance to chalk up another victory. The Red flyers were not cowards, but were acutely aware of the limitation of their kit and their chances of achieving anything worthwhile. We can be fairly confident of at least eight aerial victories, with maybe more either not recorded or taking place over the winter of 1919–20.

At the end of the campaign the squadron had picked up numerous medals and awards and many of the aircrew were to go on to have very successful RAF careers, reaching Air rank. Sadly one of the characters of the conflict, Flight Lieutenant Sam Kinkead, DSO, DSC and bar, DFC and bar, was to be killed in 1928 flying a Supermarine S.5 while attempting to break the 300mph barrier.

25 July	Nieuport	Tsaritsyn	DH9	Hatchett and Simmons
20 August	Nieuport	Tcherni-Yar	DH9	Cronin and Mercer
25 August	Nieuport	Tcherni-Yar	DH9	Hatchett and Simmons
17 September	Nieuport		DH9	
30 September	Nieuport	Tcherni-Yar	Camel	Kinkead
2 October	Nieuport	Dubouka	Camel	Kinkead
9 October	Albatros		Camel	Collishaw
18 October	Nieuport	Feskouatka	Camel	Kinkead

Chapter 5

EMPIRE SQUADRON

Egypt and Sudan, 1920–1939

RAF Helwan, 1921, with DH9As outside hangars.
Author's collection

Empire Squadron

Egypt and Sudan, 1920 – 1939

With the end of the First World War, the new RAF was under threat. It had proved the importance of air power, but with huge cuts in budget, the Army and the Royal Navy were questioning the need for a third arm, as they were concerned that this would impact on their share of the resources available. They also contended that the strategic air threat had been removed and the government's own assumptions, as far as future planning was concerned, was that there would be no war for ten years. Air Marshal Sir Hugh Trenchard, the then Chief of the Air Staff, needed to identify a role that the RAF could make its own, and prove its value as a cheap way of enforcing the government's will over the vast tracts of the Empire. He argued that a handful of squadrons based at strategic points in the Empire could police huge areas, and maintain order with localised offensive actions when required. Furthermore, if that wasn't enough, aeroplanes could be used to transport ground troops to the area far quicker than anything the Army or Navy could do with their own resources. This would save money by reducing the need to have garrisons located in remote areas. The treasury was convinced and Trenchard won the day when the 'Trenchard memorandum' was endorsed by the House of Commons in December 1919.

The RAF would be reduced from a total war-time strength of c. 280 squadrons to a peace-time establishment of 34, 22 of which would be based overseas in Egypt (10), India (8), Mesopotamia (3), and Malta (1). The RAF was soon able to demonstrate its usefulness, as promised, in British Somaliland against the 'Mad Mullah', where air power had proved its ability to patrol and pacify a huge area without the need for ground forces. In Great Britain, where the Mad Mullah had long been a source of irritation, news of the swift victory was well received in Parliament and the country. The cost of the 1920 operation was put at £77,000 and Colonial Under-Secretary Leo Amery described it as 'the cheapest war in history'. Trenchard and the newly established RAF were greatly encouraged by the outcome. It was estimated that the cost of employing ground forces to carry out the same task would have cost around £6–7 million.

Another factor of the Trenchard air force was the loss of the role of observer. As seen during the First World War and the campaign in south Russia, the squadron's aircrew would be made up of a pilot and an observer, usually both officers, one to act as pilot and the other to take the photos, communicate the fall of shot, drop the bombs and operate the flexible gun defence. It was decided that this latter role was superfluous in the new RAF, as well as NCO pilots. The pilots would be trained in navigation and the chap in the back seat would be a ground tradesman who had volunteered for extra flying duties, for the additional sum of 2s a day with an extra 6d if qualified as a gunner. This was not to be sniffed at when the basic rate of pay was 4s a day. There was to be no centralised training and this would be provided at squadron level. This policy meant that for 47 Squadron the back seater was often a trained rigger or fitter who was supplementing his pay. In the circumstances of the reliability of the aeroplane and the terrain over which they flew, the chances of a forced landing at some point were high; having somebody on board with those sorts of skills was probably an advantage. In the squadron's records these men would be noted as passengers, which rather belittled their important role.

On 1 February 1920, 206 (Bomber) Squadron, based at Helwan, south of Cairo, and under the command of Squadron Leader G.R.M. Reid, DSC, MC, was renumbered as No. 47 (Bomber) Squadron, RAF. 206 Squadron was a former RNAS unit that had served on the Western Front as a bomber squadron and had moved to Egypt in June 1919. It was equipped with DH9 and DH9A aeroplanes. Of course, at this time there were still the remnants of 47 Squadron serving in Russia, but not officially. The new 47 Squadron had a permanent home and the historic number was preserved. Around this period the squadron, along with most other RAF squadrons, adapted an unofficial badge. The 47 Squadron version showed the stepped pyramid of Zoser with the sun setting behind it over an RAF eagle and with the motto Sans Peur (Without Fear) below. The temple could be seen from the aerodrome at Helwan, which lay to the east. This was to be replaced by the current badge, which shows the head of a demoiselle crane, a migratory bird that is found in both Russia and Sudan, over blue and white waves to represent the Blue and White Niles and the Latin motto Nili Nomen Roboris Omen (The name of the Nile is an Omen of our Strength), which was approved by King George VI in November 1938.

The squadron's role was working for the governments of Egypt and Sudan, at that time British mandated territories, and was employed in mapping and plotting this vast area for the first time. It was to trail blaze its way down the Nile and further, carrying out photo-reconnaissance, policing, customs control, anti-slavery patrols and cargo and people carrying. It was also called upon to 'put a bit of stick about', enforcing Cairo's and Khartoum's will on intransigent tribesmen, sometimes requiring bombing raids on far-flung tribal villages. The unfriendly climate, inhospitable ground and frequent unreliability of the aeroplanes added to the risk. Moreover, coming down in this area where some of the locals may be less than welcoming, especially if they had recently been the object of bombing, was of significant concern to the aircrews. They would have to rely on their own charm and personality and the ubiquitous 'Gholli Chit', a piece of paper that promised the recipient a reward should the bearer be returned to the government safely and, more specifically, with his manhood intact.

In May 1920, three aeroplanes were tasked to catch a gun-running camel train. The flight moved down the Nile to Beni Suef, some 60 miles south of Cairo, to be based on a commandeered Nile riverboat. During the day the aircraft would patrol the local area and return to the riverboat as the light faded, landing on a piece of suitable land. Navigation was fairly simple; all they had to do was find the river and then the boat. During one of the sorties a crew found the 'gate' in the Great Dune. The Great Dune runs north to south for some 300 miles, from the coast to the Bahariya Oasis, and is largely impassable. The 'gate', lost since Napoleon's time, was the

Top: Fairey IIIF being lowered on to the Nile. *Townson via author*

Above: Fairey IIIF come to grief. *Townson via author*

only easily crossable point in the soft sand In September, Observer Officer B.C.S. Byrne was killed when the DH9 (D9824) he was flying in stalled on take-off from Almaza; the pilot survived.

A new task came to the squadron in 1921. After the First World War the RAF and the Air Ministry began to consider the possibility of setting up a mail service from Egypt to India. It was also pointed out that by flying the mail it would remove the requirement to send all such communications by sea, which could take anything between eighteen and twenty-eight days. Another benefit of this would be to route-prove a way for rapid reinforcement, should trouble arise in either part of the Empire. However, the Treasury were not keen to approve the £100,000 cost for the airfield works required. The feasibility of such a route was demonstrated in 1919 by Lieutenant Colonel A.T. Wilson, the British Civil Commissioner for Mesopotamia, who flew in a DH4 from Baghdad to Port Said in Egypt so he could join his ship and attend the Paris Peace Conference. His journey took five days, involved three forced landings and three changes of aeroplane. By May 1920 Wilson was able to make the flight from Baghdad to Cairo in a single day, with refuelling stops at Ramadi and Damascus.

Also in May 1920, Trenchard pushed the case for the mail route to Winston Churchill, then the Colonial Secretary. Trenchard also favourably pointed out that there was revenue to be made from carrying the mail, a bonus that no doubt the Treasury did not ignore, and thus HQ RAF Middle East was given the immediate go-ahead to start planning the course. A significant consideration was the need to avoid the French-controlled territory of Syria, the route that Lieuteant Colonel Wilson had used, and thus it had to be over British-controlled land only.

The distance to be covered was around 850 miles, from Cairo to Baghdad, about the same as London to Warsaw, and fraught with difficulties. From Cairo to Amman in Jordan the planners had to contend with the Dead Sea at 1,286 feet below sea level before climbing into the Jordan hills at 3,000 feet

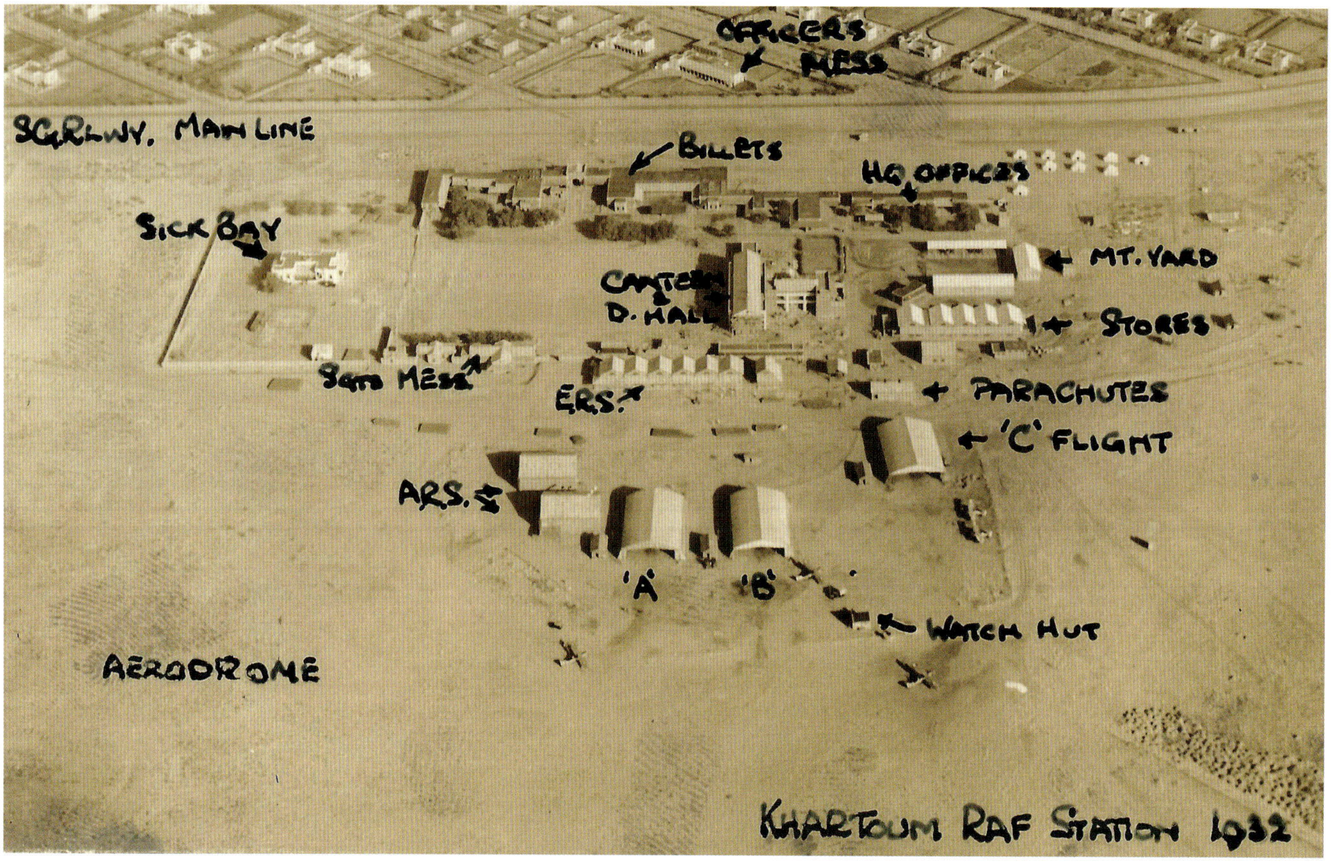

above sea level. The 540 miles from Amman was mostly uninhabited desert, comprising an arid plateau some 2,000 feet above sea level covered in small tough bushes and boulders, with a large area of black volcanic rock. Then came 120 miles of plain, rising to 3,000-foot-high hills. The way then descended into the valleys of the Euphrates and Tigris rivers. Dotted along the course were deep wadis, mud flats and large shallow lakes that filled with rain.

The aeroplanes that would have to fly this route were unreliable, which would lead to inevitable forced landings, and their range was insufficient to cover the distance and to be able to carry a useful load; stocks of fuel would have to be left at preprepared landing strips. Navigation and wireless were either non-existent or so primitive as to be of little use. The standard navigational technique was map-reading, but no accurate maps existed and furthermore there were few landmarks on which to plot an aeroplane's position.

An initial survey was carried out in April 1921 from the eastern (Baghdad) end of the route, led by Major Holt, and a series of landing grounds (LG) were prepared at roughly 50-mile intervals, marked by the numbers I to IX (although they would use 8 instead of VIII). Another team left Amman heading east on 10 June comprising three Rolls-Royce armoured cars and six Crossley tenders under the command of Squadron Leader W.L. Walsh. They were to be supported by DH9As from 47 Squadron This party was also to establish suitable LGs, which would be lettered A to R (I and Q were deliberately omitted to avoid confusion.)

Squadron Leader Walsh's team marked their course by dragging a chain harrow behind one of the tenders, and the landing grounds were denoted by the simple expedient of driving one of the vehicles round in circles until a defined boundary was created. Later, the route would be marked by a ploughed furrow created by a Fordson tractor dragging a plough. Walsh met up with Major Holt to the east of El Djid. Both teams reached Baghdad on 26 June, the three 47 Squadron aeroplanes having arrived on the 22nd, which date the Air Ministry regarded as the opening of the route. The first full test came when three DH9As of 30 Squadron left Baghdad at 04.30 hours on 30 June, reaching Heliopolis at 19.45 the same day.

No. 47 Squadron completed the first Cairo to Baghdad flight, with Air Vice Marshal

Left: RAF Khartoum, 1932.
Townson via author

Bottom: Fairey IIIF on the Nile with RAF launches.
Townson via author

Salmond as passenger on 9 July. The first official mail left Baghdad on the 28th and the service was opened to private mail on 8 October. A regular service was soon established, with aeroplanes departing on Thursdays, fortnightly in each direction so the westbound flight could connect with the mail ship at Port Said. Letters could be back in London within ten days of leaving Baghdad. A surcharge of 1s per ounce was charged, later reduced to 3d. In addition to 47 and 30 Squadrons flying DH9As, 216 Squadron supplied twin-engined DH10s based at Kantara in Egypt. All this work was carried out in addition to the squadron's usual duties.

The DH9As could only carry one passenger and, although they had a theoretical cruising speed of 110mph, the machines were not new, and when loaded with extra petrol tins lashed to the underwing bomb racks, a spare wheel under the fuselage and various other bits of luggage, tools and spares tied to convenient parts of the airframe, they would be lucky to reach 80–90mph. Mail was stowed in the rear cockpit, behind what had been the observer's seat.

Regulations required that at least two aeroplanes should make the trip together, as a wireless operator and fitter should always be on board, but the actual number taking part was dependent on the load to be carried and any priority passengers. Flying from Cairo to Baghdad with the prevailing winds would often be done non-stop, but flying the other way would usually require a refuelling stop. The tanks would have to be topped up, the fuel carefully filtered through chamois leather to keep out any impurities, and all this would all this need an overnight stop at Amman.

In the first twelve months of operations, 4¼ tons of private and official mail were conveyed, representing some 175,000 pieces of correspondence, the amount having increased tenfold by Christmas. Nos 30 and 47 Squadrons continued to fly the route until April 1922, but by now it had been proved, and with bigger load-carrying aeroplanes becoming available the task was taken over by 70 Squadron operating twin-engined Vickers Vernons, the first of the RAF's real transport aircraft, and 216 Squadron, which had re-equipped with Vickers Vimys. The task was also shared with 45 Squadron also with Vernons. The RAF continued to carry the mail on this route until 1926, when the role was taken over by Imperial Airways.

The squadron lost an aeroplane and crew when Flying Officer S.H. Potter and Corporal H. Lake were killed in a flying accident on 14 August 1921.

The year 1923 began with a show of force against a miscreant tribe near El Rumel. This mainly amounted to low flying with lots of noise and, if really necessary, a few flares and the occasional bomb. Usually the very sight of aircraft quelled any trouble. Not until some years later, when the natives became used to the airborne threats, did it become necessary to bomb villages and livestock.

In the spring, Squadron Leader Henderson crashed a DH9A when a wandering camel strolled into his touch-down point. Once again 'Lucky Hendo' who had a bit of a reputation for bending aeroplanes, escaped unscathed. As they say, any landing you can walk away from is a good one, any landing where they can use the aeroplane again is perfect!

While the usual training sorties carried on each day, there was always the additional experimental trials. New altimeters had been fitted to all the aeroplanes, which gave accurate readings to over 20,000 feet. This was fine, except in the attempts to try out these instruments the crews were finding the DH9As hard to handle. Worse still, the airmen were having difficulty breathing at height and, of course, their hot-weather flying suits – donned in temperatures of around 30 degrees – were totally ineffective at the minus 10 degrees encountered at altitude. Clothing could be rectified, although they then took up more space in the already cramped cockpit. Engines, however, were more of a challenge as new, replacement Rolls-Royce Eagles or Liberty types were hard to come by in Egypt, and therefore the only reasonable answer was to limit the operating altitudes. There were experiments with breathing apparatus, but again lack of space forestalled their use. Some hopeful tests were carried out with a less bulky bottled air mixture supply, but this was unreliable, and with the aeroplanes limited to 15,000–18,000 feet for short periods only and with little need for regular high altitude flying, it was decided to grin and bear the discomfort.

Another trial involved attempts at a snatch system. Two rifles, with bayonets fixed, were rammed into the ground, a rope tied loosely between them and a message bag attached. The pilot then flew as low as possible with the observer hanging over the side of the aircraft, dangling a hook in an attempt to grab the loose rope and haul the message bag on board. It took considerable skill to achieve and its practical use was limited, but did make for an impressive demonstration at displays and competitions.

The early months of 1924 were uneventful apart from a number of forced landings. The first was near Quella in February. The crew walked away from the broken machine towards the railway and caught the first train to base. There, tired and dirty from their experiences, they washed, shaved and changed into clean uniforms, and only then reported the abandoned aeroplane to the adjutant. The following month a DH9A ditched in the Nile, but the crew were able to swim to shore.

In July night flying was introduced. For almost all the aircrew this was a new and somewhat daunting prospect, requiring keen concentration and good night vision, the only landing aids being flares to mark the landing area. Inevitably there were several heavy touch-downs in which aeroplanes were damaged, one of which was more serious when the pilot managed to rip the under-

Below: Army cooperation photos of Khartoum taken by 47 Squadron.
Townson via author

Right: Fairey IIIF wrong way up on the Nile, 1930's.
Townson via author

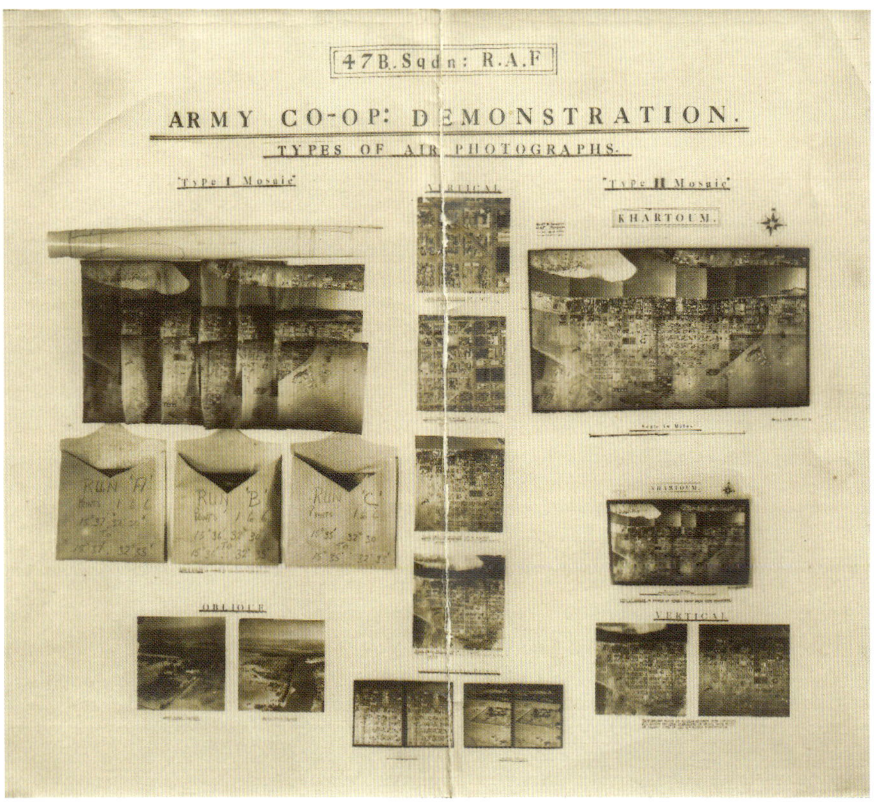

carriage off, coming to a sliding halt in a cloud of dust some 200 yards after it hit the ground; but luckily with no injury to the crew. Another accident occurred when, on a night bombing exercise, while fumbling for the reserve fuel cock, the crew inadvertently released their bomb load over the camp; again, fortunately nobody was hurt. However, later a local who had strayed into the night bombing range was killed.

August and September 1924 brought a number of detachments to Khartoum, Omdurman and El Obeid, usually only comprising a couple of DH9As and ground crew for a few days. The squadron was also tasked by the Egyptian government to provide a photographic mosaic of Cairo and surrounding areas for mapping and planning purposes. In October, there were outbreaks of local unrest around and in Khartoum. All the squadron's aeroplanes were recalled, bombed up and put on standby; however, local government forces restored order and the squadron's intervention was not required.

At the beginning of 1925 the squadron took part in another long-distance pioneering flight, flying from Cairo to Kano, Nigeria. The three aeroplanes were led by Squadron Leader Arthur Cunningham, and flew the 6,500 miles in under 85 hours. A remarkable feat when one considers the flimsiness of the machines and the almost complete lack of navigation and wireless aids available.
At many of their numerous stops en route – necessary as the DH9A had an endurance of just over five hours, and in their overladen state this would be reduced – they were the first aeroplanes ever to be seen by the locals and attracted huge crowds of curious people. Everywhere, as Squadron Leader Cunningham reported, they were greeted by a 'wonderful display of happy and colourful people'. These pioneering flights were to pay great dividends during the Second World War, as routes for flying reinforcement aircraft to Egypt for the Desert Air Force.

By now the squadron was spending much of its time in the Sudan, with more and more regular detachments south to Omdurman Bridge close to Khartoum and carrying out Army cooperation flights, mapping and weather research, all of great interest to the Sudan government. At the same time the government were getting concerned about smuggling and gun running in the Red Sea, and it seemed only a matter of time before the squadron moved south permanently.

In June the squadron acquired a new type of aeroplane, but this was not to be officially on squadron strength as it was allegedly acquired from an Aboukir scrapyard for several bottles of scotch. The machine was an Armstrong Whitworth Siskin III, a single-seat fighter. Two Siskins had been sent out to Egypt for tropical trials in the latter half

of 1925 (J7818 and J7179), so one of these could have been temporarily borrowed by the squadron, rather than rescued from a scrapyard, as both aeroplanes returned to the UK between September 1925 and January 1926.

In October 1925 Squadron Leader R.S. Maxwell became CO, and for the next two years the unit continued to be based in Egypt, with its parish spreading down to Khartoum and across to the Red Sea.

On 10 August 1926 the squadron suffered a fatal crash. Flying Officer H.G. 'Crasher' Slater, so called by the riggers because of his regularity of heavy landing and usual destruction of the tail skid, stalled on take-off; the aeroplane (DH9A E928) nose-dived into the ground and exploded, killing Slater and his passenger Aircraftman First Class Harvey.

The year 1927 was one of change for 47 Squadron. On 12 October a new OC arrived, Squadron Leader P. Cox, and four days later the movement orders for Khartoum arrived. In December the unit took delivery of the first of its Fairey IIIFs, initially to replace one of the DH9 flights, finally becoming fully equipped when the second flight converted to IIIFs in June 1928.

The Fairey IIIF was another of the RAF's stalwarts of the interwar years, a two-seat general-purpose machine, powered by a 570hp Napier Lion XIA engine, giving a maximum range of 400 miles (1,520 miles with overload tanks) and a maximum speed of 120mph at 10,000 feet. It was also developed as a three-seater for the Fleet Air Arm. By 1932, when production ceased, over 560 had been built. They served with three squadrons at home and five overseas.

Stretching 1,800 miles from the border of Egypt almost down to the equator, Sudan, the largest country in Africa, covered a million square miles. The northern half was mainly arid deserts sparsely populated by Arabic-speaking Islamic peoples, changing as one moved south to a land of heavy seasonal rainfall, many rivers, immense areas

Clockwise from top left: Fairey Gordon over flooded countryside. *Townson via author*

Fairey Gordon taking off from the Nile. *Townson via author*

Fairey Gordon K2734. *Townson via authors*

47 Fairey Gordon K2645, stalled on take off. *Townson via authors*

of swamps and tropical forests inhabited by black native tribes who spoke their own languages and had their own traditions. The south was dominated by the Sud, a permanent swamp about the size of Wales depending on the time of the year, which fed the White Nile.

Administered by the British, civil law was the responsibility of fourteen provincial governors and many widely scattered district commissioners, with minor posts filled by Sudanese officials. Military authority was in the hands of the Sudan Defence Force, locally raised with British officers and senior NCOs and two battalions of the British Army stationed in barracks at either end of the bridge over the Nile at Khartoum.

The expat British population were mostly employed by the government and worked on the railways or in agriculture; otherwise they were engaged by the import/export agents Gellatly Hankey and Contomichaelas-Dark. The hotels at Port Sudan and Juba and most of the intermediate rest houses were state run.

Khartoum itself was a relatively modern city situated at the junction of the Blue and White Niles. It had wide, tree-lined boulevards and from the air looked like a Union Jack with these roads meeting at the middle, albeit this layout also meant that the streets could be more easily covered by artillery and machine-gun fire from one point. Although surrounded by desert the extensive irrigation from the Nile gave the city lush vegetation and parks, including a zoological gardens. The imposing Governor's Palace stood by the river and in its gardens there was a brass plaque to mark the spot where General Gordon had been cut down.

Across the Nile stood Omdurman, where the local native population lived, a teeming city of 100,000, living in single-story mud-brick houses with workshops, producing goods in ivory, brass and silver and providing the menial workforce for Khartoum.

Outside Khartoum, metalled roads were all but non-existent and travel south was by river, even if many only became navigable

Clockwise from top: Fairey Gordon K2645 on the Nile. *Townson via author*

Fairey Gordon over Khartoum. *47 Sqn Archives*

Refuelling a Fairey Gordon. *47 Sqn Archives*

Camouflaged Fairey Gordon for operations in South Sudan, 1937. *Townson via author*

in the rainy season. Trains ran infrequently and slowly on the single-track line linking Khartoum, Wadi Halfa and Port Sudan. And the Imperial Airways aeroplane on its weekly Cairo to Cape service made overnight stops on its way north and south. Thus, travel to most parts of this vast country was slow, primitive and uncomfortable. 47 Squadron was able to change this, at least for government officers or other VIPs.

The move to Khartoum was not without difficulties. When the squadron arrived at its new home, Said Pasha barracks in Omdurman, the Army was still firmly at home, and had no confirmed date for moving out, so the unit personnel were forced to live under canvas. Moreover, upon inspecting the aeroplane hangars, they were found to be full of lorries, and so the brand new Fairey IIIFs were either housed outside or in temporary Besseneaux hangars. This location was to become a major staging post for all types of aeroplanes passing through in all directions, making the squadron regular hosts for numerous VIPs and assorted travellers.

The Fairey aeroplanes were slightly larger than the old tired DH9As, but, more importantly, had been designed for the general-purpose role and thus did not suffer the same problems of stuffing new kit into overly cramped cockpits, and in late 1927 trials began with long-range HF communications equipment, using Morse code and short-range voice communications installed in the aeroplanes. This was a welcome upgrade for the crews, both in their own patrol work where previously they had no way of communicating with base to alert them of any problems or intelligence, but also for the long-range proving flights.

The first trial on a long-range flight was soon undertaken when four of the IIIFs flew to Nigeria. Throughout the journey they were able to send a daily situation report back to HQ. As Sergeant W. Ross noted in his log book, it was 'a very comfortable feeling'. But he went on to say: 'I see the day when we shall lose control of our own destiny.'

At the end of November two flights, one of DH9As and one of IIIFs, were sent on active operations against the Lau Naureres tribe, who were becoming restless. The operation, known as Patrol S8, was to go on for some months. The tribespeople lived in an inaccessible region of the Nuba mountains and the aeroplanes' effectiveness was greatly restricted by the lack of suitable landing grounds or access to fuel and provisions. The operations continued against the Lau Naureres, but the personnel involved were living in poor conditions in grass huts and were plagued by mosquitoes, which caused malaria. This prompted the investigation of an effective antidote. Quinine was the new drug of choice. It didn't prevent the initial infection, but did suppress the symptoms, as long as sufficient supplies were available.

During the squadron's time in Sudan over 100 landing grounds were to be created to provide access to all parts of the country, with 22 floatplane moorings selected, especially important in the south where the seasonal rains made land operations impossible. Every landing ground was visited periodically to ensure it was being properly maintained: clearly marked, safe for landing and take-off and petrol and oil stocks checked at places where they were kept. These were stocked by the Shell Company by any means available, ranging from camel to canoe. Some landing grounds also included facilities for storage of bombs and ammunition.

Flights were allowed six weeks per annum for bombing and air gunnery practice, but for the rest of the year machine guns and mountings were removed and bomb racks converted to carry plywood baggage lockers. During the year flights of two or three aeroplanes carrying their own airman riggers and fitters who doubled up as aircrew, were away for up to four days at a time, making overnight stops at a government rest house if possible, otherwise wherever and whatever shelter could be found.

Except on strictly local flights full desert equipment was carried, including emergency rations – 5 gallons of drinking water, screw pickets with rope lashings, collapsible wheel chocks (no breaks), ground signalling strips (no W/T carried), cockpit and engine covers, tools and spare spark plugs. If going away for a few days the crew would also carry mosquito boots and small kit including slacks and white shirt for wear after dark.

Take-offs were usually at dawn when the air was comparatively cool, but at intermediate landings when refuelling was required, temperatures could be very high and the task of refuelling the aeroplane from 4-gallon cans was time-consuming and difficult. The fuel tanks were in the top of the wing, and as there were no fuel pumps at any of the remote airstrips, the fuel cans would have to be passed by hand up to the airman (rarely the pilot) perched on the wing, which would often lead to spillages, and then the fuel had to be carefully poured into the tank through a chamois leather filter. When the squadron received Vickers Vincent aircraft this was even more of a tedious task and would require three men: one on the ground opening the fuel cans, who would pass to the man on the ladder, who would then have to lift it up to the man on the wing, which was some 12 feet above the ground and probably slippery with petrol spillages. It was even more of a challenge when the aeroplanes were on floats, with the whole thing rocking every time somebody moved. After all this the engine would have to be hand started, the ground crew using a hand crank to wind up the starter motor to a pitch sufficient for contact to be called and the engine to burst into life, hopefully first time. The crewman would then have to extract the starting handle, his head probably no more than a foot away from the spinning propeller blade and restow it. This was made all the more precarious with the Vincent as he would be balanced with one foot on a small step next to the engine and the other on the leading edge of the wing, with his free hand grasping on to anything that might offer purchase.

Before leaving the aeroplane at night the crew would carry out the daily inspections and take care of any necessary maintenance, change the spark plugs and make sure no oil had accumulated in the bottom of the engine, which would make starting the engine the next morning much more difficult. The

Clockwise from top left: Gordons Vincents and Vickers Walrus over the Nile, 1939. *47 Squadron Archives*

Vickers Vincent. *47 Squadron Archives*

Vickers Vincents in formation over the meeting of the White and Blue Niles, 1939. *47 Squadron Archives*

machine would then have the engine and cockpit covers fitted and picketed down for the night.

Navigation was always a problem, not helped by the lack of specialist navigation training given to pilots, and thus flights would try to fly about 1 mile to the left of any road, track, railway or river running in the right direction; this, it was hoped, would help any search party sent out should the aeroplane be reported overdue.

District commissioners were, on the whole, pleased to see the airmen, as their nearest fellow DC could be over 100 miles away, and in return for the hospitality the crews would bring along a bottle of whisky or some other rare delicacy such as kippers from the Khartoum Nile cold storage facility, simple pleasures but much appreciated.

It was a bad year for the squadron's safety record in 1928, there being some seven crashes and thirty-one forced landings, and a IIIF was written off when one of the above crashed into it. In these accidents three pilots – Flying Officers Cheshire, Ricks and Mammesham – and two aircrew passengers – Aircraftman First Class Arnold and Leading Aircraftman Barme – were killed and four others, including two civilian passengers, injured.

In February 1929 the Rt Hon. David Lloyd George, the wartime prime minister, visited the Sudan and nine of the squadron's aeroplanes were dispatched to escort his ship into Port Sudan. Over the next few days the unit played host and tour guide to Lloyd George and his party. He flew almost every day and took a deep interest in the squadron's role, especially its anti-gun-running and smuggling patrols along the coast. In the spring operations were commenced against another intransigent tribe, the Ajwong, and this too was to take up a lot of the squadron's time in the coming months.

A plague of locusts was reported in September. This was not an infrequent occurrence, but the intensity of this event had not been seen for some years. Calls were received from the governments of the Sudan and Abyssinia to assist,[49] and the squadron's aeroplanes were used to spot and track the clouds of insects, reporting their movements by wireless. This gave the government agents on the ground time enough to build large fires to divert their path. When possible, and the insecticides were available, squadron aeroplanes attempted to spray the clouds of locusts from tanks attached to the underside of the fuselage. One of the squadron armourers even

Vickers Vincent, Squadron silver.
47 Squadron Archives

developed an insecticide bomb with a timed fuse, designed to explode in the cloud, but no records exist of its use. The assistance the unit provided was greatly appreciated and the promise was made to do the same the following year.

In March 1929 the squadron took part in another long-distance proving flight, this time heading south to South Africa. The aeroplanes used tended to come from the pool reserve and were therefore not the best available, which seems curious considering the tasks being undertaken. The machines were often in need of major services and overhauls, which were beyond squadron facilities, and crews were sceptical as to their reliability. This concern was to prove tragically well founded when Fairey IIIF SR1146, piloted by Flight Lieutenant Bennett and with passenger Leading Aircraftman Turner, developed a major engine problem and crashed into the jungle, killing both men.

July saw the final exit of the Army from the squadron's aerodrome and after some nineteen months under canvas the unit personnel and aeroplanes could move into their permanent home.

Squadron Leader Howard-Williams became the new OC in February 1930, for what was to become an eventful period in the squadron's history. As mentioned above, Khartoum was a popular staging post for aeroplanes carrying out long-distance flights and in March of that year an Italian, Count Colliborio, landed to refuel. He was warned of the dangers of flying solo and without radio over these parts, where navigation aids were non-existent and there was unpredictable weather. However, he chose to ignore the warnings and a few days after he left Khartoum he was reported missing. The squadron spent some days searching for him, but no sign of him or his Fiat aeroplane was found.

The squadron had a royal visitor in March when the Prince of Wales, the future Edward VIII, arrived for a two-week tour of East Africa. The squadron were his hosts for the entire time and he was flown on numerous tasks around the area and then down to Uganda and Kenya. He befriended many unit members and in his letter of thanks to the squadron OC expressed his sympathy for the loss of Flight Lieutenant Barron and Leading Aircraftman 'Tarzan' Davis who had been killed when Fairey IIIF S1210 had crashed just days after the prince's departure. Barron had written off IIIF J9163 the previous year, while attempting to take off in an overloaded aeroplane, but in that instance he and the observer, Corporal Carter, had walked away not seriously hurt. This time, also in an overladen plane, Barron had been taking off from Wadi Halfa on 21 April when he spotted a sandstorm ahead; he tried to climb above it, but the load shifted in the aircraft and it crashed.

By this time the squadron needed a mascot and a lioness named Belinda seemed to fit the bill; the aeroplanes were powered by Napier Lion engines so it seemed logical. The lioness was popular within the unit, but she did smell a bit, and finding enough suitable food for her and her veracious appetite was challenging. She did not last long, having been acquired for the Squadron at the end of May, but was reported as missing by the end of July and assumed to be adorning the home of a recently posted-home officer. Two lion cubs were found as replacements, but if anything the smell was worse. They too were soon noted as missing, and it was decided to forgo a replacement.

During 1930 some of the IIIFs were temporally fitted with floats and these were used as part of an extensive survey of the Nile, including the Mongalla region near Juba, which contained vast flooded swamps, where the ability to land on the water was of great advantage. The aeroplanes returned in August to resume the war against the locusts.

September saw the squadron again tasked with carrying out one of the long-range flights to West Africa, but, as previously mentioned, the aircraft allocated for the mission were not in the best of conditions and, despite the sterling efforts of the squadron ground crews, their reliability was suspect. Further, the maps issued were of doubtful accuracy; fortunately the planes were fitted with short-range voice wireless telephones that were to prove invaluable.

The misgivings about the aeroplane's reliability was well founded, and during the flight mechanical and other faults led to twelve forced landings. The most serious occurred about 150 miles east of Kano in Nigeria when IIIF 1170 suffered a burst oil cooler. Flying Officer Fowler managed to glide the unpowered aeroplane safely on to a small track, but as well as the unserviceable (u/s) engine, the lower mainplane and tailplane were damaged, and the voice W/T broken. However, neither he nor his passenger Sergeant Mill were hurt. Squadron Leader Howard-Williams, leading the flight, had seen them go down and signalled that he would send a recovery team as soon as he got to the next stop at Maiduguri.

Once landed Howard-Williams sent a message back to base, including a strong-worded comment about the state of the aeroplanes supplied for the flight, and set about organising a local rescue party. Fowler and Mill, lost in very deep jungle, managed to find some locals and arranged for some runners to take messages onward to Howard-Williams. It was found impossible to reach the downed aircrew with vehicles – the dense jungle and swamps blocked their path – so a runner was sent back, telling the men to find a suitable landing strip.

With the help of about 500 locals the IIIF was manhandled some 25 miles through the jungle to a promising location, where Fowler and Mill coordinated their helpers to create a relatively clear area 200 yards long and 60 yards wide. Sergeant Mill immediately set about trying to repair the aeroplane. The next day Howard-Williams arrived with a mechanic and supplies of spares and food. They then set about completing the repairs and, four days after the initial forced landing, the aeroplane was able to fly out of the jungle and continue its journey. Not surprisingly, both Fowler and Mill subsequently had bad cases of malaria and Fowler had to be repatriated back to the UK. Eventually the flight was able to complete its journey to Lagos.

By 1931 restive natives were getting used to

the sight and sound of the squadron's aeroplanes and their effectiveness in kowtowing the locals was diminishing. It seemed that the tribes were also getting more fidgety and the unit had to resort to being more aggressive in its role, starting to bomb villages and livestock. However, this active use of bombing may also have aided the squadron in winning the Middle East bombing competition held in March. The accepted method was to drop one bomb on each pass, but Corporal 'Speedy' Hill came up with a more effective method and dropped the lot in one pass in the straddle method, which usually ensured that at least one bomb either hit the target or counted as a near miss. Although it wasn't really within the spirit of the competition – even if not actually against the rules – the Squadron nevertheless came away with the trophy. It was just a case of showing its initiative, and a flexible attitude to the rules, attributes it had always been happy to exploit.

During the early 1930s Imperial Airways was investigating and exploring new routes to join the distant parts of the Empire, using either landplanes or seaplanes. In June, 47 Squadron was requested to carry out a detailed survey of the west coast of the Red Sea for suitable landing sites and anchorages; it was also apparent that this survey work could be expanded to include the identification of potential military sites, such as invasion beaches and defence positions.

Squadron Leader Howard-Williams was keen to introduce or develop kit that would be of use to his crews, and in October a number of float-equipped aeroplanes were sent to Port Sudan to test new life jackets and a different style of rubber survival and utility dingy. Unfortunately due to high humidity and heat the new gear did not work well, also because the dingy had to be very tightly packed; when recovered it was found to be either punctured or just a large solid rubber blob, which sank.

The OC's tenure with 47 Squadron nearly came to a premature end in late 1931. When taking off, a sudden, vicious sandstorm blew up that tossed the squadron leader's aeroplane around like a cork; somehow he managed to bring the machine down in what is best described as a controlled crash. Walking away from the wreckage he lit his pipe, turned to his passenger and said: 'Hodgen, that's the end of a damn fine aeroplane.'

Nile surveys were the order of the day for the beginning of 1932, relieved by a few days at Heliopolis for an RAF display. Much of the patrol work was concerned with customs patrols and checking suspicious vessels for gun running or drug smuggling in the Red Sea. The procedure when a likely vessel was spotted was for one IIIF to alight beside it while the second remained airborne and circled to watch for any items thrown overboard. The surface aeroplane would then send over the other crewman with a government official to search the boat, usually no larger than a dhow.

However, these intercepts were not always carried out without incident. In one case the surface aeroplane managed to corner the dhow in a small cove, but in his excitement the pilot had failed to notice a submerged coral reef, which ripped through one of the floats, fortunately without sinking the aeroplane. The dhow fled and it took a team of engineers six days to repair the aeroplane.

The king of the Belgians arrived at the end of March and Howard-Williams acted as his personal pilot, taking him all over the area and down to Kenya and Uganda. The king was a very keen game hunter and worked on the principle that 'if it is in range it is in season', but for this hunt he was only carrying a camera.

For the next couple of years the squadron continued in its general reconnaissance role; aeroplanes were fitted with floats for the rainy season and they ranged far and wide over their territory, which was four times the size of France. Imperial Airways used Khartoum and the adjacent Nile as a staging post for their Empire routes, which brought in regular mail for the men stationed so far from home. From 1933 the squadron started to trade in its Fairey IIIFs for Fairey Gordons, basically a IIIF with a 535hp Armstrong Whitworth Panther radial engine. Some were simply converted from existing IIIF airframes. This rather ruined the pleasing lines of the IIIF, but brought benefits of range and endurance, and a better take-off performance at maximum load. It was also capable of being fitted with floats for the rainy season, and now the squadron, with the assistance of a new slipway into the Nile, could convert the Gordons from landplanes to float planes and get them in the water in 35 minutes, a saving of almost 2 hours.

During 1935 events to the east of Sudan in Abyssinia, modern-day Ethiopia, were taking a disturbing turn. This part of East Africa had been an Italian objective for many years and through the first half of the 1930s there had been a number of border incidents between Italian Somaliland and the neighboring Abyssinia, which culminated in an Italian invasion in October 1935. The squadron was put on a heightened alert, but did nothing to intervene. The League of Nations imposed sanctions on Italy, but these were ineffective as they did not include oil or ban it from using the Suez Canal and thus Italy could move its forces south. During the winter there was little contact between the opposing forces, but in the spring of 1936 Italy renewed its attack and pushed the Abyssinian army back. The Italians used the full force of a modern Western power – tanks, bomber aircraft and the use of gas, against an army that had no answer to them. Abyssinia soon came under full Italian control and Mussolini set about persuading the poor and disposed of Italy of the benefits of 'a place in the sun', with promises of good farming, plentiful cheap labour and markets for their products back home.

With the conclusion of Italy's invasion and occupation of Abyssinia, 47 Squadron returned to its usual tasks of army cooperation: visiting its landing grounds, bombing, gunnery and navigation exercises and survey work; one of the perks of this was that crew members often got to name geographical features after themselves.

In July 1936 the squadron received the first of its Vickers Vincents, which started to replace the Fairey Gordons. The Vincent had been a private venture by Vickers to meet an Air Ministry specification for a general-purpose aeroplane, by converting the Vildebeest costal defence torpedo bomber. Its main advantage was range; by removing the torpedo equipment and making provision for a 100-gallon fuel tank under the fuselage, it gave a range in excess of 1,000 miles, nearly double that of the Gordon. It was also a larger aircraft and capable of holding all the equipment that was required, including desert survival kit and a wireless. It carried a crew of three and could convey a bomb load of just over 1,000lb. All the Vincents built were sent overseas. The first squadron to receive them was No. 84, stationed at Shaibah in Iraq in January 1935.

The Vincents did not replace all the Gordons on 47 Squadron – they could not be converted to float planes and thus a flight of Gordons was retained to undertake that particular work.

The Vincent performed admirably in its role, but it did have a number of idiosyncrasies that made the job a little less pleasant. One was communication between the crew. The pilot was separated from the other two crew members, the wireless operator (WOP) and rigger or fitter, carried in the back, by a tunnel, and passing messages was done by the pilot indicating he wanted the WOP by waggling the wings, and the WOP could tug on the elevator cables. Communication between aeroplanes in flight was by 'zogging' – the crew member would hold out his arm outside the cockpit and wave it up and down in Morse code, very strenuous for long messages. But these problems were far outweighed by the difficulties brought about by the simple need to perform bodily functions. A tube and funnel was provided but, no matter how careful one was, the slip-stream always blew the urine back into the aeroplane, which was bad enough for the wireless operator, but it also went forward up the tunnel and on to the pilot's legs. The only solution was for the whole formation to land and, with the engines left ticking over, everybody could take advantage of the open spaces to relieve themselves.

Imperial Airways continued to stage through Khartoum, but by now the Handley Page Hannibal landplanes had been replaced by the Short Empire flying boats. KLM and Alitalia also used the aerodrome. Record-breaking flyers as well passed through, including Amelia Earhart on her round the world flight, which ended in her, her co-pilot and the aeroplane disappearing over the Pacific. One intrepid pair was the Lewins; 63-year-old Brigadier A.C. and his wife – in a single-engined Miles Whitney Straight (G-AEZO) – were on their way to Kenya when their aeroplane disappeared flying south from Khartoum in October 1937. After some days of searching, including by Imperial Airways aircraft, they were found alive and well on the upturned wreck of their machine; they were rescued and returned to Khartoum in one of the squadron's Vincents.

The life for the young men posted to this remote part of the Empire was a curious combination of home comforts and life over-seas. The squadron was largely self-sufficient, with its own headquarters, workshops, W/T station, stores, sick quarters and so on, all housed in permanent buildings just outside the boundary of Khartoum. The aeroplanes were looked after by the ground crew, fitters and riggers etc., only having to be flown north back to Egypt and the maintenance base at Aboukir for major overhauls.

All personnel were housed within the station, except the officers who had a mess and bungalows across the road just outside the wire. There was the traditional range of social and formal functions and the 'colonial' society of the British abroad with its strict pecking order of social status. Those officers without the equivalent income level were treated as 'Honorary Grade Three', by virtue of holding the king's commission.

For the men the posting was for three years unaccompanied. Dick "Buck" Taylor arrived in 1939, but his experiences would have been little different for drafts that had arrived at Khartoum any time during the 1930s. He set sail from Southampton on the troop ship *Somersetshire* in February and eventually reached Port Sudan after a voyage across the Mediterranean and through the Suez Canal: 'When we took our KD (khaki drill uniforms) out of our kit bags and changed into it, you had never seen such a sight. ... Nothing tailored, shorts below the knees, tunics too big, black boots instead of shoes, topees too big.' From Port Sudan it was a two-day rail journey to Khartoum, finally arriving at about six in the evening. 'A Sudanese came out of the camp gate leading a donkey, accompanied by two others with brooms. The Warrant Officer in charge of our party was asked to mount the donkey and slowly he was led in and under the camp gate. All the time the two other Sudanese were sweeping the road in front of the donkey to ensure that the donkey did not trip up and that the new draft arrived safely. As we walked under the archway we saw the Squadron on the roof and they rained hundreds of beer bottle tops down on our topees.' The daily routine of squadron life meant being 'woken up by the billet boy at half past five with a mug of tea and a chunk of fruit cake and work by six o'clock'.

Buck Taylor was an aircraft rigger: 'Breakfast, eight to nine, and with Topees, back to work until one o'clock. A light meal, tiffin, and a quick shower and into bed. All shutters of the billet had to closed by eight o'clock in the morning, with six big fans in the ceiling trying to keep us cool. Peace reigned until four in the afternoon when the sportsmen got up to pursue their different pleasures.'

Pilot Officer Graham Reese 'Digger' Magill joined the unit in April 1938 from 211 Squad-ron and recalls:[50]

47 Squadron consisted of three flights of Vincents and one of Gordons. The Gordons were converted to float planes (great fun) for part of the year to enable them to operate in the upper Nile areas during the rainy season.

The flights were commanded by a flight lieutenant or flying officer according to the squadron strength at the time. If I remember correctly, each flight had five aircraft with others held in the station's maintenance organization.

Pilots were definitely allocated to flights as evenly as numbers would permit. Overseas squadrons had a higher proportion of NCO pilots than did the home based units. … 47 Squadron had eight [NCO pilots in early 1938]. Incidentally, those NCO pilots I knew were of the highest quality and those who survived the early stages of the war were soon to be commissioned.

Initially air gunners were 'recruited' from airmen of any trade within the station, given gunnery training and a pittance of extra pay to fly part-time in that role in addition to their normal duties. The badge of distinction was the 'flying bullet' worn on the uniform sleeve.

Observers were different. They were recruited from the various trades and sent on specific navigation, bombing and armament courses prior to posting to units according to their role. They wore the original 'O' Observers half wing – the flying arse-hole!! Pre-war Khartoum we had three, one was an ex-wireless operator, one an ex-aero engine fitter and the other an airframes man. Later the numbers increased with the introduction of commissioned observers and gunners. The observers were full-time aircrew but on detachment at other times of shortage the ex-tradesmen were known to help out to a considerable effect. They were a very good lot.[51]

For the men of 47 Squadron there was entertainment to be had from the open-air cinema at the barracks and the bars at the Grand Hotel (officers only) or the Gordon Hotel (open to other ranks). The Grand was also used for the overnight stays for the passengers of the Imperial Airways flights. Initially these would be by flying boat, which would alight on the Nile, but later by landplanes, which would land on the aerodrome shared with 47 Squadron.

An additional source of income could be obtained, as a bounty of £20 for officers and £10 for other ranks was paid to those who took and passed local examinations in colloquial Arabic, and this was always a popular and lucrative diversion. Some ground crew were also known to supplement their income by servicing private aeroplanes as they passed through.

In the mid-1930s the RAF undertook one of its fairly frequent reorganisations and the rank of seargent major was abolished; those holding that rank were promoted to warrant officer. One of the reasons for this was the realisation that in a 'pilots only' officer set-up there was a need for senior NCOs to take on the roles of squadron engineering officer and squadron armaments officer, and with many overseas squadrons there was no officer in the nominal role qualified to take this responsibility, so this was passed on to warrant officers, who could then qualify for promotion to flying officer and thus there was a need to back-fill this rank.

Other changes included the introduction of short-sleeve 'romper suits', which ended at the knee, to replace the unsuitable blue boiler suit used in the UK. The heavy Wolsley pith helmet was replaced with the much lighter 'tea planter' type. Both were much appreciated by the ground crews working in the heat.

Being more than 1,200 miles from headquarters in Cairo, 47 Squadron was able to run its own affairs without too much interference from above, and if the top brass did decide to head south for a visit, there would be ample warning of their arrival, and they could be hustled away on the threat of impending sandstorms (haboobs) that could blow up at any time, causing the complete shutting down of the aerodrome, and rather uncomfortable living conditions.

In June 1939 the squadron took delivery of the first of its Vickers Wellesleys. This by squadron standards was a leap forward, a single-engined monoplane bomber with retractable undercarriage. It used the geodetic structure designed by Barnes Wallis, which gave it strength but was light, imbuing the aircraft with a long range and endurance. It carried a bomb load of 2,000lb in panniers under the wings and was armed with a forward-firing 0.303 machine gun, with another machine gun in the rear cockpit. Although it had a much better performance than the Fairey Gordons and Hawker Audaxes it was due to replace in the light bomber role, it soon became obvious that its lack of speed and defensive armament would make it easy meat for the new German fighter, the Bf109, that was beginning to enter service, thus it was soon withdrawn from home service. However, the aeroplane's exceptional range, 1,100 miles (specially modified Wellesleys of the Long Range Development Unit established a distance record of 7,158 miles after 48 hours in the air in November 1938, flying from Egypt to Australia), was seen as perfect for service in the Middle East and East Africa where it was assumed it would stand a better chance against the far less capable Italian fighters.

The Wellesleys that arrived at Khartoum were genuine hand-me-downs, many in a poor state of repair and in need of major servicing, which could only be done back at the main depot at Aboukir in Egypt. The crews took some time to get used to the new aeroplanes and in the first couple of months there were a number of accidents: L2640 suffered an engine failure on 28 August 1939 and force-landed in a swamp, where it was abandoned; L2699 overshot on landing, swung, and its undercarriage collapsed on 3 October; L2700 crash-landed 3 miles west of Jebel Aulia on 16 October; and K7776 crashed on landing at Khartoum on 18 October. Magill says: 'It was an easy aeroplane to fly and, in general there were no real problems in converting to type. Unfortunately we had one fatality. A Sergeant Pilot in my flight [Sergeant. W.R.T. Shelley Wellesley in L2702, 13 September 1939] spun in on his first circuit of the airfield. Although well briefed beforehand we could only assume that he was concentrating too hard on the new hydraulic controls for flaps and undercarriage, let the airspeed fall away and spun without any hope of recovery at that height. Another spectacular incident involved a pilot of less than distinguished natural ability who came in to land much too fast, charged across the airfield and disappeared into the sanitary farm beyond the boundary amidst a veritable cloud of flying lavatory buckets. No water-borne sewage then.'[52]

Chapter 6

TAKING ON THE ITALIANS

East Africa, 1940–1941

After the declaration of war on 3 September 1939, the squadron moved on to its war footing and spent much of its time practising dispersing aircraft and ground crews to a number of prepared emergency airfields closer to the border with Ethiopia. Although war had not been declared against Italy, this was the direction that any threat was likely to come. Aircrews were still getting used to the Wellesleys and new aircraft would be delivered frequently to bring the squadron up to strength. The crews also needed extra training, and the changes to aircrew status that had been introduced had to be integrated into squadron life.

The Italians had gone to great lengths to encourage colonialists to move to Ethiopia after it had been occupied, but even so they were still very much isolated from the homeland and could muster only one division of regular troops, although these were well trained, equipped and led and would prove tough opposition in any future fighting. The regulars were supported by 'Blackshirt' battalions, equipped as territorial units of local volunteers, mostly older than the average front-line solider, lacking in equipment and training, but in defending their new home they were to prove tenacious and determined.

The bulk of the army was made up of locally recruited, native battalions, but these presented significant organisational headaches in trying to maintain a workable racial mix, as many tribes were hostile to each other on sight. The units had Italian officers and senior NCOs and were often useful in attack, if well led; but in defence they proved vulnerable to artillery and air attack, not being comfortable with the European way of war. At the bottom of the pile came the 'Banda', native skirmishers and scouts with Italian officers and used for local policing duties.

The usual engineer, medical and administrative arms, with a few pieces of artillery, armoured cars and tanks ancient and modern, supported the army. In total the Italian ground forces amounted to some 280,000 men. By June 1940, once reserves had been called up, the total stood at 330,000 troops. However, they were badly restricted in what they could achieve due to a critical lack of transport and decent communications, and trying to cover a vast area of mostly mountainous country.

On paper the Italian air force (Regia Aeronautica) was of sufficient size to provide a decent level of air support, but, as with the rest of the military, much of the equipment was out of date and obsolete by mainland European standards. The most important aircraft was the Caproni Ca.133, a trimotor monoplane with fixed undercarriage. It had been designed in the early 1930s with colonial duties in mind and could be used as a bomber or troop transporter, comparable to the RAF's Bristol Bombay. However, the designers did not consider that it would face fighter opposition and, as such, its defensive armament was poor. The dedicated bombing force was made up of Savoia-Marchetti SM.81s and 79s. The SM.81 was a trimotor fixed undercarriage aircraft that had seen useful service during the Spanish Civil War; it could carry a bomb load of 4,000lb and had a range of 1,250 miles. Yet it was poorly protected and would need fighter escort to be able to operate in areas defended by fighters. The SM.79 was the best bomber available, again a trimotor aircraft, but of more modern design with a retractable undercarriage. It was fast, by local standards, at 270mph and had adequate defensive armament; however, the bomb load was only 2,750lb and it had a range of 1,250 miles. Fortunately there were only twelve SM.79s available in the region in June 1940. The SM.79 was to excel as a torpedo bomber in the Mediterranean during the war. For short-range reconnaissance and army cooperation the Italians had the IMAM Ro.37Bis, a single-engined biplane equivalent to the Fairey Gordon.

The Italian fighter force consisted of two types, both biplanes with fixed undercarriage. The Fiat CR.32 had first entered service in 1932 and was now just about obsolete. It was under-gunned with only two 12.7mm (about 0.5in) machine guns, but these little aeroplanes were rugged and manoeuvrable and the machine guns packed a bigger punch than the British 0.303s. The other fighter was the Fiat CR.42 (Falco), probably the best biplane fighter in anybody's air force at the time. It had a top speed of 272mph, not great by the standards of the monoplane fighters in other air forces, but it was very manoeuvrable, being able to out turn most opposition, a useful advantage in a dogfight and was a stable gun platform. Like the CR.32, however, it was under-gunned, only having two 12.7mm machine guns. It had entered service in early 1939.

Camouflaged Vickers Vincent, 1940. *Jarvis, via author*

It was in Africa Orientale Italiana (AOI) that the nimble Italian biplane performed best.

In 1940, three squadriglie stationed in Italian East Africa – Ethiopia, Italian Eritrea and Italian Somaliland – were equipped with CR.42s. The 412a – the most experienced squadriglia – was based in Gura (with the 414a Squadriglia) and in Massawa. The 413a Squadriglia was in Assab.

No. 47 Squadron had a good opportunity to see what they were up against, as on a number of occasions the Italian bombers and transports staged through Khartoum on their way to Ethiopia, before hostilities commenced. Buck Taylor recalls helping to refuel the Italian bombers; when they left the following morning 'we noticed that the camera door was open and they were taking shots of everything in Khartoum; the army camp and the air force'.

The RAF was no better equipped. By June 1940 it had assembled three Wellesley squadrons; 47 Squadron had moved up to its war station at Erkowit in May 1940, in the Red Sea hills on the railway from Port Sudan (50 miles north) to Khartoum (330 miles south-west), 30 miles west of the Red Sea and 100 miles north of Eritrea. No. 223 Squadron was based at Summit nearby and 14 Squadron was at Port Sudan. This was rather grandly referred to as the 'advanced striking force' under the control of 254 Wing. No. 47 Squadron's Vincent D Flight was split off for army cooperation duties. Air defence was provided by nine Gloster Gladiators of 112 Squadron based at Summit. The Gladiator was more than a match for the CR.32, but struggled against the CR.42 where the Italian aircraft's better speed and manoeuvrability was a distinct advantage. Also the Gladiator's four 0.303 Brownings lacked the punch of the Italian's 12.7mm (equivalent to 0.5in). The Gladiator's endurance of about 2 hours also meant that it was not suitable for escort on most sorties.

Across the Red Sea in Aden at Khormaksar was a small force comprising 8 Squadron, equipped with one flight of Vickers Vincents and one of Blenheim 1s, and 203 Squadron, with Blenheim IVs, some of which were fitted with a ventral gun pack carrying four 0.303 Brownings and known as Blenheim IVFs. The Blenheims were quick by bomber standards (260mph) and could carry a 1,000lb bomb load, but it was soon shown in the Battle of France, when acting as day bombers, that they were horribly vulnerable to fighters. No. 94 Squadron was at Sheikh Othman with a flight of Gladiators, and was joined in June by two more Blenheim squadrons, Nos 39 and 11.

To the south of the Italian forces in Kenya the RAF had nothing, but fortunately Rhodesia and South Africa were able to make up some of the deficit. This was a real hotch-potch of types, including a few Hawker Hurricanes, with the main strike force comprising 11(B) Squadron SAAF, equipped with twenty-four ancient Hawker Hartebeests, a two-seat bi-plane light bomber of early 1930s vintage, developed from the RAF's Hart bomber, and 12(B) Squadron SAAF with thirteen twin-engined Junkers Ju 86s. The Ju 86 had originally been designed as a bomber in the 1930s. Those delivered to South Africa had been converted for civilian use, but were now changed back to their original role. The SAAF also had a few Hawker Fury biplane fighters and a lone Fairey Battle single-engined light bomber. As the campaign developed, more aeroplanes would be added to both sides, but none of these, with the exception of a few Hurricanes, were to be of modern types.

Ground forces comprised three British Army infantry battalions and twenty companies of the Sudan Defence Force, a total of about 9,000 men in Sudan, 1,475 men of the Camel Corps in British Somaliland and a further 8,500 troops in Kenya.

There was a small Armáe de l'Air detachment in French Somaliland, consisting of four Potez 631 twin-engined modern reconnaissance bombers, eleven Potez 25 TOE army cooperation biplanes, a type that first saw service in 1926, three Morane 406 modern single-engined fighters and two Potez 29 single-engined biplane and general liaison aircraft. They were to take little or no part in the forthcoming conflict as, after the fall of France, their allegiance was to the Vichy government.

This was the extent of the forces available to both sides. They faced each other across an inhospitable region about the size of western Europe, from deserts in the north to arid grasslands in the south. Much of the area was mountainous and over 5,000 feet with peeks in excess of 10,000 feet, cut through by impassable ravines and thorny scrub. To the east were vast plateaus and intense stifling heat, to the west dense tropical forest. It was a conflict about as far removed from that going on in western Europe as one could get. An almost complete lack of modern aircraft, few maps – and those that were available of dubious accuracy – and no navigation aids. Neither was there RDF (radar) to provide early warning; the best available method was a man up a tall tree with a pair of binoculars and a field telephone. Poor radio communications, especially ground to air, and a critical shortage of spares and stores added to the list. On the ground, the forces were largely made up of inadequately equipped colonial troops, hindered by an almost complete lack of suitable or reliable transport to cover the vast distances involved. In these circumstances it was probably best to wait for the enemy to come to you; armies could stumble about the region for years without making contact.

In June 1940 the war in Europe was going badly for the Allies. France had all but been defeated, and the British Army had left most of its kit and a lot of its best trained men on the wrong side of the Channel. In the Mediterranean, the British and French navies were confident that they could keep the sea open for convoys, but this was all to change rapidly when Italy entered the war on Germany's side, seeing the opportunity for easy gains and reclaiming parts of southern France, and declared war on the evening of 10 June.

The RAF was the first to react and at first light the following day eight 47 Squadron Wellesleys took off to bomb the Italian base at Asmara in Eritrea. The target was found and bombed, but Italian AA fire hit Wellesley K7730, piloted by Pilot Officer B.K.C. Fuge, which crashed in Italian territory and the crew were taken prisoner. 47 Squadron was followed into action by the SAAF (officially some 6 hours before South Africa formally declared war on Italy) in the south and later in the day 14 Squadron carried out its first raid. Other squadrons undertook reconnaissance sorties. The Italian air force carried out a single aircraft raid on Port Sudan and sent three S.81s to bomb Aden that night; one S.81 returned early and another struck a hill on its homeward flight, killing the crew. Now the gloves were off and the activity rapidly increased. The next day there were numerous raids and reconnaissance flights made by both sides. Eight 47 Squadron Wellesleys attacked Asmara again and although intercepted by fighters only one Wellesley was slightly damaged; another Wellesley was hit on the ground on 15 June when the airfield at Erkowit was bombed by two S.81s, and on the 17th another by RAF Gladiators, which attacked it in error, and the aircraft was forced to make an emergency landing, fortunately without injury to the crew.

The 47 Squadron Vincents were in action on the 21st. Three aircraft of D Flight had moved forward to an advanced landing ground at Malakal the day before, and carried out a raid on an Italian outpost at Asosa just across the border in Ethiopia. Vincent K4683, flown by Pilot Officer J.E. Dennant, ran out of fuel on the return journey and had to force land. The aeroplane was undamaged and on the 24th fuel was flown in and a temporary air-strip built to allow Dennant to fly the Vincent out and back to Malakal. The same day an armistice was signed between Italy and France.

No. 47 Squadron suffered its second Wellesley loss on the 25th when L2696 failed to return from a reconnaissance sortie to cover Asmara, Gura and Massawa. The aircraft piloted by Sergeant F.A. Saunders came down shortly after overflying Asmara, due to technical problems, and the crew set fire to the aircraft before being captured. On 30 June the squadron sent a detachment of seven Wellesleys back to Khartoum, from where five aircraft carried out a low-level bombing and strafing run on Italian troops at Metemma on 2 July.

During the attack Wellesley K7777 was hit by ground fire and crashed. The pilot, Pilot Officer C.G. Bush, was killed and the wireless operator/air gunner, Sergeant J.W. Davidson, died the following day.

By mid-July 47 Squadron Wellesleys were flying combined raids with the Wellesleys of 14 Squadron to Massawa airfield. Some of the 14 Squadron aircraft had been up-gunned and now carried four Lewis guns, plus the single forward-firing Vickers. On 12 July 47 Squadron's base at Erkowit had its name changed to Carthago. During a combined raid on Asmara on the 16th two 47 Squadron Wellesleys collided in mid-air during an attack by fighters; Sergeant W.C.H. Style's aircraft, L2641, crashed, killing the crew, while the other aircraft, K7771, managed to return to Carthago where it was written off.

Italian ground forces had made some gains by the end of July, and crossed the border into Sudan. The airfield at Kassala became a target for 47 Squadron raids, now close enough to benefit from the escort of Gladiators. As August opened, the tempo of operations did not diminish. On the 3rd the Vincents of D Flight were formed into an independent unit, 430 (Army Cooperation) Flight, which also was equipped with five Gloster Gauntlet biplane fighters. In the same month 203 Group, RAF, was set up under the command of Air Commodore L.H. Slatter (a 47 Squadron 'old boy' who had served with the squadron in Russia) to control all RAF air units in Sudan.

On 4 August ten Wellesleys from 47 and 14 Squadrons attacked naval facilities at Sheikh Said Island, coming at them from the landward side, with Blenheims of 45 Squadron flying in low from the sea. Despite intense AA fire, the raid was a success and no aircraft were lost, although many returned with some form of damage.

On the ground, the Italians were making inroads into British Somaliland and, despite air support being provided from Aden, it was only a matter of time before the position became untenable and had to be evacuated.

Newly arrived Wellesley still wearing previous squadron codes, Khartoum, 1939.
Jarvis, via author

47 Squadron continued to carry out bombing raids on Italian targets throughout the following weeks. In the early hours of 16 October a 430 Flight Vincent, piloted by Flight Lieutenant Mitchell operating from the 47 Squadron forward operating base at Gaderef, attacked Tessenei airfield. Unfortunately, on his return flight he was followed by an Italian Ca.133, which was able to report where the Wellesleys were operating from. The Italians immediately organised a strike. An SM.79, personally piloted by Generale Piacentini, took off from Tessenei at 05.25 hours leading nine CR.42s of 412 Squadriglia. The SM.79 bombed without much effect, but the fighters then strafed the airfield and destroyed all eight 47 Squadron Wellesleys and two 430 Flight Vincents. Desperate calls were made to the fighter detachment at nearby Azzoza, but the line had been cut. Pilot Officer Chopping, the adjutant of 223 Squadron was inspired to write the following poem:

The Ides of Gaderef

Ho trumpets sound the war note
Ho lictors clear the way
The knights will ride in all their pride
Along the streets today.
Today the doors and windows
Are hung with garlands bright
And from Asmara down to Addis
The beacons flare with light.
So long as Mussolini
His place of pride shall fill
The proud Ides of Gaderef
Shall have such an honour still
Gay is the day of the march on Rome
Adowa's day is gay (1)
Cut the proud Ides when the squadron rides
Shall be Rome's proudest day
For on this day was ended
A fourth Punic war
And before the might of Roman Arms
Carthago bowed down once more (2)
All hail to Piatcentini (3)
Who humbled cartage's might?
All hail the gallant seven
Who helped him in the fight?
The gallant knight Cascara
And Macaroon so brave
Sagrada from the banks of the Po
And Count Spaghetti grave.
The bold Chianti brother
Made up this little band
Who swept with fire and pillage
The Carthaginian land.
In seven stout Roman Fiats (4)
The knights took off that day
And in his fleet Savoia (5)
Piatcentini led the way
For across the border
On Gaderef aerodrome
The martial tents of Pelly Fry (6)
Defy the might of Rome
Heedless the Carthaginian
Swills down his ham and eggs
Soon, soon he'll taste a bitterer cup

Wellesley taxying.
Jarvis, via author

**And drain it to the dregs
For he trust in the South African (7)
To guard him from the raid.
He little knows the fatal gap
Which cuts him off from aid.
Now looking down from high aloft
Upon the scene of peace
Brave Piacentini gave the sign
And pulled the bomb release.
At once a rain of biting fire
Falls on the surprised foe
And the Fiats sweep like eagles
Upon the prey below.
Sir Pelly's Wellesley that was once
Now sits between Sagrada's sights
And is raked from nose to tail.
The mount of Brave Magill is now (8)
Cascara's easy prey.
And a pair of burning Wellesleys mark
Macaroon's victorious way.
Spaghetti cries in wonderment
'Why what is this I see
Those box like two winged monsters (9)
That stand beyond yon tree?
Are they savage idols
Worshipped of ancient time
Or skeletons of mammoth beasts
From a prehistoric time?'
What ere they are he fires at them
And, to his great surprise
The pride and joy of Mitchell (10)
Goes flaming to the skies
The haughty face of Carthage now
In the lowly dust is laid,
While Walker rings up frantically (11)
And tries to summon aid
'To arms, to arms South Africa!'
For in the night, a stealthy spy
Has cut the telephone
'A horse, a horse!' brave Witty cries (12)
And quickly spurs away
Too late he rides, for Carthago
Has already lost the day.
As Piatcentini gazes down
On the roote of the foe
He sees a thing untouched
In the flame and smoke below.
'Why that belongs to our foes of old
The deadly 223. (13)
We'll leave it as a tribute
To a gallant enemy.'
So stands the sole survivor
Of Cartago's fiery fate
Chance lights, prime mover, item one (13)
In solitary state
The work is done
The day is won
Carthago is destroyed
Mussolini's bosom swells
And Hitler's overjoyed
But Khartoum sits in sackcloth
With ashes on its head
The AOC sits all alone (15)
And staff creep round in dread.
For he is reading a signal
And his breast fills with remorse,
'The Mayfly for today sir – (16)
One serviceable horse.'**

(1) Adowa – probably means Aosata, Italian Viceroy of East Africa.
(2) Carthago – 47 Squadron's airfield.
(3) Piacentini – Italian air commander, East Africa.
(4) Fiat – CR.42.
(5) Savoia – SM.79.
(6) Squadron Leader J.E. Pelly-Fry, 47 Squadron OC 15/08/40–01/01/41
(7) No. 1 Squadron SAAF with Gladiators and based nearby.
(8) Flight Lieutenant G.R. 'Digger' Magill, OC after Pelly-Fry.
(9) No. 430 Flight Vincents.
(10) Flight Lieutenant A.B. Mitchell.
(11) Squadron pilot.
(12) Pilot Officer Witty, later shot down on 6 December and died in captivity.
(13) 223 squadron, also equipped with Wellesleys
(14) Chance Light – armoured flood light.
(15) Air Commodore Leonard Slatter
(16) Mayfly – daily return of available aircraft.

How this light-hearted poem would have been viewed if it had fallen into the hands of senior RAF officers back at headquarters, may have had an adverse affect on Pilot Officer Chopping's future prospects and postings, one suspects not in a positive way.

The South Africans of 1 Squadron tried to square the score the following day and attacked the Italian airfield at Barentu with three Gladiators. They caught three CR.42s preparing to take off and set them on fire; they then turned to strafe an S.79 and five

Ca.133s on the airfield, claiming the destruction of all. However, Italian records do not confirm this, only noting the loss of the fighters. General Heath sent the South Africans a present of champagne; 47 Squadron were not so impressed, still surveying the smoldering remains of about half the squadron. Replacement aircraft came from 14 Squadron, which was re-equipping with Blenheim IVs.

On 6 November British ground forces opened their first offensive of the war with artillery and air support as they pushed towards Gallabat. The Italians, initially taken by surprise, reacted swiftly to the air threat and within the first hour five Gladiators had been shot down without a single loss being inflicted on the enemy. The British and Indian troops continued to push forward, but most of the tanks were knocked out or damaged, and on the rocky ground the infantry were vulnerable to the Italian bombers, which were thrown into the defence. The British had lost local air superiority, but by the end of the day the ground forces had taken Gallabat Fort.

The next day, 47 Squadron Wellesleys, escorted by South African Gladiators, were over the front, but the Allied forces were too weak to make a decisive impact. The Gladiators successfully kept the CR.42s away from the bombers, but while distracted an Italian bomber force got through and pounded the ground forces at Gallabat and it was decided that holding the fort was untenable so the British withdrew to the surrounding hills. Another ground assault further north, near Kassala, also ran into trouble, and, after coming under intense bomber attack, fell back.

47 Squadron's detachment at Sennar sent four aircraft to attack the village and fort at Burie on the morning of 6 December, one aircraft returning early with engine trouble. The remainder of the force continued on its mission, but were intercepted by CR.42s and Wellesley K8521, flown by Pilot Officer Witty, was shot down; the crew bailed out and were subsequently captured.

During December an offensive was launched by imperial forces from Kenya. In the meantime 47 Squadron had moved to Gordon's Tree near Khartoum, but maintained detachments near the front at Blackdown, close to the railway line about 15 miles east of Gaderef. At the end of 1940 the Italian air force was still a formidable foe, although the delivery of reinforcements was difficult and on 1 January 1941 it could field about 132 serviceable aircraft, with another 125 in various states of disrepair. Also the balance of types was moving to more modern aircraft with the availability of S.79s and CR.42s having increased, although the Ca.133 still made up the largest single type available. Most of

Previous page:
47 Squadron 'A' Flight, Khartoum, 1940.
Jarvis, via author

Left: Wellesley KU-C in flight, 1940.
Jarvis, via author

Right: Attack on Kassala, 17 August 1940.
Jarvis, via author

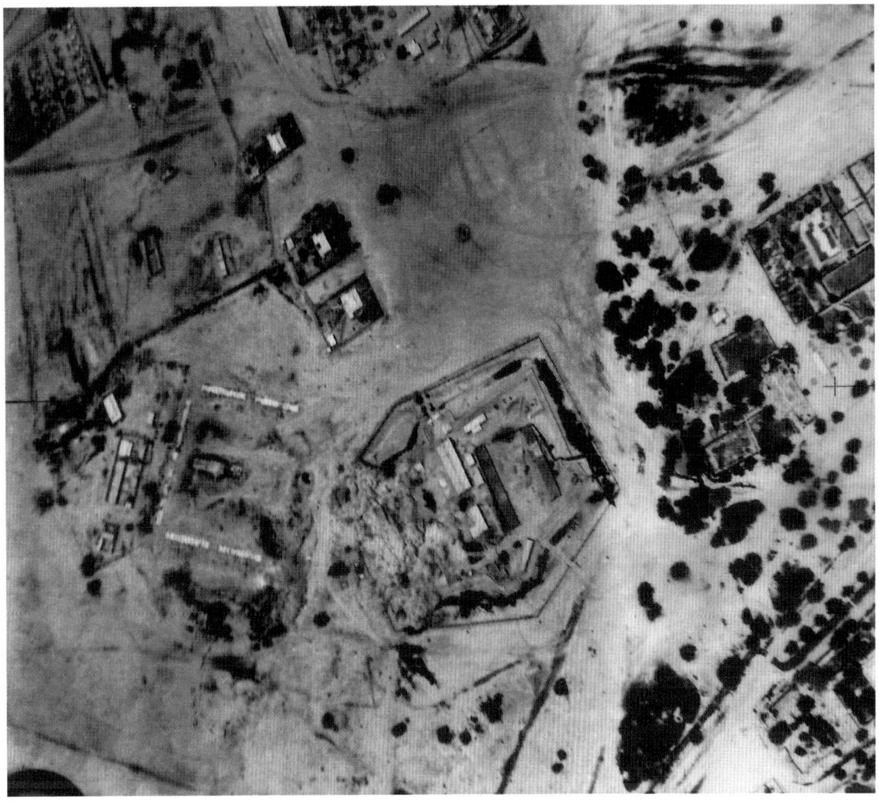

the aircraft were based in the north and west (about 75%), which were facing the 203 Group squadrons.

For the RAF, in numbers it was at least reaching parity, and it did not face the same problems of reinforcement, with more modern aeroplanes beginning to arrive. However, the Wellesleys of 47 and 223 Squadrons still made up bulk of the long-range bomber force. No. 223 Squadron was almost entirely operating at night, while 47 Squadron was carrying out some long-range – 500 miles plus – raids into Ethiopia in support of Ethiopian patriotic forces preparing to rise up in aid of the exiled Haile Selassie who was awaiting the opportunity to re-enter his country.

In preparation for a new British ground assault to retake Kassala, 47 Squadron moved six Wellesleys to Blackdown. The British started their offensive on 20 January, but the Italians had evacuated Kassala the day before. 47 Squadron used its aircraft to attack the airfields at Barentu and Agordat and the Caproni workshops at Mai Edaga. On the 20th a 47 Squadron Wellesley flew Haile Selassie from Khartoum to Umm Idla on the border with Ethiopia, while in the north the British offensive continued, making progress against the Italian defenders despite regular interference from Italian bombers and fighters.

Operations continued throughout the month and into February. On the 6th two 47 Squadron Wellesleys carried out a road reconnaissance from Barentu to Adi Ugri, but were intercepted by CR.42s of 412a Squadriglia, both aircraft being shot down. The Allied forces continued to advance into Ethiopia and Eritrea. During this period of intense air fighting the Italians had lost fifty-three aircraft destroyed and twenty-three damaged, about 75% of its front-line strength at the beginning of the year, with little hope of the losses being replaced. Some 95 men were posted dead, wounded or missing. They were losses that could not be sustained for much longer, but throughout the conflict the Italian air force fought with tenacity and aggression.

In Eritrea the Italian forces were holding out in the strong defences that were made possible by the natural fortress at Keren, but they were unable to break out and were kept under regular air assault. By the middle of March sufficient British and Indian ground forces had been built up to plan for a final raid. The operation started at 07.00 hours on 15 March and throughout the day the Blenheims and Wellesleys of 14, 47 and 223 Squadrons maintained regular bombing attacks, dropping some 38,800lb of bombs in support. The next day the sorties continued, but one of the 47 Squadron assaults was intercepted by five CR.42s, shooting down K8527, the aircraft of Pilot Officer Leuchars.

Only the pilot was able to bail out and the observer, Sergeant S.W.J. English and WOP/AG Sergeant C.W. Minn were both killed and are buried in Keren war cemetery.

Reinforcements arrived at the squadron the next day in the form of a Free French Blenheim IV (Z9583) of GRB1, which was attached to the unit for a period. On 18 March the squadron lost another Wellesley, K7786, when it was caught on the ground by strafing fighters at Agordat. On the ground heavy fighting continued as the British and Indian infantry tried to force their way through the Italian defences.

No. 47 Squadron was fully committed to operating from Agordat as the battle to take Keren reached a climax, and was flying numerous sorties over the battlefield in support of ground forces. On 25 March it flew sixteen, but Pilot Officer Kennedy's aircraft (K7715) was intercepted by two CR.42s and in the ensuing exchange of fire the air gunner, Sergeant D.A. German was mortally wounded and the aircraft set on fire. Kennedy, in a desperate attempt to put out the flames in the wings, dived vertically – it would either work and blow out the flames, or just accelerate the process by which the wing structure burned through and detached itself from the rest of the aeroplane, with fatal results. Fortunately the plan worked and Kennedy was able to nurse the aircraft back to Agordat, where it crashed on landing to join a quickly growing pile of written off Wellesleys dumped on the airfield.

Keren eventually fell on 27 March and approximately 40,000 Italian prisoners and 300 guns were captured, while those Italians who could withdraw were subjected to strafing attacks from assorted Vincents, Gladiators, Lysanders and Hardys, with some Hurricanes joining in. One of the 430 Flight Vincents was shot down. By 1 April Asmara, the Eritrean capital, had fallen. The Italians had lost some 3,000 men and the colonial troops were deserting in droves. However, the naval units at Massawa made a last desperate sortie to raid Port Said and Suez. The flotilla was detected and attacked by combined RAF and FAA aircraft with Royal Navy ships. None of the Italian destroyers made their intended target, all being sunk, run aground or scuttled. At Massawa most of the remaining shipping, both navy and civilian, were scuttled.

In Ethiopia, Addis Ababa was soon to fall and in early April the fighting was all but over. On the 17th 223 Squadron headed for Shandur in Egypt for conversion to Marylands, and handed over its remaining Wellesleys to 47 Squadron, which returned to Asmara on the 24th. However, the fighting was not quite over and isolated Italian units continued to hold out, their hope being that a successful campaign in North Africa and Egypt would

From left: Vickers Vincents, Sudan, 1940. *Jarvis, via author*

Buck Taylor, Khartoum, 1939/40. *via Buck Taylor/ 47 Squadron*

Somewhat weathered Wellesley in flight, 1939/40. *Jarvis via author*

force the British to abandon East Africa. In the north they occupied Dessie, a fortress facing the imperial troops advancing south from Asmara. To the west was another fortress at Gondar. There were also scattered units around Addis Ababa and in the south, but these were being contained by patriot bands. Much of the imperial forces had been hastily sent to Egypt to strengthen the defences after the British Army had been driven back by the newly arrived Africa Korps, and in Greece the position was also looking desperate. This meant that in the north the only air assets available were 47 and 237 Squadrons (Gladiators), with the Blenheims of the Free French Flight and three Ju.52/3ms of 51 SAAF Flight.

These mopping-up operations were to continue until the end of November. 47 Squadron was heavily involved in the bombing of the fortress at Gondar and on 2 July another Wellesley and crew were lost when L2713 (Pilot Sergeant A.G. Brown, observer Flight Sergeant S.A. Elsy and WOP/AG Flight Sergeant D.G. Barbonne) was shot down by two CR.42s, all the crew being killed; they are buried at Asmara war cemetery. At this time it was only Gondar that was holding out, but it contained some 25,000 troops and the imperial forces lacked the strength to take it. Moreover, the heavy rains that fell between July and September made all movement virtually impossible. Consequently, the RAF and SAAF were given the task of keeping the Italians bottled up until more suitable weather conditions would allow an assault. 47 Squadron was also tasked with dropping supplies to ground forces.

In August at Asmara, as recalled by Buck Taylor, a ground crew were awaiting the arrival of a Wellesley from Addis Ababa:

We sat outside the hangar listening for the approaching drone of the aircraft; Asmara

was over 7,000 feet up and when the aircraft staggered up over the edge of the plateau it seemed to have already started its approach.

The normal crew were pilot, navigator and rear gunner, but on this trip a passenger had replaced the gunner. I mounted the step opening the heavily loaded spring Perspex canopy. Looking into the fuselage, I saw a young army captain gathering his kit together. I turned to the form 700 and was debriefed by the pilot Flying Officer James, a young bachelor. This done he turned and shouted towards the mid fuselage window position.

'Sling down my hat Bonner.'

Bonner was a navigator, a sergeant married with three children. Neither answer nor hat arrived. James jumped onto the step, put his head through the window and peered fore and aft. No navigator. He turned to the passenger.

'Where's the nav?'

He bailed out about 300 miles back.'

'He what? What the hell for?'

'I don't know. He came through the tunnel, clipped his chute on his chest, put a bag of desert rations over his shoulder, a water bottle over the other said 'Excuse me' opened the hatch and bailed out'

'What did he do that for?'

'Don't ask me. I thought he might be on a secret mission.'

A few days later Sergeant Bonner turned up with quite a growth on his chin. He had been picked up by Abyssinian tribesmen who had taken him to a British forces outpost; from there he had hitched transport back to Asmara and the squadron. He explained what had happened. After departure from Addis Ababa James had, instead of climbing to his briefed height, decided to have a bit of a change and fly along the valleys. But Bonner, mindful perhaps of his paternal responsibilities, had other ideas. He knew the capabilities of the Wellesley, cruising at 140 knots, one little Pegasus in the front, rate of climb at 10,000' about zero and did not fancy the idea of suddenly being confronted round the next bend by a mountainous cul de sac. The conversation had gone something like this:

Top: Crashed Wellesley. Note the long canopy. Believed taken in 1941. *Jarvis, via author*

Below: Wellesley taking off, Karen, 1941. *Magill via author*

Opposite page: Bombing Italian airfield, 1940. *Jarvis, via author*

Nav to pilot: 'Come on get on top above these mountains.'
Pilot to nav: 'Who is flying this kite?'
Nav to pilot: 'Either you get up or I get out.'
Pilot to nav: 'Go away' (or insert suitable expletive).
Nav to army officer: 'Excuse me sir.'

The final assault was scheduled for the second week of November, with 47 Squadron providing the RAF element to support the SAAF. British forces attacked on the 13th, but were driven back, and more forces were brought forward to strengthen the advance. It seems that from somewhere a rumour had started that fifteen German aircraft had arrived in the area and four 47 Squadron Wellesleys, led by the recently appointed OC Squadron Leader D.M. Illsley, DFC, set off to find and destroy them. The rumour proved false but on the sortie Illsley's aircraft (L2659) suffered a broken oil pipe, which caused the engine to seize, and Illsley tried to make an emergency landing over a hill 4 miles west of Kilo 148 on the Adi Quala–Adua Road, stalled and crashed. Illsley was killed but the other two crew members (Sergeants K.V. Rann and L.V. Martin, RAAF) survived but were injured.
At dawn on 27 November a huge artillery barrage opened up on the fortress and 47 Squadron was in the air most of the day providing support. By the end of the day Generale Nasi had surrendered and over the following days messages were dropped to isolated Italian units instructing them to surrender. In all some 11,500 Italians and 12,000 native troops were captured, along with large numbers of guns and stores. So ended a long, hard campaign, which, although only comprising relatively small forces, covered a vast area. From 47 Squadron's perspective it cost the lives of 20 aircrew, with a further 15 being taken prisoner – although all these were released as the camps they were being held in were soon liberated – and the destruction from all causes of approximately 48 Wellesleys.
In December the Squadron moved to Egypt and for four months was left with no aeroplanes to call its own until the operational echelon was formed in April with Wellesleys.

Attack on Italian position, Asmara, 19 February, 1941.
Jarvis, via author

Chapter 7

SECOND CLASS AEROPLANES, FIRST CLASS PERFORMANCE

North Africa, 1942–1943

With the ending of hostilities in East Africa, 47 Squadron moved north to Kasfareet on the great Bitter Lake, but to all intents and purposes it was disbanded as an operational squadron as it possessed no aircraft. After moving the ground crew to various landing grounds in Egypt during the early months of 1942, an operational echelon was established on 16 April at LG89, approximately 25 miles south of Alexandria, under the command of Squadron Leader E.B. Grace and equipped with Wellesleys. The air echelon became part of 235 Wing, which had established itself at Ramat David in Palestine in the naval cooperation role. Alongside the Wellesleys were 700 Squadron FAA with Walruses, 13 (Hellenic) Squadron and the Free French Nancy Flight, both equipped with Bristol Bisleys (Blenheim Mk Vs).

The role of the operational echelon was coastal patrol and anti-submarine surveillance and it moved to St Jean, Palestine, in July. On the 4th of this month one of the Wellesleys spotted a submarine off the coast and attacked, but with no reported success. On the 10th another submarine was attacked. The Wellesleys were useful in that their endurance allowed them to carry out long patrols, but they had no onboard aids to help detect their targets, relying on the use of the Mk 1 eyeball, which all crew members had been equipped with two from birth, and the shallow clear waters of the eastern Mediterranean, meaning that even submerged submarines could be spied. For attack they relied on 250lb anti-submarine bombs or depth charges, with the ability to carry four in the under-wing panniers.

At 12.18 hours on 26 August Flight Sergeant Moore observed a U-boat between Port Said and Gaza and dropped his four 250lb depth charges. A large air bubble was seen after the explosion, followed by air bubbles for 40 minutes. The C-in-C of the Mediterranean Fleet decided that the U-boat had probably been sunk; however, no U-boat or Italian submarines were reported lost around that time in the area. In September, the air echelon moved to Shandur and came under the operational control of 203 Squadron – operating Maryland, Baltimore and Blenheim V aircraft – which was carrying out a similar role. During September the air echelon carried out thirty-two sorties.

On 30 October a Wellesley (K8531) piloted by Flight Sergeant R.J. Moore, with Pilot Officer Ward as navigator and Flight Sergeant Dempsey as gunner, had just taken over a patrol from a Hudson. A Sunderland had spotted and attacked a U-boat in the area the night before and it was still being hunted, when, at 12.34 hours, the Wellesley pilot spotted a periscope, signalling to nearby destroyers he attacked and dropped three 274lb Torpex-filled depth charges on the diving submarine from approximately 30 feet. These weapons were much more effective than the old depth charges and were the first to be released in anger by 235 Wing aircraft. A large oil patch was noticed, although whether this was as a result of the attack has been open to conjecture. Moore summoned the destroyers to the scene, and remained in the area until 16.13 hours, when he was relieved by another 47 Squadron Wellesley (L2712) flown by Pilot Officer B. Osborn. The submarine (a Type VIIC U-559) was then subject to further attack from the destroyers.

Beauforts Shallufa, September 1942, newly delivered to the squadron.
Sullivan, via author

At 22.40, after some 10 hours of constant depth-charging, Kapitanleutnant Hans Heidtmann gave the order to set timing charges to scuttle the boat and surfaced close to HMS *Petard*, which immediately opened fire on the stricken U-boat. The crew abandoned the U-boat, but it would appear that the scuttling charges failed to go off. Seizing a rare opportunity, three men from *Petard* boarded the boat. Lieutenant Fasson and Able Seaman Grazier went below and recovered the code books and Enigma machine and passed them up to Boy Seaman Tommy Brown; sadly the U-boat suddenly sunk and Fasson and Graizer were lost. They were both awarded posthumous George Crosses. Brown received the George Medal, but it was discovered that he had lied about his age on enlistment and was only sixteen, and therefore was discharged from the Navy and sent home. He was killed two years later in another act of selflessness when trying to rescue his younger sister from a house fire.

The recovery of the Enigma machine and code books were a godsend to the people at Bletchley Park, who had been unable to read U-boat signals since the introduction of the Triton code (called SHARK by the code-breakers) and the four-wheel Enigma machine in February 1942.

The air echelon returned to Egypt in November, but was to have no further success and on 3 March 1943 was finally disbanded at LG07 about 25 miles west of Mersa Metruh and some 5 miles south of the coast.

In the meantime, on 8 September 1942 the main party of the squadron had been re-established at Shandur on the Great Bitter Lake from elements of Nos 39 and 42 Squadrons and equipped with Bristol Beauforts. The Beaufort was a twin-engined monoplane air-craft with a crew of four. It was Coastal Command's standard torpedo bomber from 1940 to 1943. The prototype had first flown in

October 1938 and it entered squadron service in November 1939. While it was a huge leap forward from the Vickers Vildebeest biplanes (the Vickers Vincent's torpedo-carrying relative), it was soon shown to be vulnerable when operating anti-shipping strikes in the North Sea. This factor resulted in heavy casualties and was largely responsible for the calculation that stated that the chances of surviving one operational tour was less than one in six, and two tours one in thirty-three. The aircraft were progressively up-armed with additional defensive guns, but the Beaufort was hampered by the choice of the Bristol Taurus engine. During the late 1930s airframe design was moving ahead much quicker than the design of the aero engines, which tended to be rushed into production in a desperate attempt to keep up. The Taurus was one such type and was handicapped by too little time in development before being bolted on to aeroplanes; it suffered from dangerously high running temperatures, which led to frequent engine failures. However, in the summer of 1940, with the imminent threat of invasion, these vulnerable aircraft could not be withdrawn to allow development of the engine and losses continued to mount.

It was not until late 1941 that Bristol were satisfied with the engine in the guise of the Taurus XVI, but also another solution had been found in ordering the American Pratt & Whitney Twin Wasp engine and fitting it to the airframe in what was to become the Beaufort Mk II. In early 1942 Coastal Command in the UK started to consider a replacement for the Beaufort and looked to the development of the Beaufighter as a torpedo bomber, also it was felt that the need for torpedo bombers was more urgent in the Mediterranean and Far East, and squadrons started to move overseas.

No. 47 Squadron more or less hijacked aircraft and aircrew from 39 and 42 Squadrons on their way through to the far east. This had the advantage of giving the squadron a core of experienced Beaufort crews, but, unfortunately, the aircraft tended to be rather worn-out Mk Is fitted with the less reliable earlier Taurus engines; for 47 Squadron the story was ever thus and no different to most of its aeroplanes acquired in the First World War or the Wellesley in 1939.

One of those who transferred to the unit was Eric Farrington-Birchall, a wireless operator/air gunner who had already served at least one tour with 42 Squadron in the UK until posted overseas in August 1942. The crew collected a new Beaufort from the Bristol works and set off on the long haul via Gibraltar to Malta, arriving there after some 17 hours' flying time. There the Beaufort was passed on to 39 Squadron, who exchanged it for one of their own war-weary Mk 1s for the final leg to Egypt, where they arrived, just, in early September. Eric was to remain with 47 Squadron throughout its time with Beauforts until, having completed some two and half operational tours, he was posted back to the UK when 47 Squadron converted to Beaufighters in June 1943.

The re-established 47 Squadron had a new boss, Wing Commander Richard Sprague, DFC. He had previously commanded 208 Squadron in 1940, an army cooperation squadron flying Lysanders in North Africa, and then 221 Squadron, an anti-shipping Wellington squadron, although he had only been in that post for a month before being sent to 5 Middle East Training School (METS) for torpedo training. On taking up his new command, 47 Squadron started to work up on the new aircraft and role. It was part of 201 (Naval Cooperation) Group, which comprised eleven squadrons, including three belonging to the Fleet Air Arm. The group operated a variety of aircraft types, providing support to naval units and shipping strikes. On 24 October 47 Squadron was sufficiently trained to take on operations and the first eight Beauforts left Shandur and moved west to a forward airfield at Gianaclis, about 25 miles south of Alexandria, in an area dotted with landing grounds (LGs) that were basically sufficiently flat bits of desert to land an aeroplane, but with very limited facilities, everything being mobile and without permanent resources. The LGs tended to be clustered close to established roads or railways, which not only helped with supplying the units but was also a useful navigation feature in a relatively featureless sand and rock desert.

The British situation in North Africa in October 1942 was desperate. The see-saw battles that witnessed advances and retreats along the North African coast in the previous two years had seen the front now temporarily stabilised along the line running south from the railway halt at El Alamein into the Qattara Depression only some 50 miles west of Alexandria. In August General Montgomery was given command of the 8th Army; he ordered no further retreats and set about reorganising his forces. By October new equipment, including 300 Sherman tanks and reinforcements, had arrived. The Desert Air Force (DAF) was being strengthened and now had a superiority in numbers, if not performance, of about 5:3. The German and Italian forces, under Rommel, were at the limit of their supply lines, everything having to come by road from the nearest usable port facilities at Tobruk, about 250 miles behind the lines. These roads were being frequently interdicted by Allied aircraft and the Long Range Desert Group.

The day 47 Squadron moved forward, Montgomery opened an offensive along the coast road, but mines and mud held up the advance. Further congestion in those paths cleared through the minefields made the exploitation of any advantage difficult.
The DAF was in action from before dawn carrying out strikes in support of the ground forces. By this time the DAF was a formidable force, comprising around 70 British and Dominion squadrons and flights with the support of two USAAF bomber groups and one USAAF fighter group as well as other units from Allied countries such as Greece and France.

47 Squadron was in action on 25 October when four of the squadron's Beauforts, carrying torpedoes, with four Bristol Bisleys (Bristol Blenheim Mk Vs) of 15 SAAF Squadron and an escort of six Beaufighters from 252 and 272 Squadrons, went in search of a merchant vessel, which was not found. However, a number of F-boats were spotted and Wing Commander Sprague and two of the

Beauforts attacked. In spite of this, the pilot of the fourth Beaufort held back. Pilot Officer Ralph Manning, an experienced Beaufort captain, believed the draught of the F-boats was too shallow for the torpedoes to do any damage, they would simply pass under the vessels without exploding, and he did not attack and brought his torpedo back.

These naval barges (Marinfahrprahm – MFP to the Germans) were used in large numbers to ferry men and supplies around the Mediterranean. There were two types, of 200- or 280-tons displacement and about 164 feet long, but with a draught of only 6 feet. They carried fearsome AA defences comprising 88mm, 37mm and 20mm guns; travelling in small groups they presented a constant headache to the RAF. 47 Squadron encountered them frequently and learned, at their cost, to treat them with respect.

The following day orders were received to attack a convoy approaching Tobruk. The convoy consisted of three merchant ships escorted by four Italian torpedo boats (the *Partenope*, *Lira*, *Ciclone* and *Calatafimi*). These vessels were not the same as what the Allies would call a torpedo boat, being more in the role of destroyer escorts, ranging in displacement from 800 to 900 tonnes and around 270 feet long. They carried significant AA armament, comprising 20mm and 13mm guns, as well as 100mm main armament. The merchant ships consisted of the *Tergestea*, an Italian freighter of 5,890 tons carrying fuel and ammunition, the *Dora*, a German vessel of 584 tons, holding some 400 tons of military stores, and – the prize target – the *Proserpina* (the former French Beauce), a tanker of 4,869 tons transporting a precious and vital 4,533 tons of fuel for the Luftwaffe, the Panzerarmee and Italian forces. The convoy commander was Capitano di Corvetta Gustavo Lovatelli flying his flag from the *Partenope*. Air cover was provided by relays of three to five aircraft, which would be increased as the convoy got within range of Tobruk.

The *Proserpina* and *Dora* had left Piraeus, Greece, at 06.34 hours on 24 October, and were joined by the *Tergestea*, which had left Suda, Crete, at 09.34 hours on the same day. The convoy set sail for Tobruk on the morning of the 25th, which they were scheduled to reach some 32 hours later on the afternoon of the 26th. The braking of Axis codes had given early warning of the convoy's departure. The convoy was shadowed by RAF Maryland reconnaissance aircraft and plans were put into place for an assault. During the night of the 25th/26th long-range Wellington torpedo bombers of 28, 221 and 458 (RAAF) Squadrons raided the convoy, and although torpedoes were dropped, no hits were recorded.

In the morning, the convoy was joined by its first relay of air cover and was making good progress. Just after midday, with the vessels only 50 miles from Tobruk, eighteen B-24 Liberators, of the 98th Bomb Group, USAAF, flew from their base in Egypt and attacked from 20,000 feet in three waves. Bombs were seen to land close to the ships and hits were claimed, but the convoy still did not slow down. Two hours later and now only 30 miles from Tobruk, the *Proserpina* developed engine trouble and dropped out of the convoy; the *Calatafimi* stayed with the troubled vessel to provide defence. Desperate and rapid repairs got the tanker going again within 30 minutes. The convoy was now less than 3 hours' sailing from Tobruk and, benefiting from fighter escort, and would soon be protected by shore-based AA guns.

At Gianaclis an attack force had been assembled comprising eight 47 Squadron Beauforts and six 15 (SAAF) Squadron Bisleys, with an escort of four Beaufighters from 252 Squadron and five from 272 Squadron, which would have the duel role of keeping the fighters away and supressing the flak from the escorting warships.

It is said that Wing Commander Sprague, although squadron OC, did not lead the raid, but instead passed the duty on to Flight Lieutenant R. Gee as he was the most experienced Beaufort pilot. However, in correspondence with the author, Pilot Officer David Heden who was Sprague's navigator, was under the impression that the OC did head the attack.

The Beauforts were each carrying a Mk XII torpedo of some 1,610lb slung under the fuselage; these could be fitted with either a contact fuse, or a Duplex fuse that not only worked on contact but could be set off by a ship's magnetic field, and thus would still explode if it ran too low and passed under the ship's hull. But these had proved less reliable and it is more likely that the contact fuse was fitted. Torpedo dropping was a particular skill, which required the weapon to be released within certain tight parameters. Too high and the torpedo would enter the water at too steep an angle and dive straight to the seabed, too low and it could skip off the surface. If the torpedo was dropped too far from the target, it would run out of power and simply sink before getting to the ship. Too close and the fuse would not have time to set and it would fail to explode on contact. All this was known to the crews and had been practised over and over again, but, for many, this was only the first or second time it was being performed in action, with the added distraction of flak and the pressure to make sure it worked. It had been stressed to the crews the absolute importance of making sure the tanker, at least, was sunk.

The Bisleys were carrying four 250lb general-purpose bombs fitted with delay fuses to ensure they did not explode immediately under the attacking aircraft or bring the following aircraft down. These would be delivered at very low level to increase the possibility of a hit, and again it would be into the face of fierce AA fire.

The plan was that, as soon as the convoy was found and identified, the Bisleys would fly ahead of the Beauforts and drop their bombs on the ships as the Beauforts released their torpedoes, the Beaufighters also adding to the confusion. Everybody was hoping that the enemy navy gunners would have too many targets coming at them at different heights, approaches and speeds and that the 20mm cannon fire from the Beaufighters would keep their heads well down.

The first 47 Squadron Beaufort (piloted by Flying Officer A.A. Maclean in aircraft /D)

Attack on the *Proserpina*, October 1942. Two 47 Squadron Beauforts have just passed over the vessel. The splash on the left is possibly the SAAF Bisley of Lieutenant Dunstow. *Heden, via author*

Below: Beaufort /F after the attack on *Proserpina*, October 1942, showing damage to tail. The officer is David Heden. The photo also shows the extra free mounted Lewis gun in the turret. *Heden, via author*

left Gianaclis at 12.30 hours and was followed by the rest of the group. One of the South African Bisleys took off late because of technical issues and, realising it could not catch up, returned home early. The Beauforts led the formation, with the Bisleys behind. The Beaufighters kept station slightly higher and weaved gently to keep pace with their slower charges. By 14.40 the formation was approaching Tobruk and came under sporadic and fairly inaccurate AA fire from shore-based batteries. Turning north-west they soon spotted a large group of F-boats, which also opened fire, but this was not the target they sought, and turned away to continue their search. At this point the presence of the formation was being reported, local air defences alerted and fighters scrambled.

At 15.25 hours, the Beaufighters, flying slightly higher, spotted the convoy and waggled their wings to signal to the rest of the strike force. This was the leading section of the convoy and comprised the *Dora* in the lead followed by the *Tergestea*. The seaward flank was guarded by *Partenope* and *Ciclone* with *Lira* bringing up the rear. Air cover was provided by two Ju 88s, two MC202s and a Bf109. The Beaufighters climbed to intercept these as the Beauforts and Bisleys turned towards the convoy. They were attacking from the east and into the setting sun. The ships reacted immediately, throwing up a fierce curtain of AA fire. Each pilot made their own choice of target, most going for the *Dora*, probably assuming that as it was in the lead it was the tanker.

The first section of three Bisleys, led by Lieutenant James Lithgow, overtook the Beauforts and coming at a very low level dropped their bombs. All the aircraft were hit by flak, but the second aircraft, piloted by Lieutenant A.B. Gooch, struck the *Dora*'s mast and spun into the sea. The navigator, Lieutenant A. McL. Johnson, was killed, but Gooch and his gunner, Air Sergeant R.E. Twigg, managed to reach their dingy and were picked up by the Italians and became POWs.

The Beauforts were next. Five aimed their torpedoes at the *Dora* and one went for *Tergestea* – all missed. Wing Commander Sprague's aircraft (DE108/F) was badly hit, losing much of its rudder, but he was able to keep the damaged machine in the air. The Beaufort of Flying Officer H.J. Davidson (DW834/C), a Canadian, new to the squadron and on his first operational sortie, was also hit; the aircraft flipped on to its back and crashed into the sea, only the navigator, Pilot Officer T.H. Jones, surviving to become a POW. The other two crew members, Sergeant S.B. Gitsham (RAAF) and Sergeant S.R. Pugh, were killed with their pilot.

Two of the Beauforts did not attack – those flown by Pilot Officer Manning and Flying Officer N. Hern-Phillips. They were not convinced that either of the ships was the prime target. No doubt some questions went through the minds of the other 47 Squadron crews when it seemed, for the second time, Manning had failed to press home a strike. Thus, with the two remaining Bisleys of Major Pidsley and Lieutenant Dustow, they continued their search. A few minutes later Manning spotted the *Proserpina* with its escorting *Calatafimi* on its sea-ward flank.

Hern-Phillips had been hit during the earlier assaults and lost his torpedo, so only Manning's was left. The Beauforts and Bisleys were spotted by the Italian crew and the tanker captain was no doubt fully aware of the importance and started to turn the ship towards the attacking aircraft to present as small a target as possible. Manning also turned close to land and his aircraft strayed over the coast, coming under fire from AA guns, but at least the Beaufighters were keeping the fighters away. The Italian captain kept a careful eye on the circling Beaufort while the destroyer continued with AA fire. The tanker started to reverse its turn and, for a moment, it would be virtually stationary in the water. Manning, seizing his opportunity, flew straight at the target at the recommended 80-foot altitude and 140 knots and took careful aim, but instead of releasing the torpedo at a range of 1,000 feet, went nearer to make sure of a strike.

The two Bisleys streaked overhead on their bombing run into intense flak and a Beaufighter dived on to the *Calatafimi*, raking the ship with cannon fire. Major Pidsley reached the tanker first and released his bombs, diving back down to sea level after passing the ship; his aircraft was repeatedly hit by cannon fire, but remained flying. Lieutenant Dustow followed, but was so low that the Bisley struck one of the ship's masts and spun into the sea; none of the crew survived. Manning was last to reach the tanker and, as he passed, the delayed-action bombs exploded and his Beaufort was hit by part of the ship's superstructure.

By this time the remainder of the force had caught up with the action and Pilot Officer Francis, the navigator in Flight Lieutenant Gee's aircraft, was able to watch the torpedo run true through the clear Mediterranean waters. It struck the tanker on the starboard side, but there was no explosion. The torpedo had been dropped so close that it had not had sufficient time to arm itself. For what must have seemed like an age the torpedo bumped along the side of the still turning tanker, continuing to arm itself until it reached the stern, where it exploded. There was a large sheet of flame followed by clouds of black smoke and soon the crippled tanker sank, taking with her fifteen of her crew of seventy-seven and Rommel's last hope of reaching the Suez Canal.

The surviving aircraft from the strike group, three Bisleys and seven Beauforts, turned for home, but the battle was not yet over. Above them the Beaufighters had been engaging the enemy fighters in a running battle; they claimed one Ju 88 damaged, but a 272 Squadron Beaufighter had been lost, the crew ending up as POWs, and another 272 aircraft was damaged, but able to make it safely back home.

A number of Italian MC202s broke off and attacked the bombers, but were beaten off. Wing Commander Sprague's aircraft was hit again, one bullet striking the reserve hydraulic tank, dripping hydraulic fluid on to David Heden's head. He recalls: 'At first I thought the liquid round my neck was blood! Our rear gunner, a Canadian called Steve (Sergeant L.R. Stevenson), hand held, why I can't remember, a machine gun, and drove them off like a good-un, and got his picture in the Cairo papers as a result.' Eventually the Italian fighters, either short of fuel or ammunition, broke off their attacks.

There was to be a final tragic drama on the return flight. Lieutenant Leisegang's Bisley, which had probably been damaged either during its raid on the convoy or by Italian fighters, started to weave and slid under the Beaufort of Pilot Officer Garriock (DE110/G) and then climbed, colliding with the aircraft; both planes plunged into the sea with no survivors. The depleted force arrived back at around 18.00, five and half hours after taking off. No. 47 Squadron had lost 25% of its aircraft, seven men killed and one POW. The South Africans had faired even worse, losing three out of five aircraft, with seven men killed and two POWs. Later that day, the convoy was attacked again by three Wellingtons of 38 Squadron. One Wellington was lost but the *Tergestea* was hit by at least one torpedo and exploded, sinking at the entrance to Tobruk harbour with all hands lost. Major Pidsley and Flight Lieutenant Gee were awarded DFCs for their actions that day, but despite a strong recommendation from Wing Commander Sprague there was nothing for Pilot Officer Manning.

Further attempts were made by the Italians to get much needed supplies through to North Africa, but, because Ultra was able to read the coded transmissions, very few ships of any worth made it. On 1 November three 47 Squadron Beauforts were sent to intercept the supply ship *Ostia*, 359 tons, which had left Benghazi two days before in company with another ship that was sunk on 31 October. Pilot Officer Frederick Pile attacked the ship, which he hit with a torpedo. The vessel sunk rapidly.

During October 44% of all Axis supplies dispatched by sea had been lost to air or sea assault, amounting to some 54,800 tons. In desperation, the Luftwaffe was ordered to supply the much needed fuel by air, as ordered by Generalfeldmarschall Kesselring 'day and night down to the last crew and the last aircraft'.

On the ground, the Battle of El Alamein was reaching its conclusion and on 2 November Rommel signalled his headquarters in Berlin with an assessment of the situation, finishing with the view that 'in spite of heroic resistance and excellent spirit of the troops, the gradual annihilation of the Army must be faced'. Two days later he requested Hitler's permission to retreat, but before receiving a reply, which he could assume would have been refusal, Rommel ordered his forces to fall back. What could have turned into a rout, if Montgomery had taken the gamble of pushing forward and trying to cut off the retreat, was avoided as Montgomery feared a trap and the Axis forces were able to make an orderly withdrawal. It would be another six months before the final German units surrendered in North Africa.

With the lack of coastal shipping targets, 47 Squadron's role changed to convoy escort and anti-submarine patrols. On 5 November Beaufort DE119 belly-landed at Gianaclis after the undercarriage refused to lock down due to the failure of the engine-driven hydraulic system and also the loss of the manual emergency backup system, but Flying Officer T.K. Lockhart and his crew were able to walk away without injury. However, on 18 November, 47 Squadron lost its OC when Wing Commander Sprague was killed in a flying accident. The aircraft (DE118/S) was on a flight from Shallufa to Gambut carrying a torpedo; about halfway back the pilot, Sprague, was studying a map with the navigator Sergeant Augustinus, in preparation for some low-flying practice. The aircraft lost height and hit some high ground at 12.45 hours. Three of the crew, including the passenger, managed to get out of the aeroplane before the torpedo exploded, killing Sprague and Augustinus. Both are buried in El Alamein war cemetery.

The surviving crew members, Sergeant Lake, Flying Officer Collier and Leading Aircraftman Isbell, collected some food and water from the remains of the aircraft and headed north. After walking for the rest of the afternoon, they came across an abandoned German lorry where they made camp for the night. The next day they continued north until they encountered a group of Arabs mid-morning, whom they joined. They stopped for lunch and as Isbell records: 'Arabs made curried duck and bread. Tea and cigs all round. Gave them our photographs, had a shooting competition.' With their kit loaded on to the Arab's camel they continued on their walk until halted by a sandstorm in the evening and made camp. By this point they had run out of their own cigarettes and had to move on to the Arabs' Italian cigarettes. The following morning they discovered a German lorry 'with ammo, rifles, goggles, food, paper, grenades etc. held a looting party'. Soon after, they found an Italian lorry and staff car and added to their

Above left: Beaufort DE119 after wheels up landing, Shandur. The pilot sitting on the engine is Pilot Officer Lockhart.
Roger Hayward

Above right: 47 Squadron Officers Mess, 1942.
Daffurn, via author

collection of goodies. During the day, a number of aircraft passed over but they were unable to attract their attention. After dark they stumbled into a 'heavy barbed fence with "Achtung Minen". Not sure which way the sign should face!' Later that night they were rescued by a Royal Army Service Corps lorry, which picked them and their new found friends up and took them to a British Army camp. The three men returned to the squadron a few days later, none the worse for wear after their 60-hour trek through the desert. A few days later Sergeant Campbell Ingram was killed and Sergeant Morton wounded by a booby-trap device at Gambut.

Flight Lieutenant Gooch took temporary command until the new OC, Wing Commander David Bennett, arrived at the end of the month. Also during November, six aircraft were passed on to 39 Squadron and departed to reinforce Malta. Five crews, including Manning's, left the squadron to continue their journey to the Far East and were replaced with new crews arriving from 5 METS to bring the squadron back up to its full establishment of twelve crews.

The second-hand nature of the squadron's Beauforts led to continued issues with the aeroplane. A number of aircraft were becoming unserviceable due to the poor performance of the Taurus engines, which had to be fitted with additional filters to keep out the sand and dust, always prevalent on the desert landing grounds and which slowed the aircraft down. This was also not helped by the installation of Air to Surface Vessel (ASV), Radar, the aerials of which, projecting from the wings and nose, further impaired the machine's performance. In an attempt to counter this lack, the Perspex canopy for the turret was removed.

Added to this was the character of the new OC Wing Commander David Bennett, who

W/C TAYLOR, D.F.C.
47 S
W/C SPRAGUE, D.F.C.
W/C (JIMMY) LEE-EVANS, D.F.
47 S
"GLEN"
"POP"
"LES"
"GUNS"
"GREMLIN"
ENGINEER EVANS.

did little to endear himself to the members of the squadron. He had come from a training establishment in the Kenya highlands and was considered to be – like many from that part of the world – slightly mad. He insisted that all squadron personnel took part in PT, including officers and aircrew, whose idea of hard exercise was probably limited to an evening stroll, hands in pockets, from their tent to the mess.

As the army advanced so did the air force, moving from one dusty landing ground to another. No. 47 sent a detachment forward to Al-Berka, just south of Benghazi, towards the end of the year, where they could watch the almost nightly bombing of Benghazi harbour, being far enough away to feel safe. That is, until one night when a stick of 250kg bombs hit the airfield. Fortunately nobody was hurt, although the Irish cook, after being partially buried, swore he would become a conscientious objector and return home, but never got around to it. The action did, however, make people pay a lot more attention to the digging of slit trenches, which became much deeper very quickly.

The year 1943 got off to a poor start, with the loss of Beaufort X8934 flown by Flight Sergeant D.M. Boon, who went missing on a cross-country flight on 10 January. No wreckage was found and he is commemorated on the memorial at Alamein. No other members of 47 Squadron are recorded by the Commonwealth War Graves Commission (CWGC) as having been killed on that day, so he may have been flying solo or with a crew from another squadron.

Four days later another Beaufort (DD999/K) was lost on a night navigation exercise north-west of El Abaiar Jall; all the crew of Flying Officer Pile, Flying Officer Daly, Sergeant Hallsworth and Sergeant Angus were killed. The cause of the loss was not known, but engine failure was suspected. Engine failure also led to the next aircraft casualty on 22 January. The pilot, Sergeant Douglas, returning from an anti-submarine patrol, lost power from the port engine and struck the ground in darkness. The machine caught fire, but, due to the exemplary actions of the fire crews, none of the crew were seriously hurt. The Operational Record Book makes specific mention of the actions of Leading Aircraftman Beadon, who rolled away the depth charges from the burning aircraft, no doubt preventing an explosion and any further injury. Two days later another Beaufort was written off when Squadron Leader Gooch lost his undercarriage while landing Beaufort DE122/D in the dark at LG227. January had cost the squadron five aircraft and five aircrew.

On 6 February three crews were sent by flying boat to South Africa to collect three replacement aircraft. They would be staging through neutral territory, so were required to wear civilian clothing and were issued with passports. However, on reaching the airfield in South Africa nobody was expecting them, knew who they were or had any Beauforts, so the crews had to wait – which considering the pleasant climate, plentiful food, no blackout and the hospitality of the local British expats was worth the delay. They eventually got away on 6 March, arriving back in Cairo on the 15th, where the aircraft were promptly declared unserviceable.

The squadron practice was to rotate crews every couple of weeks, until it moved forward to Misurata West in March 1943. The state of the aircraft was not progressing and getting spares for the Taurus was proving a bigger

Left: 47 Squadron personalities, 1942. *Daffurn, via author*

Below: Beaufort W6496/S LG227, February 1943, newly delivered to the squadron. *Sullivan, via author*

challenge as time moved on. Some planes had to be cannibalised just to keep the others flying. There was a natural reluctance by crews to accept aircraft they were not entirely satisfied with, much to the disappointment of Bennett, who would berate crews for showing undue caution, with an underlying hint that they may be 'lacking moral fibre' (LMF), an accusation that could ruin a man's RAF career and was tantamount to an accusation of cowardice, although Bennett never went that far.

Accidents continued to plague the squadron. A Beaufort /Y hit a landmine on 10 February and was written off. March was relatively quiet, but April was to be another bad month. On the 10th, Beaufort DE112/R spun into the ground due to engine failure soon after take-off from Misurata, killing Flight Sergeant Barber and his crew. The next day DD978/X also crashed on take-off but without injury to Flight Sergeant Travell and his crew. Flying Officer Ken Painter suffered a similar problem on 15 April when his aircraft (DW879/N) crashed soon after take-off, again without loss of life. Painter's log book states: 'Air test after engine repairs. After 4–5 minutes flying from take off starboard engine cut at 500' – belly landed with port engine – aircraft complete write off 1,000 lb depth charges did not explode no fire owing to cutting switches before crash. No injuries to self or crew.' Flight Sergeant Hollis suffered severe vibration in the port engine, and another aircraft (DW811/P) was written off. On the 24th Sergeant Barber, a member of the ground crew, taxied DW829/M into DD986/B, causing severe damage to both machines. He was placed under close arrest, charged and sent for court martial, though one feels that many of the aircrew would have offered up a quiet prayer of thanks. During April, because of the poor availability of aircraft, the squadron duties were taken over by a detachment of 454 (RAAF) Squadron with Baltimores.

Four more aircraft were lost in May, the last being DW880/J. Pilot Officer Daffurn, who was scheduled to pilot this aircraft, made his views clear that it was unfit to fly; he was, however, overruled by Squadron Leader Jimmy Lee-Evans, who took Daffurn's place but kept Daffurn's crew. Soon after take-off an engine failed and Lee-Evans was forced to ditch 2 miles off the coast. The crew paddled to shore, no doubt mumbling under their breath about their very temporary pilot.

Bennett handed over command of 47 Squadron to Wing Commander Taylor on 10 May. As an end to the story of Wing Commander Bennett, in 1996 the squadron was approached by his widow with a request that his ashes be scattered from one of the squadron's Hercules planes. Bennett had told his wife that he had only ever felt free while in the air and she wanted to 'set him free'. He had died in December 1991 at Southampton, but his wife had retained his ashes. It was a rather unusual

request, but, out of respect for a former OC, the squadron and the OC at the time, Wing Commander Graham Crawford, set about organising the event, and on 1 May 1997 Wing Commander David Edmund Bennett's ashes were scattered from Hercules XV188 at 11.35 hours over the sea, approximately 5 miles north of Lynton in Devon.

Taylor arrived to be surrounded by rumours of the demise of the distrusted Beaufort and conversion to Beaufighters. This soon grew to a certainty that the aircraft were waiting for them at the delta. Unlike most RAF rumours this one proved to be correct and at the end of May the first pilots left for Beaufighter conversion. Although good news for the pilots and navigators, it left the other two members of the crew surplus to requirements and they were to be dispersed to other units, breaking up some close teams who had been flying together for over seven months.

Below left: Ground collision between two Beauforts, 24 April 1943. Sergeant Barber placed under close arrest. *Daffurn, via author*

Above Beaufort DW835/M with Popeye nose art. *Daffurn, via author*

Right: Beaufort DW879/N, crashed after engine failure on take off, Misurata, 15 April 1943. Pilot Flying Officer Ken Painter and the crew uninjured. *Ken Painter/ 47 Squadron.*

Below Beaufort DW830/T, showing ASV aerials in wing leading edges. Misurata, 1943. *Daffurn, via author*

Chapter 8

GO IN AND SINK; TORBEAUS

Tunisia, 1943

47 Squadron aircrew, Tunisia, July 1943.
Heden, via author

At the beginning of June squadron pilots and navigators were sent back to the Canal Zone for conversion to Beaufighters. The aircraft the unit were to operate was the Bristol Beaufighter TF.X. Developed from the Beaufort it was a two-crew, twin-engined, low-wing monoplane specifically aimed, in this mark, for anti-shipping operations. The plane was powered by two Bristol Hercules XVII fourteen-cylinder two-row radial air-cooled engines adapted for low-level use, and each rated at 1,665hp for take-off. According to the pilot's notes, the aircraft had a maximum speed of 400mph (345 knots, 640kph) clean; a more reasonable speed would be 303mph (265 knots, 485kph) at 1,330 feet (400m). The economical cruise was 200mph (175 knots, 320 kph), giving a range of approximately 1,470 miles (2,350km) and an endurance of 7 hours, although most of the sorties that 47 Squadron carried out were between 4 and 5 hours, giving a good margin for reserve.

The aircraft packed a considerable punch, with four 20mm Hispano cannons mounted in the belly of the fuselage with 283 rounds per gun, and, although on many Mk Xs they had been removed in the quest for range, some planes retained the six 0.303 machine guns in the wings (four starboard and two port). Additional armament comprised a single Lewis, or more usually Browning, 0.303 machine gun in the navigator's compartment, more of a scare gun than an effective weapon against Luftwaffe fighters (at this stage of the war the Italian air force was little in evidence, even though at the time of the armistice in September there were in excess of 100 fighters in the region, but many of these were either obsolete or unserviceable), lacking the range or weight of shot to do much damage. The belly and wing guns were fired from a button on the control column, and the torpedo launched via a button on the throttle controls on the port side of the cockpit. As the torpedo dropped, the nose camera automatically took a photograph.

In the torpedo role, in which they were often referred to as Torbeaus, the aircraft carried an 18-inch 2,000lb Mk XII Aerial torpedo, slung on clutches under the fuselage, thus effectively blocking the pilot's and navigator's escape hatches. This weapon was a copy of the naval torpedo and not specifically designed to be dropped by high-speed aircraft, but when fitted with a timber air tail and released within specific parameters it was a very effective weapon.

Bob Milne, a pilot who joined the squadron on 25 August 1942, provides a useful description of Beaufighter operations:

If an enemy ship was sighted we hoped that we would not be seen until we climbed to 150 feet to launch the torpedo. Prior to that we would fly at 50 feet to avoid radar detection, but no lower because slipstream trails would show on the sea where enemy fighters could see them from above.

The type of ship would be judged and its speed assessed. If the wake behind the ship was of equal length then it would be at its cruising speed, maybe 7 knots for an old merchantman or 10 knots for a modern vessel. Warships would of course be faster.

Having estimated the speed we would get into position for dropping the torpedoes. Ideally two Torbeaus would approach head on, two out to port and another two to starboard. If the ship continued straight ahead then four aircraft would have good positions but the other two would need to turn to improve their approaches. If the ship turned then the two Torbeaus straight ahead [would] have good positions but the other four [would] have to turn to improve their positions. At every attack at least two Torbeaus should have good approaches.

After climbing to 150 feet ... the pilot estimates when he is at a range of 1,000 yds with wings level, level fore and aft and a speed of 180 knots. Then he aims ahead of the ship using a bar on the windscreen marked off in knots from the centre to left and right.

After launching the 'fish' the Torbeaus had to continue flying ahead because its turning circle would approach 1,000 yds and be a sitting target for the anti-aircraft guns on the ship. In order to avoid collision, the aircraft on the starboard side fly under the bow of the ship and those on the port side fly under the stern.

If attacked by fighters they

would usually fly at right angles across the flight path at about 1,000 feet. Then they would turn onto the tail of the Beaufighter, diving towards it. ... The observer on the Beau would call out the action i.e. – turning in –1,000 yds – 800 yds – and at this stage the pilot would execute a steep turn on the water. Hopefully the 109 has to break off the attack as it is heading down to the water. After several such attacks the 109 is short of ammunition or fuel and is obliged to return to base.

On the whole the aircraft was a considerable advance on the Beaufort and much more popular with both air- and ground crews, being more reliable and able to take a fair amount of punishment. However, it was not without its vices; it tended to sink rapidly and lacked rearward defence, further, when the cannons were fired it was likely to upset the P4 compass.

On the ground since the battle of El Alamein, the Axis forces had been pushed back out of Egypt and through Libya, Tobruk was retaken within a couple of weeks and Tripoli on the 23 January 1943. On 8 November 1942 Anglo-American forces had landed in French Morocco and Algeria in Operation TORCH, and advanced eastward. Two days later the Germans marched into southern France, toppling the Vichy government. The Allied forces in Algeria made rapid advances, meeting little resistance from the French, and by mid-November had reached Tunisia, but here they met much sterner opposition as the Germans had rapidly reinforced their forces, sending elements from three divisions based in Italy to form the 5th Panzer Army in Tunisia. After a series of inconclusive engagements over the winter the Germans counter-attacked at Kasserine Pass and pushed the Americans back 50 miles. To the east Montgomery had reached the German defensive position known as the Mareth Line. After fierce fighting on both fronts the Axis defences were broken in May and on 13th the last units surrendered and North Africa was in Allied hands. Nearly 250,000 German and Italian soldiers were taken prisoner, including the army commander, Generaloberst Hans-Jurgen von Arnim, Rommel having been invalided home on 9 March.

With North Africa in Allied hands, attention turned to Italy and 47 Squadron was sent west to Protville II, an airfield about 15 miles north-east of Tunis, arriving with its new Beaufighters on 22 June 1943. The airfield had been carved out of farmland and comprised a 6,000-foot runway of rolled hard silty clay loam. It was surrounded by low hills, which was a bit disconcerting. Again, there were no permanent structures and the squadron was back to living in tents. It had taken the ground crews four days by road convoy to make the journey. The air-field was shared with the Beaufighters of 39 Squadron, which had arrived from Malta on 1 June and 144 Squadron, which had left the UK with fifteen Beaufighter TFXs, but bad weather had delayed them and eventually only eleven aircraft arrived, on 18 June, one having crashed and three other delayed due to technical issues.

47 Squadron was now part of 328 Wing, 242 Group Northwest African Coastal Air Forces (NACAF). The wing was initially made up of three Beaufighter torpedo fighter (TF) squadrons (Nos 39, 47 and 144), two Wellington torpedo bomber (TB) squadrons (221 (detachment) and 458 RAAF), a Marauder TB squadron, No. 14, and three general reconnaissance (GR) squadrons – 13 (Bisley), 52 (Baltimore) and 608 (Hudson).

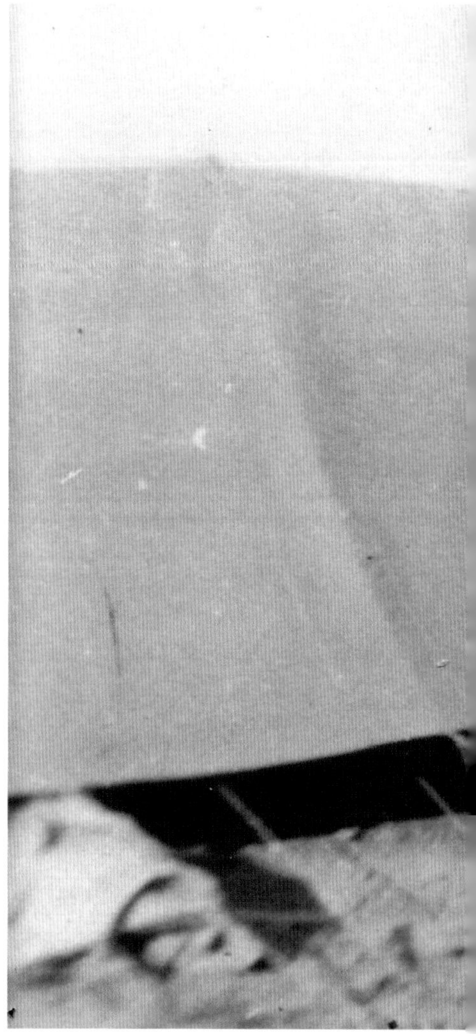

Bob Milne and Rod Lowman in flying kit, outside the aircrew accommodation, Tunisia, 1943. *Lowman*

No. 144 Squadron was to return to the UK in August. The role of the group was anti-shipping, with the various squadrons carrying out long-range strikes to Sicily, up the western coast of Italy and around the islands of Sardinia and Corsica. The sorties were referred to as 'armed rovers' and usually consisted of two elements: one of torpedo-carrying Beaufighters to take on the shipping, with another section flying Beaufighters without torpedoes but with the task of flak suppression, using their cannon fire to keep gunners' heads down.

The names of those crews on operations the following day would be posted the night before, with standby at 06.00 hours. A briefing would be given, indicating the targets they were looking for, location, take-off time etc. The flight leader allocated crews a specific role, either as torpedo carriers or anti-flak. Aircraft would be loaded and crews would carry out their final checks. On days when they were at immediate readiness in case the Italian Fleet was threatening to sortie, this could mean sitting in their aeroplanes for hours on end, slowly being broiled in their own sweat under the North African sun. The other Beaufighter squadrons would be going through the same process and usually at least two squadrons would be flying each day. Later, up-to-date information would come through from reconnaissance aircraft and if nothing was found or the weather was poor, the op would be scrubbed, torpedoes taken off the aircraft and the crews could return to their tents to wait to see if their names were on the list for the next day.

The squadron was soon in action, Squadron Leader Lee-Evans leading a strike on 21 June, the day before their formal arrival at Protville. The four Beaufighters found and sunk a merchant vessel off Sardinia, although two of the aircraft were damaged by return fire, and on the flight back to base Warrant Officer Whitington was fired upon by a USAAF B-17, but all aircraft returned safely. Two days later three aircraft made a torpedo attack on what they reported was a tanker, which sunk after a large explosion; however, it turned out to be a former French vessel, *Pescagel*, a trawler of about 1,100 tons, which had been converted to the submarine chaser UJ2212 on transit from Naples to Palermo. Beaufighter JM206/A was hit by return fire and with the port engine in flames, crashed into the sea. The crew, Pilot Officer Ian Robertson and Pilot Officer William Joy, were killed.

On 25 June, Lee-Evans led another 'rover' attacking a merchantman, but although a hit was claimed, the vessel remained afloat; on the flight back a Heinkel He-115 twin-engined float plane was found and dispatched by Lee-Evans. Another Beaufighter was lost on the 28th, but apparently not due to enemy action when JM212/M flew too low and struck the water. The navigator, Sergeant Deacon, was killed but the pilot, Warrant Officer Travell, was posted missing, and does not appear in the CWGC register, so one can only assume he survived. An 'armed rover' was dispatched in the early morning of 2 July, but about 30 minutes into the sortie, Flight Sergeant Carroll's plane ditched. The crew were seen to get out of the rapidly sinking machine and reach their life rafts. The sortie was scrubbed and while one aircraft returned to base to alert the rescue services, Flight Sergeant Hare circled the two men. Both were picked up by air-sea rescue services and despite their experience were back with the squadron quickly.

Another aircraft, JM324/B, ditched the following day after being hit by flak during an operation led by Wing Commander Taylor against armed trawlers south of Sardinia. The crew of Flying Officer Charles Ogilvie and Sergeant Williams were picked up by an air-sea rescue Walrus and back with the squadron, somewhat sunburned, on the 6th. Facilities at Protville were slowly improving and by early July the unit were up to full strength. However, living and working conditions were trying; daytime temperatures could get up to 30 degrees plus, making the airframe too hot to touch and crews sitting in the cockpits waiting to take off would sweat profusely. Flight Lieutenant David Heden, a squadron navigator, records in his diary the pleasure of a 'stand up' bath in a canvas bath tub after coming back from a sortie, although a few days later 'I passed an extremely unpleasant night as most of the time was spent hanging on to the tent in a 40/50kt gale. Daffurn [Heden's pilot] and I really thought we'd had it – but it managed to stay up somehow.' The following morning many tents had not been so resilient and everything was covered in a film of dust and sand.

On 8 July all three Beaufighter squadrons were briefed on the possibility of having to take on the Italian Fleet and there was a full dress rehearsal with all squadrons putting up twelve aircraft and forming up. It was announced that from the following day, between 06.00 and 06.30 hours, fourteen crews (twelve to go, two reserves) would be on immediate standby to attack the Italian Fleet should it decide to venture out from its home ports. An escort of USAAF P-38 Lightnings was promised. In the morning the crews were ready as ordered, but the call did not come. The Allied invasion of Sicily (Operation HUSKY) commenced on 10 July, and the three Beaufighter squadrons were put on an immediate state of readiness. Heden records: 'We were all certain that the fleet would come out today, but they seem to be as windy as they've always been and so we spent 13 odd hours on standby for nothing. Everybody is pretty keyed up and if they do come ... I hope it's soon.'

The next day it was decided that some aircraft could be released and Wing Commander Taylor led six Beaufighters against two merchantmen with a warship escort reported off the east coast of Sardinia. The five aircraft attacked out of the sun from 100 feet into an intense flak barrage. Strikes were seen on both ships, one of which was reported to be sinking by the stern, but Taylor's aircraft, LX796/F, was hit and crashed into the sea killing Taylor and his navigator, Flying Officer Frank Whitlock. Both 39 and 144 Squadrons also carried out raids during the day. No. 144 Squadron found the convoy that 47 Squadron had attacked earlier, now down to one merchant ship, which would support the report that 47 Squadron's torpedoes had done for the other ship.

Jimmy Lee-Evans was promoted to wing commander and appointed OC on the 17th and threw a party to celebrate this and the squadrons' recent success. A few days later there was further good news with the announcement of immediate DFCs to Lee-Evans, Painter and Reneau.

The Beaufighter units continued to be on standby during the week and every now and again there would be a 'Fleet's out panic, which was beginning to get on everybody's nerves.' In the meantime, 'rovers' were going out each day. On the 14th there was an eight-aircraft strike led by Squadron Leader Powell against a convoy north-west of Corsica. David Heden and Lionel Daffurn were part of this operation, flying one of the anti-flak Beaufighters: 'We left the MV sinking with two torpedo hits out of four dropped ... Daffurn gave the 2 MVs good squirts with the cannon. Painter and Ogilvie got a Ju 52 between them on the way up.' The MV was the ex-French 6,013-ton *San Francisco*, which was sunk.

Painter was flying one of the torpedo Beaufighters and his diversion to attack the Ju 52 was not looked upon sympathetically on his return and he was told he would be court-martialled for leaving the sortie before attacking the convoy. However, Painter's navigator had managed to catch a superb photograph of the torpedo dropped by Warrant Officer Whitington at the moment it hit the ship, showing a huge white plume of water against the side of the vessel, and this was quickly released by the RAF and published in many local and London papers. The court-martial threat was quietly dropped.

Another crew were lost on 20 July during an operation up to Livorno (often referred to as Leghorn in British contemporary records) on the Italian west coast north of Rome. The eight Beaufighters led by Flying Officer Gordon 'Spanky' Reneau (as an aside, Reneau got his nickname for an apparent likeness to George 'Spanky' McFarland, a child actor from the 1930s who regularly appeared in the Hal Roach 'Our Gang' comedy films) found and attacked three heavily laden barges, which were assaulted with cannon fire leaving one in flames. The aircraft of Flying Officer Selwyn Hunt and Flying Officer G.A. Corbin (JM320/E) was forced to ditch off the coast, but both men were seen to make it to their dinghy. They were out of range of

Right, from top:
Beaufighter Mk.X engine running up, Tunisia, 1943. *Daffurn via author*

Beaufighter ready for operations with torpedo under the fuselage. *Sullivan via author*

Beaufighter on its way out on a shipping strike with torpedo under the fuselage. *Sullivan via author*

Allied air-sea rescue services and they were not spotted until the next day and eventually picked up by an Italian minesweeper. They were held in an Italian POW camp, but after Italy surrendered in September they were transferred to Germany. On the way north by train, Hunt was able to escape and, with the aid of a sympathetic Italian family who sheltered him through the winter, he was able to reach Switzerland in early June 1944. Corbin was not so fortunate and ended up in Stalag Luft III at Sagan (where the 'Great Escape' happened in March 1944) where he was to be joined by a number of other 47 Squadron aircrew until liberated in 1945.

Wing Commander Lee-Evans led his first 'rover' as squadron boss on 24 July, taking eight Beaufighters up the Italian coast. An unescorted ship was spotted near the island of Ponza and two aircraft were detailed to attack, one with torpedoes and the other to provide covering fire. Warrant Officer Thompson hit the ship amidships, which exploded and sank quickly. However, the vessel was the *Santa Lucia*, a small Italian ferry of 452 tons and went down with heavy loss of life. Of the approximately eighty-five passengers and crew, no more than five survived. In 2007 this author was contacted by an Italian documentary maker who had been looking into the events surrounding the incident. Mr Maiorino, the film-maker, had been in touch with the captain's daughter and the Italian navy and there were a number of conspiracy theories around the circumstances of the sinking.

First the ship was deliberately targeted in an attempt to spread fear among the civilian population, with a subsequent fall in morale, and the fact that the attacking Beaufighters opened up with cannon fire was to force the passengers into the ship and destroy lifeboats. Second, the raid was a deliberate attempt to kill Mussolini, who was sent to the island of Ponza, which the ferry served. Third, it was part of the pre-invasion strikes before an amphibious landing on the coast between Rome and Naples planned to take place in August.

None of these theories stood up to much investigation, and the story of the sinking of the *Santa Lucia* was one of the ship being, for its passengers, in the wrong place at the wrong time. The ferry was camouflaged and also carried a gun on the prow, although how effective the weapon and its crew were is open to question. The formation of eight Beaufighters came across the vessel on an 'armed rover'. Wing Commander Lee-Evans split the two aircraft off to attack, as what looked like a bigger ship had been spotted a bit further ahead. The assault was fairly standard, the anti-flak Beau leading the way, using cannons to keep the gun crew's heads down, followed by the Torbeau, flown by Warrant Officer Thompson, carrying out

Left: Heden, Daffurn, and Robertson.
Heden, via author

Squadron anti-shipping strike, 1943.
Sullivan, via author

a copybook strike. The reason why the ship exploded with such force has not been determined. Sergeant Tony Crawford, the navigator in the second Beaufighter remembers: 'The ship simply disintegrated – a really tremendous explosion tossed both bow and stern high in the air, and then there was nothing; I vividly recall that violent explosion.' And wrote in his diary: 'Obviously an ammunition carrier, or rather it was but ain't no more.'

The Allies had no idea that Mussolini was about to be fired, and he didn't turn up at the island until 28 July; the idea of an amphibious landing this far from any fighter cover was out of the question. The Allies had landed in Sicily on 10 July, and did not complete operations there until 12 August. Although Eisenhower had been ordered by the Combined Chiefs of Staff on the day of the attack on the *Santa Lucia* – the same day that Mussolini was sacked – to prepare for a landing on the Italian mainland as soon as possible, it was not until 3 September that a landing was made, and not at Salerno until 9 September.

At the end of July 144 Squadron was posted back to the UK. The operational pace for the two remaining squadrons did not let up and on the 29th eight Beaufighters led by Squadron Leader Powell attacked a small convoy comprising an MV escorted by a destroyer and two motor torpedo boats (MTB). David Heden was flying with Lionel Daffurn in one of the Torbeaus: 'The anti flak a/c broke left for the DR [destroyer] and we came in from the right. Daff's torp hit amidships and there may have been a second hit. I saw the DR being covered in cannon bursts and that can't have been in very good shape when we left!' Lionel Daffurn in correspondence with the author said: 'As I went in to attack, I saw the destroyer being shot up. After dropping the torpedo I crossed in front of the ship and my navigator yelled "She's hit! She's hit!" I looked back and saw smoke pouring from the vessel amidships.' A second hit was scored by Flight Lieutenant Russell Hastings. The MV, estimated at 6,000 tons, but later identified as the MV *Alfieri* of 4,573 tons, was left 'low at the stern with her rails awash and listing to port', as was quoted in an RAF PR statement issued two days later.

The aircraft of Flying Officer Stewart Cowan (JM401/N) was flying as part of the anti-flak section when it was hit by AA fire and had to ditch. He and his navigator, Sergeant Antony Crawford, promptly exited their rapidly sinking Beaufighter and scrambled into their dinghy. Six hours later they were picked up by an Italian air-sea rescue float plane and taken to the mainland. Cowan was 'a big tough Canadian and will be as mad as hell at being a PoW!' according to David Heden. Cowan was to be true to his reputation. While being transported to Germany by train in late September he and George Purt, a Royal Engineers lieutenant, escaped via the roof of the cattle truck they were being held in. They had left the train near Anversa, some 70 miles east of Rome, and decided to head south in the hope of meeting up with Allied forces advancing north.

Cowan had twisted his knee badly in the escape and walking was both difficult and painful, but they both benefited from the kindness and bravery of Italian civilians who sheltered and fed them on their way south. However, they had a number of encounters with German forces, but with determination they continued southwards, until after forty days on the run they were startled to be challenged: 'Halt! Who are you guys?' But someone with a Canadian accent had uttered those words – they had made it through the German lines and into the forward position of the Canadian Hastings and Prince Edward Regiment. Cowan was sent to the UK to recover and then back to Canada; he remained in the RCAF and retired as a wing commander in 1969. The full story of Cowan and Purt's adventures are in the book *Forty Nights to Freedom* (1984) written by Gladys E. Smith, George Cowan's sister.

All the aircraft returned to Protville, but for Daffurn this was to be his last 'rover' with 47 Squadron; he was officially tour expired after forty-seven sorties. A party was required, which duly happened, made rather more comfortable with the furniture 144 Squadron had left behind.

No. 47 Squadron's next 'rover' was on 2 August when Lee-Evans, with David Heden as his regular navigator now that Daffurn had left the squadron, led eight Beaufighters towards Sardinia. They found a burning ship with a warship and five MTBs milling around. As the vessel did not appear to be sinking Lee-Evans decide to attack with cannon fire, but one of the Beaufighters (JM224/G) was hit by flak and seen heading south with an engine on fire. The pilot, Flying Officer Reneau, successfully ditched the aircraft and he and his navigator, Sergeant S.H. Hutton, climbed into their dinghy. They were adrift for two days before being picked up by the Italians. They were held in Italy until the armistice, when they were put on a train to Germany. Reneau was able to make good his escape from the train just north of Trento and, after walking for a week through the Alps, he made it to Switzerland. It would appear from the stories of Hunt, Corbin and Reneau that 47 Squadron aircrew objected to train travel and would disembark at the earliest opportunity, maybe to avoid paying the fare! Hutton did not have the same opportunity as Reneau and spent the rest of the war in Stalag Luft IV.

On the same 'rover', the Beaufighter (JM323/A) of Sergeants Kemp and Fisher was

posted as missing. It had also ditched in the same area, but the location was not spotted by any of the other crews. They drifted in their dinghy until picked up by the Italians in the evening, taken ashore and locked up with an RAF Wellington crew who had been shot down earlier. The next day Reneau and Hutton joined them, looking a bit sunburned from their two days adrift. Soon they were transported north to Campo PG 54, about 25 miles north of Rome, where it would appear they were split up – probably as Reneau was an officer and he may have been taken to a different camp. When the Italians capitulated in early September there seems to have been a certain amount of confusion and a couple of days later Kemp, with four South Africans and three American airmen, simply walked out of the camp and headed for the hills where they split up, Kemp finding himself in a group of three. Despite German search parties they remained at large until 19 October, when they were recaptured and locked in a castle in the middle of the town of Palombara. The building also housed 3,000 German soldiers under training. They shared a cell with two RAF aircrew. Remarkably they were able to escape again, this time making a rope from bed sheets, clichéd but effective. Kemp badly sprained his ankle, which slowed them down, but with the help of friendly Italians, the group tried to make their way south, collecting other escapees on the way. They tasted freedom until 5 May 1944, when they were rudely awakened by 'Jerry knocking on our front door with hand grenades'. There were to be no further escape attempts for Kemp, who was transported to Germany and arrived at Stalag Luft VII in July 1944.

The following day 47 Squadron were in action again, flying a 'rover' between Italy and Sardinia, taking off at 16.00 hours. A small convoy was spotted off the east coast of Corsica and the aircraft immediately

Below: Torpedo drop, 14 July 1943. The photo is taken at the point the torpedo is dropped, and the cross marks straight ahead, which is the point the ship will be when the torpedo contacts.
Sullivan, via author

attacked; no hits were reported with torpedoes but one of the MVs was emitting smoke from the stern. The flight turned for home. Cliff Sullivan from Australia was navigator for Sergeant Whittington: 'Immediately after the attack we headed for home, just us, Temple and Ambrose on the port side in close formation at about 500 feet. For no apparent reason Temple and Ambrose's port engine burst into flames – their plane rolled to port, turned upside down and dived into the sea. It instantly became apparent that a small ship about a mile away in the Strait of Bonifacio [between Corsica and Sardinia] had registered a lucky shot on their aircraft. My pilot was furious and did his block and dived at the ship firing his four 20mm cannon. It and a nearby smaller ship kept firing at us in this short space of time. We were not hit and left the ship in a shambles and lots of smoke.' Sergeants Albert Temple and William Ambrose were both killed in their Beaufighter JM388/X. Ambrose had attended Thetford Grammar School in Norfolk in the 1920s and on 10 November 2000 his loss was commemorated during a special service at the school.

Over the next two weeks the squadron was regularly sent out to hunt for shipping. By early August it had been reduced to thirteen crews out of an original establishment of twenty-one in its first six weeks of operations, and thus could not maintain its earlier intensity. There were also the regular fleet standbys to contend with. No. 39 Squadron was also very stretched, having lost a number of crews and aircraft during the period. On the 12th a 39 Squadron 'rover' was bounced by German fighters over the bay of Naples; one Beaufighter was shot down and another returned with a dead navigator. The Germans had started to evacuate Sardinia at the end of July and were trying to move their forces back to Corsica and Italy, which provided plenty of trade for the two Beaufighter squadrons. This was not without loss, although ten new crews arrived on the 17th but would need conversion to the Beaufighters as they had come from flying Bisleys. As there were no dual Beaufighters, conversion was done by an experienced pilot explaining the controls and flying characteristics and

Tanker on fire, 1943, after being hit by 47 Squadron torpedoes.
Heden, via author

Bottom: 14 July 1943 torpedo hit on *San Francisco*, merchant ship, 6,000 tons. Warrant Officer Whitington and Sergeant Sullivan.
Sullivan, via author

then standing behind the new pilot while he did his first flights before going solo. Dummy attacks were made on a wreck off the coast to give the new crews practice. For the experienced airmen these flights were viewed as an entertaining diversion; Heden commented: 'It's all very nice and easy and nobody shoots at you!' The same day about twenty Ju 88s raided Bizeta on the coast about 20 miles away, but they provided a spectacular display from the AA fire.

In Sicily the ground offensive had been pushing the Axis forces back to Messina, and by 17 August they had completed their evacuation of the island and it was in Allied hands. Preparations could now commence for the invasion of the mainland; in the meantime the Italian government was carrying out desperate negotiations with the Allies to get out of the war.

Two 47 Squadron Beaufighters were badly damaged by fighters during a 'rover' on the 19th and were lucky to make it back to Protville, where they crash-landed. On the 24th Flying Officer Hayden's Beaufighter hit a schooner's mast and was damaged; turning for home he was pursued by two single-engined fighters, but he was eventually able to shake them off and ditched the aircraft 7 miles off the coast of Tunisia, where he and the navigator Sergeant Collier were picked up by a high-speed rescue launch. This was one of the new replacement crews on their first operation.

Around this time some of the Beaufighters were beginning to be fitted with ASV to help find surface vessels. The receiver was squeezed into the navigator's compartment for him to operate/brake and aerials added to the forward edge of the wings and nose, which unfortunately interfered with the aircraft's performance. Also, because of the Beaufighter's usual low-level operational height, range of the kit was limited due to sea clutter appearing on the screen and enemy jamming.

The squadron was taken off operations for a week from the 26th, given two days' leave and then training, although this largesse from the RAF was viewed with a degree of suspicion by the aircrews. What were they being trained for? Not attacking Italian battleships was the hope. Much of the week was taken up with practising maximum-effort ops, with twelve aircraft from each squadron up at the same time, to include practice attacks on Royal Navy cruisers. David Heden makes the point in his diary that the stress of the unknown was beginning to play on people's minds but 'I hope the damn fleet does come out this time. … Anything would be better than just waiting.'

On the last day of the stand-down the squadron threw as big a party as limited resources allowed. There were a large number of American and British guests, including thirty young women, mainly nurses, which must have been a pleasant distraction for the men. One has to remember that on the whole aircrew would have had an average age of about twenty-one; they were a long way from home, wives and girlfriends, and for many they had known nothing apart from war since leaving school, and their long-term prospects were not good. Not surprising men very much outnumbered women, who were much in demand and could afford to be picky, but as one 47 Squadron pilot commented to Heden as the nurses left the party to go to another one: 'They ain't half going to feel the draft [sic] when the war is over.'

Operations were back on for 2 September when Squadron Leader Powell led a ten-aircraft 'rover' up the Italian coast. They were hunting two merchant ships reported between Leghorn and Bastia in Corsica, but nothing was found. On the way back the formation spotted two Siebel ferries; these were landing craft of about 150 tons, which had been originally designed for the planned Operation Seelöwe, the invasion of Britain in 1940. They could carry about 450 men or ten vehicles or up to 100 tons of cargo, and were armed with 40mm and 20mm anti-aircraft guns. Their wide beam made them very stable gun platforms. Their shallow draught also made them unsuitable for torpedo attack. With its simplicity of design, sturdy construction, good seakeeping and the ease with which it could be disassembled and shipped via rail to virtually any point on the

Continent, the Siebel ferry proved a highly useful and adaptable amphibious vessel for transporting troops, vehicles and supplies across open water wherever needed by German forces. It was also easily configured to serve a variety of special purposes, from minelaying to convoy escort.

The Beaufighters attacked with cannon, but two of the aircraft were shot down. Flight Lieutenant Hastings's aircraft (LX802/D) crashed in flames and he and his navigator, Flight Sergeant Francis Hill, were killed. The other aircraft was flown by Sergeant R.A. Forbes with his navigator, Sergeant A.C. Dingwell, who were on their first op with 47 Squadron. They ditched, both managing to escape the aircraft and were picked up and became POWs. The two vessels were left smoking but still afloat.

On 8 September Italy announced its unconditional surrender and the following day Allied forces landed at Salerno. The Italian Fleet had been ordered to surrender and sail to Malta. Those from Taranto in southern Italy made the voyage without incident. However, the northern fleet, which sailed from La Spezia on the morning of the 9th were not so lucky. The Germans were not about to stand by and let the Allies get hold of the warships without having a say in the matter. This fleet was intercepted by six Do 217 K2s of Major Bernard Jope's III/KG100, based at Istres in southern France. The attack took place at around 05.00 hours close to Sardinia. The Do 217 was fitted with Fritz X radio-controlled bombs. These were launched from a range of about 5 miles and guided to the target by the aircraft's bomb aimer. Each weapon was armoured-piercing, weighed 3,454lb, hit the target at a terminal velocity of nearly 630mph and could penetrate 5 inches of armoured plate. The battleship *Roma* was struck twice and blew up, sinking with the loss of between 1,255 and 1,390 of her crew of 1,920; her sister ship, *Italia*, was also hit but managed to limp into Malta with some 800 tons of water in flooded compartments.

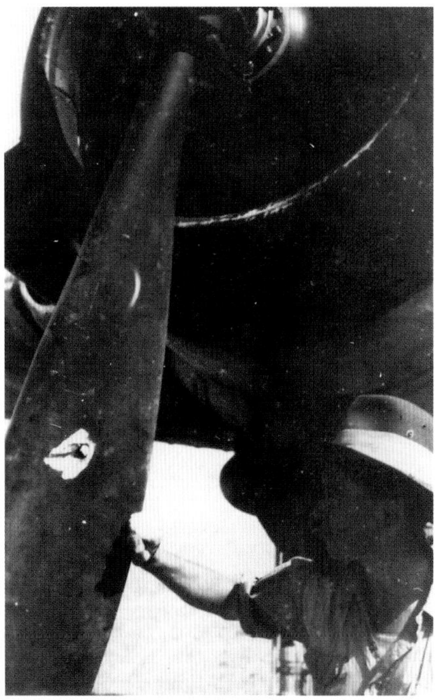

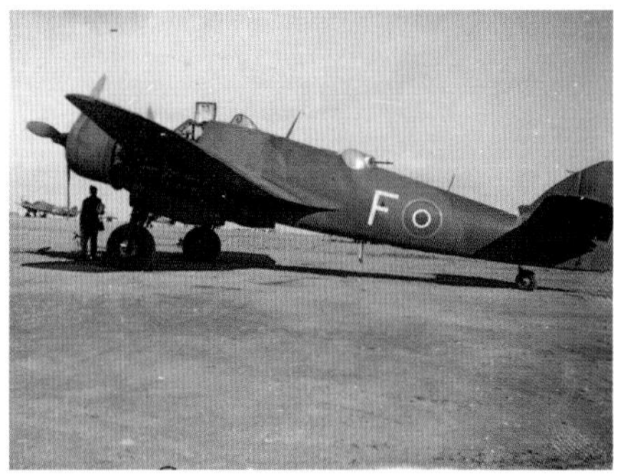

So in the end it was the Luftwaffe who took on the fleet and not 39 and 47 Squadrons.

Clockwise, from the top: Ground Maintenance, poking a Hercules engine with a screwdriver. *Lowman*

Beaufighter/ F desert airstrip, 1943. *Lowman*

Damaged propeller sustained by flak on a strike. *Sullivan, via author*

All in all things were relatively quiet on the anti-shipping front for the rest of September. On the 18th Lee-Evans led a 'rover' up to Leghorn, and an MV observed with an escort was found north of Corsica. An attack was launched and although hits were reported on the MV it was not sunk. Squadron Leader Painter's aircraft was shot down after dropping its torpedo, but he was able to ditch and after an uncomfortable night bobbing about on the sea he and his navigator, Pilot Officer Glenn-Davison, were picked up and taken prisoner. The next day they were transported under close escort to Germany (obviously the Germans had been become wary of putting 47 Squadron aircrew on trains without keeping a very close eye on them). Painter was thoroughly interrogated by a German officer, and although he stuck to the usual answers of name, rank and serial number, the officer was able to produce a document with the names of every 47 Squadron member. Painter and Glenn-Davison were sent to Stalag Luft III.

Early into the sortie Sergeant N.V. Hollis's Beaufighter (LX780/Q) suffered the loss of his port engine and had to turn back. On his return flight Hollis spotted a Luftwaffe Ju 88 heading in the opposite direction; as they passed, the Ju 88 waggled its wings – whether this was due to poor aircraft recognition on behalf of the German crew or an acknowledgment of a fellow aviator in trouble one can only surmise. Soon, however, the starboard engine began to falter and then promptly died. Hollis had set the aircraft trim up to deal with the asymmetric power of the aircraft and was unable to change this before the aircraft hit the sea, one wing down. The Beaufighter broke up on impact and Hollis was temporally knocked out; fortunately he had been thrown clear and was able to scramble into the dinghy, which had been automatically released from the wing. He was picked up the next day by an air-sea rescue launch. Unfortunately his navigator, Sergeant Patrick Cameron, was not found and was posted as missing.

With the Germans now evacuating Corsica, back to Italy, there were new opportunities for 39 and 47 Squadrons to interfere, but as much of the transport was by air it was decided to use the aircraft range and fire power as long-range fighters. On 23 September a combined 39 and 47 Squadron sortie intercepted a formation of Ju 52s and SM-82s north of Corsica; one SM-82 was shot down and two Ju 52s damaged. Later, another formation was found and attacked, one of the enemy aircraft being seen to ditch.

The next day 47 Squadron assaulted a group of twelve Ju 52s, but before they could claim any aircraft shot down they were attacked themselves by three single-engined fighters. While the Beaufighter was well armed, it was no match for the much more manoeuvrable fighters and the formation beat a hasty retreat. By now the Allies had a firm foothold in mainland Italy and the area was coming into the range of RAF and USAAF fighters, who took over the task.

With the evacuation of Sardinia and Corsica coming to an end, the Germans were confined to the mainland of Italy, and hence their need for coastal shipping was dramatically reduced and the requirement to keep two torpedo fighter squadrons in Tunisia was not necessary. Also, heavy rainfall in early October reduced the airfield to an unusable swamp. On 21 October 39 Squadron moved to Sidi Armor in Tunisia, but with detachments operating from the Italian mainland. No. 47 Squadron moved back east across North Africa to El Adem in Libya, where its new area of operations was to be over the eastern Mediterranean.

During its time in Tunisia the squadron had lost sixteen Beaufighters on ops, twelve air crew were killed and thirteen captured, of whom three subsequently escaped and seven were picked up by air-sea rescue services. The relatively good ratio between those killed and those who survived the loss of aircraft is a testimony to the basic strength of the Beaufighter, and although it may have had all the seagoing characteristics of a house brick, the roof escape hatches made exit possible. Many other aircraft were damaged by enemy fire or in accidents.

Chapter 9

DESPERATE ACTION

The Aegean, 1943–1944

47 Squadron Beaufighters on their way out on an Armed Rover in the Aegean, 1943. *Lowman*

With the fall of Tunisia and the removal of all Axis forces from North Africa, the Allied high command turned its attention to the next stage of the war in the Mediterranean.

General Eisenhower, the Supreme Allied Commander, had his sights set on Sicily as a stepping stone to Italy and the removal from the war of Germany's most significant ally. Churchill was also keen to have a go at the 'soft underbelly of Europe' and was very aware that soon the pressure to release forces and equipment from this theatre, so that they could be used for the forthcoming invasion of France, would be irresistible. He had also been stung by Stalin's implied accusations that it was only the Soviet Union that was taking on, and defeating, the 'Fascist Hordes' and that the West was doing nothing to pull its weight in the conflict.

With this in mind, and Churchill's reputation for looking beyond the obvious, his attention was drawn to the Aegean; in his opinion these islands would fall easily into the Allies' hands. The islands had been occupied by Italy since 1911. The British view was that the Italians had had the fight knocked out of them and would soon overthrow Mussolini and want to sue for peace. The Germans would be too involved on other fronts to be able to react before the Allies had a permanent foothold in the area. It would be a useful way to show a neutral Turkey which way the wind was blowing and hopefully get them to join in with the Allied cause, which would provide a very useful overland channel to Russia and mean the Germans would have to withdraw more of her forces currently facing the Soviets to shore up the Turkish border. What could possibly go wrong?

Others were more skeptical. General Sir Alan Brooke, the Chief of the General Staff, wrote that Churchill 'has worked himself into a frenzy of excitement about the Greek Islands. He refuses to listen to any arguments or to see the dangers. The whole thing is sheer madness.' To accommodate the plan, a new RAF Command was formed – Air Defences Eastern Mediterranean – and comprised four fighter groups equipped largely with Hurricane and Beaufighter squadrons, with some Spitfires. The first phase of the operation started in late July 1943 with the Hurricanes of 219 (Fighter) Group carrying out sweeps over Crete, assisting bombing raids against the communications network, but the main focus for action was to be the islands of the Aegean and would comprise a seaborne invasion supported by naval units, with the long-range Beaufighter squadrons tasked with providing air cover from bases in Cyprus and Egypt. Events took on an urgency when on 8 September Italy capitulated. Negotiations had been going on for some time with the Allies, and landings were carried out on the Italian mainland the following day. In the Aegean the British, without American aid – which had been refused on the basis that this was an unwanted distraction from the main thrust of operations against Italy – made their move.

The first objective was the island of Rhodes and approaches were made to the Italian governor to seize control of the island and neutralise it to the Germans. However, the Germans pre-empted any attempt to defect to the Allies by attacking the Italian garrison on 9 September, which was forced to surrender on the 11th. Within days twenty Bf109Gs of IV/JG27 arrived. The Beaufighter was no

match for the Messerschmitt Bf109G, the most modern version of the German fighter, armed with two 13mm machine guns and a 20mm cannon in the nose and also capable of carrying an additional 20mm cannon in gondolas under each wing (albeit this tended only to be fitted to aircraft flying against USAAF B-17 and B-24 formations). It had a maximum speed of about 320mph at sea level. Based around the islands were Arado Ar 196s of SAG125 and 126. These single-engine, two-seat float planes had originally been designed for use from capital ships, but their ability to land and take off from water was highly prized. Although not fast, at 190mph they were agile and were fitted with two 20mm cannon and two paired hand-held 7.9mm machine guns in the rear of the cockpit. Although no match for Allied fighters, their ability to be based anywhere there was a suitable bay meant they could and would be encountered just about everywhere and were treated with respect by the Beaufighter crews. As well as these defensive aircraft there were Heinkel He 111s, Junkers Ju 88 and Ju 87 bomber units stationed within easy range of the islands. The enemy also had a number of Italian aircraft flown by crews loyal to the old regime.

With the failure to secure Rhodes the British looked to occupying the islands of Kos, Leros and Samos all to the north-west of Rhodes. Kos was key, about 30 miles long and 7 miles wide it had an airstrip where it was planned to base two Spitfire squadrons to provide close air support for the ground and naval forces. Fortunately the Italian air force units already based there decided to throw their lot in with the British and on 13 September the first of the Spitfires from 7 (SAAF) Squadron and 74 Squadron arrived, followed by three Dakotas bringing in ground crew and supplies. On both occasions the jittery Italian gunners had opened fire with sporadic, but thankfully largely inaccurate AA fire. The next day 120 men of 11 Para were dropped on to the island and more Dakotas touched down. Ships also brought further men and stores, and soon British forces comprised some 1,600 men, and 3,500 Italians, although how enthusiastic for any fighting the Italians were was yet to be determined. The Spitfires maintained a standing patrol of two aircraft, even if without any radar or a reliable reporting system; interception was either going to be down to luck or as the German aircraft departed.

The Germans were not slow to react and on the 17th the first air attack took place, with Ju 88s with a Bf109 escort bombing the airfield. Over the next few days there were numerous raids and, without protected dispersals for the aircraft parked on the ground, many were damaged and Spitfires and Dakotas destroyed. It was not all one way, however, and the Spitfires were able to account for a number of the German aircraft. Reinforcements and replacement aircraft were flown in but the situation was getting desperate. By 26 September, 7 (SAAF) Squadron were down to four serviceable Spitfires and had to be withdrawn. On 3 October the Germans invaded, landing some 4,000 men by sea and air, and just over 24 hours later resistance ceased and the British and Italian forces surrendered.

On Leros, not far to the north, the Luftwaffe commenced bombing and strafing attacks against the British forces that had landed there on 15 September. Leros boasted a deep-water harbour and had been fortified during the 1930s by building numerous artillery positions, but even though there were numbers of anti-aircraft guns, they were vulnerable to air attack. More importantly, it had no airfield from which fighters could operate. British forces on the island comprised about 3,000 men with 7,600 Italians, mostly navy troops. Air cover had to be provided by the long-range Beaufighters based in Cyprus and Egypt. Supplies were delivered by sea and subject to frequent air assault and the British destroyer *Intrepid* and the Greek destroyer *Queen Olga* were sunk in the harbour in one such raid, which also wiped out large quantities of stores.

The original German plan was to invade on 9 October, but two days beforehand the Royal Navy intercepted the convoy, sinking many of the landing craft, and it would be more than a month before these could be replaced. In the meantime, the Germans kept up their bombing attacks and the Navy was forced to do fast night-time runs to deliver supplies, and then seek shelter in neutral Turkey's coastal waters during the day.

47 Squadron had moved from Protville to Sidi Armor near Tunis in October 1943, but had a detachment based at El Adem, 15 miles south of Tobruk and close to the Beaufighters of 603 Squadron and B-25s of the 310th BG based at Gambut. The whole unit made the 850-mile move from Tunisia to El Adem in mid-November. El Adem was about 370 miles almost due south from Kos, which was thus beyond the range of single-engined fighters.

When 47 Squadron carried out its first sorties over the Aegean on 26 October, the Luftwaffe's X Fliegerkorps could field over 300 aircraft, the British around 260 – 144 fighters (single- and twin-engined) and 116 bombers and torpedo bombers, mostly USAAF B-25 Mitchells and RAF Beaufighters. The USAAF B-25G Mitchells of the 310 Bombardment Group were fitted with a 75mm cannon in the nose, which, it was hoped, would be devastating against the small vessels the Germans were using. However, not only did the Germans have a numerical advantage, but being based only 100 miles away, it was within easy range of single-engined fighters who could operate over the islands for longer.

Jimmy Lee-Evans led the first 47 Squadron sortie of eight Beaufighters on 28 October, but nothing was found. The next day during a strike led by Squadron Leader Ogilvie against a small vessel and escort south of Naxos, one of the Beaufighters (JM225/W) was shot down by an Ar 196, the crew – Flying Officers John Dixon and George Terry – were killed. On the 30th 47 Squadron were operating again, this time with two aircraft escorting two B-25Gs in an attack on Naxos harbour. Again, one 47 Squadron aircraft was lost, brought down by flak, but the crew of JM317/S – Flying Officer Hayter with his navigator from 603 Squadron Warrant Officer Harper – were unhurt and able to evade capture, and returned to their respective squadrons some weeks later. As Hayter had been posted missing, as was the tradition, much of his kit was divided up among the squadron. Bob Milne took advantage of this and bagged Hayter's bed, it being more comfortable than his own. When Hayter got back to the squadron he was very keen to get his own bed back, not for the comfort it provided, but more for the gold coins that he had acquired in Tunisia and stored in the bed. Fortunately for him Milne was blissfully unaware of the riches he was sleeping with, just happy with a good night's sleep. In June 2007 the wreck of the aircraft was found on the seabed, largely intact, 34 metres below the surface. The pilot's escape hatch was open and the navigator's canopy missing. The starboard propeller was also missing and the port propeller twisted. One of the B-25Gs (42-64579) of 321st BG, 446th BS, flown by Second Lieutenant Gordon J. Black, was also lost to flak, and crashed into the sea. The surviving Beaufighter and Mitchell circled the crash site but there were no signs of survivors.

The two Beaufighter squadrons based at Lakatamia in Cyprus, Nos 227 and 252, were also operating that day, providing escort for the Royal Navy cruiser *Aurora* and three destroyers, and were heavily engaged with Ju 88s and their fighter bodyguards. In the ensuing dogfight the Beaufighters claimed one Ju 88 destroyed; however, the cruiser was hit by a bomb and had to retire to Alexandria. Two more Ju 88s were claimed by a second patrol of 227 Squadron aircraft.

As the Germans assembled their invasion fleet a hostile game of cat and mouse ensued, with the RAF and RN, but the Navy was very concerned about the vulnerability of their ships to Luftwaffe attack and the Beaufighters were too far away to be able to provide a constant air umbrella, and also could not cope easily with the escorting 109s. The British knew where the Germans were heading, but they could only island hop at night and avoid being caught in open sea during the day. The only place were they could be certain of being intercepted was the final run in to Leros.

The date of 5 November was to prove a costly day for the Beaufighters. No. 227 Squadron lost four aircraft out of five, none of the crews surviving in an engagement with Bf109s of 8./JG27 near Rhodes. In the afternoon 47 Squadron sent out three Torbeaus with an

escort of two of their own and three Beaufighters from 603 Squadron, to attack one large and two small merchantmen spotted in Livrion Bay. The raid was not a success and no torpedo hits were claimed. Two 47 Squadron Beaufighters were lost. David Heden was flying as navigator for Jimmy Lee-Evans:

'We were hit by flak over the bay and lost an engine, after a very brief discussion we decided to ditch the aircraft which was carried out successfully, I got out of the aircraft after a bit of a struggle getting past the VGO gun. The take off had been a rather scrambled affair and Jimmy, who could not swim, had left behind both his Mae West and seat dinghy. Fortunately the large wing dinghy had released, but we discovered it was full of holes and useless. This put an end to Jimmy's idea of paddling away and joining the partisans. He was like that, jolly keen. In the meantime the Beau, as promised, was sinking rapidly. We grabbed as much as we could from the dinghy and got the water bottle and large sheaf knife. Unfortunately as Jimmy got into my dinghy he sat on the knife, which punctured the thing, and it started to sink as well.

So there we were, bobbing about in the water, one Mae West between us, and no chance of reaching the shore. A German motor launch soon appeared, and Jimmy even suggested we overpower the crew, but I was not interested and anyway I had lost my revolver. The boat pulled up alongside us and we were greeted with the immortal words 'for you the war is over'. We were taken to the harbour where we were marched past the German gunners who were cleaning their guns and looking rather smug.'

Heden and Lee-Evans were sent to Germany and Stalag Luft I at Barth. The other Beaufighter was also lost to flak and again the crew – Flight Lieutenant Thomas Graham and Pilot Officer John Langdon – were rescued by the Germans and joined Lee-Evans and Heden at Stalag Luft I. During his time there Lee-Evans made a number of unsuccessful escape attempts, until eventually liberated by the Russians in 1945.

With the loss of Lee-Evans, Squadron Leader Ogilvie took over temporary command of the squadron, and on 6 November he led a strike of four Beaufighters from 47 Squadron and four from 603 Squadron to the island of

Above: Milne and Lowman, 1943. *Lowman*

Pilot Officer Bill Hayter, 1943, before being shot down. *Lowman*

Paros. Torpedoes were not carried as the intention was to attack any shipping found with cannon fire. The group spotted two large barges in Yanni Bay, which were assaulted and set on fire, but the aircraft were intercepted by five Bf109s, probably from 7./JG27, and Ogilvie's Beaufighter (JM352/R) was shot down. Fortunately neither the pilot nor the navigator, Flying Officer Mike O'Connor, were harmed and managed to evade capture, Ogilvie returning to the squadron in December. The formation then made a strike on four caiques at Naussa, but again came under attack themselves, this time from a formation of Ar 196s, which shot down 47 Squadron Beaufighter JM403/F, killing the crew, Flying Officer Lewis Rossner and Sergeant Henry Levy. No. 603 Squadron also lost a Beaufighter, but the crew successfully ditched and were picked up by a Royal Navy submarine. Another 603 Squadron aircraft was damaged and belly-landed on returning to base. Flight Lieutenant Smith took over as acting OC, but operational flying came under the command of 603 Squadron until a new OC could be appointed. A large convoy comprising four merchant ships, fifteen barges with F-lighters and E-boats for escort was detected on the 8th and twelve Beaufighters – six each from 47 and 603 Squadrons – were sent to intercept. Three of the 47 Squadron Beaufighters were carrying torpedoes. The formation ran into a storm at sea but pressed on and as they broke out of the weather the convoy was sighted and immediately attacked. Although no torpedo strikes were recorded, plenty of damage was done with cannon fire and, as a bonus, two of the Ar 196s, which were providing top cover, were claimed shot down. All aircraft returned safely. This was followed by another raid on the 10th with four Torbeaus from 47 Squadron and an escort of nine Beaufighters from 603 Squadron. An attack was made on a small vessel south of Cos, but not sunk. The formation was engaged by Bf109s from JG27 for some 20 minutes and Beaufighter LZ148/H from 47 Squadron ditched; the pilot, Flying Officer John Hayden, was killed, but the navigator, Sergeant J. McMaster, was rescued. No. 603 Squadron also lost an aircraft, with the crew being taken prisoner. During a second sweep of the day Flight Sergeant Ted Daden of 47 Squadron claimed an Ar 196 damaged.

The Germans had been slowly and cautiously bringing together their invasion fleet for Leros and by the 11th had assembled sufficient shipping to begin their move against the island. A sweep by 47 Squadron Beaufighters and USAAF B-25s failed to find anything. A patrol by Cyprus-based Beaufighters late on saw some of the landing craft, but dared not interfere because of the strong fighter escort. As 46 Squadron recorded: 'Beaufighters operating over Leros are doing so at extreme range and could not possibly provide effective air cover.' During the previous nights, Royal Navy warships had been making sorties to try and find where the fleet had been concentrating, and during the day had to retreat to Turkish waters to avoid air attack, and by now they were running short of fuel and would soon have to retire to Alexandria to refuel and replenish. The Germans made their move on the night of the 11th and at 04.30 hours the following day reached the shores of Leros. They were supported by 500 paratroopers, who landed further inland later in the day.

Leros was a far more difficult prospect for occupation than Kos; it was defended by a greater number of troops and had better-prepared defences. The British put up stiff resistance and counter-attacked to retake some positions, but they lacked support. The Royal Navy tried to intervene the next night, but lost a destroyer to air strikes, and there was no way reinforcements could be landed – whereas the Germans had the benefit of relatively secure and much shorter supply lines and almost total air superiority.

On the first day of the invasion the RAF Beaufighter squadrons were out in force, two strikes coming from the Libyan-based squadrons, accompanied by B-25s on the second sortie, during which another Beaufighter (LZ912/T) was shot down; both airmen – Flying Officer Athol Greentree (RNZAF) and Sergeant George Freeman – were killed. It was the same story the next day, more long-range sorties and another 47 Squadron Beaufighter (LZ127/A) lost. The Beaufighters were attacking gun positions on the island when they were bounced by six Bf109s of 7./JG27. One Beaufighter was brought down into the sea and the crew of Flying Officer Edgar Clary – an American who had joined the RCAF – and Sergeant Walter Finbow were also killed.

During this intense fortnight of operations 47 Squadron had lost eight aircraft and crews and, as it was the only Torbeau squadron available for operations over the Aegean, the decision was made on the 13th to send seven crews and aircraft from 5 METS to reinforce the unit. These included a number of tour-expired instructors and advanced trainees, and among them was Lionel Daffurn who had left the squadron at the end of his own tour some months earlier. The group was led by the highly experienced Squadron Leader. Stanley Muller-Rowland and they were in action straightaway. Muller-Rowland led a sweep to Leros and intercepted a group of twelve Ju 88s. They immediately attacked and broke up the formation, which promptly dropped its bombs in the sea and fled for home. A number of hits were made, and one Ju-88 was seen to fall away with an engine on fire, but Muller-Rowland's aircraft (LX928/D) was hit by return fire, setting an engine alight. Muller-Rowland successfully ditched the aircraft north of Patmos and he and his navigator, Flight Sergeant Paddy Anderson, were seen to get into their dinghy. They were able to evade capture and arrived back via Turkey some time later. Further damage was done to the enemy formation before the Beaufighters had to turn for home, low on fuel.

On the ground the Germans were beginning to take control, forcing the defenders back, and things were getting desperate, with no air support or reinforcements and under almost constant Stuka attack the Allies' position was hopeless, but they continued to resist.

On the 14th further operations were flown, but without success or, fortunately, loss to 47 Squadron. The next day the Royal Navy was able to land some reinforcements and supplies to the beleaguered forces, but this was really only serving to postpone the inevitable. The Beaufighters continued their thankless task, but were unable to make a significant impact and two of the Cyprus-based Beaufighters of 46 Squadron were lost with their crews. On the 15th more sorties were carried out and some shipping was attacked west of Kos; all aircraft retuned safely.

The date of 16 November was to be the last day of the battle on the ground. In the air 603 Squadron were first off, shooting down one Ar 196 and damaging another, without loss. Later in the morning six 47 Squadron Beaufighters with two 603 Squadron aircraft as escort were ordered to attack a Siebel ferry towing two barges that were bringing German reinforcements to the island. The ferry was protected by a strong air umbrella comprising Bf109s, Bf110s (from ZG26, a long-range fighter unit) and the ubiquitous Ar 196s. The Beaufighter crews were left in no doubt of the importance of sinking the vessel. No. 47 Squadron only had five aircraft left and so an old training aircraft (/E flown by Sergeant Bob Milne) was thrown in to make up the numbers. It also only had five crews available. Squadron Leader Geoff Powell had finished his tour and left the unit, but he had not departed quickly enough. He was found and asked to lead the strike.

The ferry was located near the island of Kalymnos and, coming in low, the Beaufighters were able to attack before being spotted by the escort. In spite of intense flak the aircraft were able to sink the ferry and shoot up the barges. By now, however, the escorting fighters had reacted and swooped down on the Beaufighters as they streaked away at wave-top level, jinking and turning to make the German pilots aim more difficult, but by the time the fighters were forced to abandon the chase, three 47 Squadron Beaufighters had been shot down. Of the six men, only Sergeant Alfred Cottle (LX883 flown by Flying Officer Tony Bond) survived. The other two Beaufighters were crewed by Flying Officer Bill Thwaites with Flying Officer John Lovell (LZ125/L) and Flying Officer John Fletcher and Sergeant Jack Dale (LX923), who had only joined the squadron the day before. The aircraft were claimed by Oberleutnant Emil Clade of 7./JG27, his twenty-first victory, Major Ernst Dullberg of StabIII/JG27, his twenty-third and Oberleutnant Alexander Ottnad of 8./JG27, his forth.

Sergeant Cottle escaped the sinking aircraft, although wounded, and made it into his dinghy. After a day and a half in the small rubber boat he was picked up by a German patrol boat and taken to Kos. Here he was handed over to local nuns to be cared for, but with few medical supplies the sergeant's condition deteriorated. The Germans seemed to have largely ignored him and thus Cottle decided to escape and headed off to join the Greek resistance. Still weak from his injuries and speaking Welsh to avoid detection (by the Germans anyway), Cottle was moved to a cave for safety. After a while the Greeks brought a young medical student to tend to his wounds, and with primitive equipment and drugs he cleaned and dressed the airman's wounds. He stayed in the cave a further week. To help regain his strength Cottle would take long walks, recording the positions of German gun emplacements and military sites in code on his bandages.

At the end of the week the Greeks took him to a beach where he was picked up with a British officer and taken in a fishing boat to safety. In May 1944 Sergeant Cottle's citation for his Military Medal appeared in the *London Gazette*, but no details were given, and unfortunately the file containing the account of the action held by the RAF would appear to have been destroyed.

The awarding of medals can be something of a difficult subject. The groups into which they fall are often fairly tightly defined, i.e. crosses to officers, medals to other ranks. Further, some medals such as the DFC are specific to events in the air; the Military Medal is only granted for actions on the ground. Thus awards of the MM to members of the RAF in the Second World War were rare, normally to the RAF regiment, and so the award of the MM to an aircrew member is almost unheard of. But 47 Squadron can lay claim to one of the less than a dozen of these awarded during the Second World War.

The three surviving 47 Squadron Beaufighters made it back to El Adem, and for leading the attack Squadron Leader Powell was granted an immediate DSO. His navigator, Pilot Officer Cyril Adams, picked up a DFC, while DFMs went to Sergeants Vic Borrowdale, George Craven and Bob Milne. So with the exception of Milne's navigator, Sergeant Lowman, all the survivors got a gong.That evening the remaining soldiers on Leros surrendered and the campaign was over. During the period from the landing on Kos on 13th September the RAF had lost thirty-eight Beaufighters. From the time 47 Squadron entered the fray in late October, twenty-two aircraft were lost, of which fourteen were from this unit.

No 47 Squadron had to be totally rebuilt; on the morning of 15 November it was likely that it had no fit aircraft or crews it could put into the air. It also had no OC, but this was soon resolved with the appointment of Wing Commander W.D.L. Filson-Young, DFC, on 23 November, together with two new flight commanders, Squadron Leader L.H. 'Porky' Skinner and Major A.R. Pears, SAAF. New crews arrived from 5 METS as the squadron got back into the business of torpedo dropping. Filson-Young was to be a hugely popular OC during the eighteen months he led the unit and is fondly remembered by all air- and ground crew who served under him; he built a squadron spirit that lasts to this day. Another key member of the squadron was Flying Officer E.T. 'Tony' Norris, an astute pre-war Latin teacher who was the intelligence officer.

Two days later the squadron moved to Gambut, about 30 miles east of Tobruk, which was to be the main operating base for the rest of its time in North Africa until it left for India in March 1944. Gambut was a typical North African airfield. Situated on an escarpment about 20 miles inland, it was a place that was windswept, with frequent dust storms and temperatures that dropped rapidly once night fell in the winter months. The runway was simple rolled sand, which would soon become waterlogged after any rain. There were no permanent facilities, everything being housed in tents of varying sizes and suitability.

The airfield was shared again with the Beaufighters of 603 Squadron and the B-25Gs of the 310th BG, and also with B-26 Maurauders of 24 (SAAF) Squadron. The squadrons formed 235 Wing of 201 (Naval Cooperation) Group.

With the ending of the fighting to hold the islands in the Aegean, the tempo of operations slackened a bit, but this also gave the opportunity for new crews to learn the ropes. Sergeant Bob Willis, who had joined the squadron at this time with his navigator Sergeant Tommy Thompson and three other crews, were soon integrated into the unit and its recent history, and Filson-Young impressed upon them the determination that was required to fulfil one's duties, a characteristic he wholeheartedly possesed.

Willis and Thompson, feeling somewhat apprehensive of their responsibilities, set off on their first sortie on the morning of 26 November, involving four Torbeaus from 47 Squadron and three B-25s from 310th BG. Willis remembers: 'The briefing was short and to the point. Any mention that we were new to the squadron together with a few words of advice were noticeable by their absence.' The target was a supply ship sailing from Piraeus to Crete, but it was not found and the aircraft returned to Gambut. However, one of the Torbeaus (LX987/D) had turned back early with engine trouble. It was never seen again and disappeared into the sea with its crew – Flying Officer F. Gregory, an American in the RCAF, and Flying Officer J. Wood. Both are commemorated on the Alamein memorial.

In December it became apparent that there were few targets left in the eastern Mediterranean that were suitable for torpedo attack, most of the shipping found being small caiques that would shelter in well-defended harbours during the day. The boats would be attacked with cannon and 100lb or 250lb bombs carried on bomb racks, one under each wing. Raids on harbours were a risky business and the trick was to come in low and fast to try and surprise the defences and get out just as low and fast. There was also the chance of heavier AA fire if one strayed too close to the well-defended islands of Crete, Rhodes, Kos or Leros, as well as being caught out by fighter patrols.

Another uneventful sweep was carried out on 1 December, but on the 4th four 47 Squadron Beaufighters found four Ar 196s near the island of Kinaros west of Leros. One was on the water with three others circling above. Sergeant Willis immediately attacked the stationary aircraft, strafing it with cannon fire and sinking it; he then climbed and opened fire on one of the airborne aircraft, shooting off one of the floats, and it crashed into the sea, although the rear gunner kept on firing to the last. The two Arados were from 2./126; the crew of the first, being on the water, were able to abandon their aircraft, but the crew of the latter were killed. Flying Officer Unwin, who was leading the patrol, kept the other three Beaufighters circling the action, concerned – as he explained to Willis when they got back – that it was a trap and there were Bf109s ready to pounce. Later, the group spotted a high-speed motor launch coming towards the scene and strafed it with cannon fire. The boat was S-boat S511, which was badly damaged and beached, two of its crew dead.

A further sweep by the squadron in the area a few days on found two Ar 196s, which were attacked, both claimed as damaged. E-boats (S-Boats to the Germans) were also spied and strafed with cannon fire, but Beaufighter LX898/W was shot down by return fire, killing the crew of Flying Officer Denis Nichol and Warrant Officer Gerald Bell, who had only joined the squadron the day before and this was their first operational sortie. As Bob Willis records: 'We hardly knew them.' Such was the way, crews came and went, your chief loyalty was to your crewman who you were likely to live or die together with; what happened to other chaps, especially new 'sprog' crews who had only just joined the squadron was unfortunate, but it was not you.

On 14 December the squadron had another air-to-air success when a four-aircraft patrol found what was reported as a He 115 twin-engined float plane, escorted by four Ar 196s. Two of the Beaufighters went after the Ar 196s, while two, flown by Sergeants Willis and Ken Thomas, went for the larger aircraft. Bob Willis recalls: 'I could see my cannon fire sparking as it hit the wing of the Heinkel. About twenty feet of the port wing came off … concentrating too hard in my eagerness to finish the job I came in too close to the enemy aircraft, forcing me to fly over it to avoid a mid-air collision. We were an easy target to the Heinkel rear gunner who hit us and set us on fire.' The enemy plane was seen crashing into the sea by the rest of the Beaufighters and would be credited to Willis, but at the time he had other things on his mind. 'With our aircraft full of smoke thoughts were quickly concentrated on our survival. The rear gunner had shot off the tip of our starboard wing and ignited the Very cartridges stored in the rear of the aircraft. … Through the smoke I could not even see the horizon or any of the instruments. It appeared impossible to fly the aircraft. Tommy [Willis' navigator] had evacuated his position in the rear. All his navigation equipment and navigation table were burnt out, but he had courageously beaten out the flames.'

The crew's thoughts turned to abandoning the aircraft by bailing out, which was never an easy task. Willis jettisoned the cockpit canopy escape hatch over his head, and immediately the inrush of wind cleared the smoke, allowing him to see his instruments; a quick check revealed that there was no damage to the engines and the aircraft appeared to be flying straight and level, so they decided to head for Gambut, where they landed some time after the rest of the formation. Their safe return was greeted with some surprise as the last the rest of the formation had seen was their aircraft disappearing over the horizon, apparently on fire, and they had already reported missing.

The aircraft they had shot down was in fact a Cant Z.506, a three-engined Italian float plane, but coming up from behind and assuming most aircraft in the region were German, it was an easy mistake to make. The aircraft was also in German markings and operated by 2./126 on a ferry flight to Crete; the Italian pilot and five others on board were killed. The rest of December was relatively quiet. The Squadron flew numerous 'rovers', but there was little trade to be found; these sorties were interspersed with convoy protection patrols and night missions. By the end of 1944 603 Squadron had converted to rocket projectiles, and 252 Squadron on Cyprus was in the process of doing the same; 227 Squadron, also on Cyprus, retained its fighter-bomber role, which left 47 Squadron as the only Torbeau unit available, although the targets suitable for these weapons were few and far between. The 75mm cannon-armed B-25Gs of 379th BS, USAAF, were also on hand. USAAF heavy bombers were bombing ports and German airfields on the Greek mainland and major islands, taking their own toll of aircraft on the ground and ships in harbour, while their escorting P-38s took a steady toll of fighters sent up to intercept the bombers.

Wing Commander Filson-Young led an eight-aircraft sweep around the coast of Crete on 3 January, but they were intercepted by three Bf109s of JG27, which shot down Beaufighter LX919/X, killing the crew of Warrant Officer Roger Barrett and Sergeant Bill Fairfield. Caiques continued to be the targets at sea and the squadron sunk a number with cannon fire during the month, although not without loss – LX863/A went down on the 22nd. The returning crews reported seeing the navigator, Flight Sergeant Peggram, getting into his dinghy, and he was picked up by a British high-speed launch during the night. But of the pilot, Flying Officer David Hume, no trace could be found and he was posted missing, presumed dead.

The following day six crews were briefed for a daylight assault on Rhodes harbour, the specific target being the German garrison housed in the old crusader fort, which overlooked the harbour. To try and increase the chance of achieving surprise, the attacking force would be allowed to approach from neutral Turkish waters. The raid went as planned and after bombing the fort the Beaufighters strafed shipping and warehouses in the docks. All aircraft returned safely, but it was obvious that bombing a fort with walls 2 meters thick was a complete waste of time.

Attack on a small Greek harbour, late 1943. *Lowman*

Flying over what is believed to be Leros, November, 1943. *Lowman*

On 30 January the squadron OC led a combined strike of six 47 Squadron Torbeaus, with two anti-flak aircraft and six Beaufighters from 603 Squadron as escort against a 2,000-ton merchant vessel reported to have left the island of Melos. The ship was found, but it had a strong escort comprising a U-boat and two flak ships. Nevertheless, the squadron dropped all its torpedoes, although none hit their target, and the aircraft of Flight Sergeants Cyril Melling and Idris Davis was shot down. Fortunately the crew were picked up by a Swedish Red Cross ship after 36 hours in their dinghies and taken to Piraeus to spend the rest of the war as POWs.

During January a number of crews were sent back to 5 METS for further torpedo training, including night attacks and assaults against capital ships. As there were no such enemy targets left in the Mediterranean, the crews were left somewhat perplexed as to the reason for the training. Since nobody was going to enlighten them, most crews simply put it down to the mysterious ways of the RAF and left it at that.

Bob Willis flying T1571/T had a lucky escape at the end of the month. When airborne on a training sortie with Leading Aircraftman Johnny Bell as a passenger, he suffered the loss of the port engine while over the sea; he managed to nurse the crippled aeroplane back to land and made an excellently executed wheels-up forced landing among the rocks and wadis. The relieved and unhurt crew scrambled from the aircraft but had to wait overnight before being rescued. Somewhat to Willis's surprise, he was soon to receive a commendatory endorsement in his logbook for his skill in executing the forced landing.

Operations continued into February and all the units were involved to some degree. A new Beaufighter squadron arrived in Libya early in this month, No. 16 SAAF Squadron, but before they could commence operation they lost a Beaufighter and crew in a mid-air collision, the other Beaufighter being able to land safely.

Filson-Young led a formation of six Beaufighters on the 7th to attack a large merchant vessel that had been reported in Khios harbour. Bob Willis recalls: 'Carrying two 100lb bombs, each aircraft bombed and strafed either the merchant vessel, which was about 1,000 tons, or the many caiques moored against the north-east jetty. As we broke away after our first attack, much to my surprise I saw large red crosses on the side of the merchant ship. I broke RT silence and called up the leader with the message "Hospital Ship". The attack was broken off. This was the Swedish Red Cross ship *Mongabarra* that had picked up Melling and Davis a week before. No serious damage was done, but many apologies were offered by the British government.

No. 47 Squadron suffered a further loss on 13 February (Beaufighter LZ240/L) when the popular and long-standing squadron pilot, Flying Officer Joseph (although always known as Arthur) Unwin and his navigator Flight Sergeant Ken Farmer, were shot down by ground fire and killed while attacking shipping at Hydra.

One of the biggest operations of recent times was launched on 22 February to attack the MV *Lisa* (formerly the *Livenza*) of 5,343 tons and among the largest merchant ships still operating in the eastern Mediterranean. She was reported to have left Piraeus and be heading for Heraklion on Crete. Wing Commander Filson-Young led the formation, which comprised six Torbeaus and two anti-flak Beaufighters from 47 Squadron, escorted by eight from 227 Squadron and two from 603 Squadron, some of which were carrying rockets. Four USAAF B-25Gs also accompanied the formation. A further six Beaufighters from 252 Squadron were intended to be part of the attacking force but they missed the rendezvous.

Approaching from out of the sun the formation found the *Lisa*, which was being escorted by two small destroyers and had air cover comprising five Ju 88s, four Bf109s and six Ar 196s. The importance of this ship, carrying 1,750 tons of fuel and 660 tons of ammunition plus other stores to the garrison on Crete, was obvious. The B-25s, arriving a few minutes ahead of the Beaufighters, drew off the escorting Ju 88s and Bf109s, claiming the shooting down of two for the loss of one of their own. The Torbeau strike was a success with at least one torpedo hitting the *Lisa*, which was sunk, and one of the escorting destroyers was badly shot up and left on fire. Considering the intensity of the flak it was with great relief that all the 47 Squadron Beaufighters returned safely. Things were not so lucky for 227 Squadron – the unit lost three of its aircraft, with five crew killed and one POW. Two of the men who perished – Flight Sergeants Appleton and Fenton – had only just joined 227 Squadron from 47 Squadron. Due to the success of the operation, Wing Commander Filson-Young was awarded a bar to his DFC.

Operations continued to take their toll of aircraft and crews and on 25 February, during an attack on a caique and a schooner led by Squadron Leader Skinner, his navigator, Pilot Officer Tuhill, was wounded in the leg by shrapnel and the Beaufighter of Flying Officer Roy Euler and Flight Sergeant C. Boffin was shot down. Both crewmen made it to their dinghies and after four days drifting in the sea they were picked up by a British destroyer. Thankfully this was to be 47 Squadron's last loss in the Mediterranean. Operations continued into March, usually sweeps around the Aegean hunting for suitable targets, often in groups of four planes. Torpedoes had been abandoned, but the aircrafts' cannon could still make a mess of what it found. On 6 March a formation of Beaufighters, led by Squadron Leader Skinner, sighted four Ar 196s drawn up on a beach. These were shot up, three of the four being claimed as badly damaged. On the 12th the last 'rover' in the Aegean took place for 47 Squadron; this was a maximum-range sweep to Naxos harbour where a 300-ton schooner and two large caiques were attacked.

The next day the squadron was taken off operations and on the 16th moved to Amiriya in preparation for the transfer overseas to India, where the reason for the training against capital ships would become apparent.

Chapter 10

NEW AEROPLANES, NEW ENEMY

Far East, 1944–1945

The Japanese and the British had been fighting in Burma for over two years. It was a very difficult country in which to wage war, with communications being forced to run north to south between the high mountain ranges and through dense tropical jungle and across deep gorges and wide rivers. The campaigning was also restricted by the arrival of the monsoons in April/May, which made movement all but impossible. The British had tried a limited offensive by the 14th Indian Division in the Arakan in 1943, but this been comprehensively defeated. However, the first of the Chindit operations – although in itself it achieved little – startled the Japanese high command into demanding a pre-emptive strike north into India. The plan was to take the strategically important bases at Kohima, and Imphal just across the border, which would give access to the far better transport networks in the area and also the huge supplies of stores that could be

used to replenish their own troops who would only be lightly supplied. The operation was planned for March 1944 to coincide with the end of the dry season, assuming that the start of the monsoon a few months later would make a successful British counter-attack much less likely. It was a huge gamble.

The offensive began in February with a diversionary attack in the Arakan, which drew off three British divisions. On 11 March the Japanese 15th Army with about 100,000 men attacked, but the British were better prepared than the Japanese expected and one of the most decisive battles of the Second World War began around the small hill stations of Imphal and Kohima.

As part of the operation the Japanese had assembled in Singapore a fleet comprising seven old battleships, two fleet aircraft carriers, six heavy cruisers and eighteen destroyers. The presence of this, what would appear on paper, substantial naval force, was of great concern to the British and the absence of an experienced torpedo strike force was something of a worry. The high command scanned what was available and soon identified 47 Squadron as the closest and, with no more targets worthy of a torpedo left in their operational area, an obvious choice to move to the Far East, to be on hand should the capital ships sortie out from Singapore. All that additional training earlier in the year would not go to waste.

Two years previously, in April 1942, a Japanese naval strike force, including five large aircraft carriers, had attacked Ceylon (modern-day Sri Lanka), which had limited air defence resources but was an important British base for shipping, heading towards India, and the Royal Navy. A lone Catalina of 413 Squadron spotted the Japanese force on 4 April, which managed to signal its presence before being shot down. Confusion as to the exact intentions of the fleet meant that orders were given for all shipping in the harbours of Colombo and Trincomalee to put to sea and scatter, but many were unable to get away in time. Early on the morning of the 5th – Easter Sunday – the Japanese launched their carrier strike aircraft. The RAF lost twenty-one Hurricanes and the Fleet Air Arm (FAA) six Swordfish in the ensuing dogfights. Air fighting continued all day, with the RAF sending out ten Blenheims from 11 Squadron to try and find the carriers. This they failed to do, which for the Blenheim crews was probably a lucky break; against the carriers with their standing air patrols it is debatable how much they could have achieved before being almost certainly shot down.

In the afternoon Japanese scouting aircraft spotted the cruisers HMS *Devonshire* and *Cornwall* south-east of their fleet and attacked with dive-bombers – within 20 minutes both ships had been sunk with the loss of 424 men. On 9 April the aircraft carrier HMS *Hermes* was also sunk. The Japanese fleet withdrew back to Singapore, delighted with their success, but the effectiveness of the raid was not as devastating as the attacks on Pearl Harbor or Darwin; the damage on the ground was not critical and the losses in aircraft could be quickly replaced. Even the loss of *Hermes* was not to have a major impact, it being the smallest and oldest fleet carrier still in front-line service, and when sunk she was not carrying aircraft or aircrews. For the Japanese the losses in aircraft and men, although not high, did still mean that three of the carriers had to return to Japan to re-equip and would not be available for operations for some months.

In 1944 the British were still very wary of the Japanese attempting a similar sortie and over the previous two years the importance of Ceylon as a base had increased, thus it was felt that the presence of a torpedo strike force available to cover the Bay of Bengal was imperative. No. 47 Squadron had stood down on 13 March in preparation for its move to southern India. A number of squadron members who had completed their operational tours, and were married, were offered the option to stay in the Middle East before being sent back to the UK, but unmarried aircrew were not given the choice. Sixteen 47 Squadron Beaufighters left the Canal Zone on 26 March on the first leg of the flight to Cholavaram, an airfield just north of Madras. The flights were accomplished in a number of stages. Some of the aircraft were sent to an RAF maintenance unit at Allahabad

Opening chapter page, top and below:
47 Squadron, Burma, 1945. *47 Sqn Archives*

47 Squadron Mosquitos lined up Burma, 1945. *Author's collection*

Opposite: HMS *Ceylon* taking evasive action during training for attacks on Japanese capital ships, India, 1944. *Author's collection*

47 Squadron ground crew, Far East, 1944/45, with a Dakota. *Lowman*

in northern India where the Beaufighters were left behind for conversion to Far East specifications, the remainder of the journey for the crews being by train.

It was not to be until the middle of May that all the squadron aircraft, stores and men were to arrive at Cholavaram, where they were joined by the Beaufighters of 27 Squadron as part of 172 Wing, 225 Group. With the constant threat of a Japanese fleet breaking out into the Bay of Bengal, six 47 Squadron Torbeaus, with six from 27 Squadron for the anti-flak role, were kept on instant readiness right through to September. The squadron continued its training over the following months, flying exercises that included practice torpedo strikes on capital ships provided by the Royal Navy; at night these would be accompanied by Liberator bombers dropping flares. It served a double purpose in that it also allowed the Navy to sharpen up its defensive skills against torpedo attack. The exercises were not without their risks and on 2 August Flying Officer James Macklem was killed flying Beaufighter NE298, which was involved in a mid-air collision with another Beaufighter. His navigator and a ground crew passenger survived. Later in the month, on the 21st, another Beaufighter (NE382) was lost in similar circumstances, but this time both crew – Flight Lieutenant A.J. Smith and Warrant Officer L. Grimshaw, MID – were killed. In both cases the other Beaufighter was able to land safely.

With the defeat of the Japanese forces in Burma and the start of the 14th Army's advance south, the perceived threat of the Japanese fleet was thought to be removed. The attention now turned to supporting the Army and the squadron was posted to Yelahanka to start conversion to Mosquitoes. Sadly, the move to Yelahanka was marred by the loss of Beaufighter NE411/D, which crashed on take-off killing the pilot, Flying Officer Roy Euler, who was flying solo.

The Mosquito is one of the iconic aircraft of the Second World War, designed and developed as a private venture by de Havilland as a fast unarmed light bomber. Its lightweight plywood structure married to twin Merlin engines gave it a superb performance. It was soon realised that it was also perfect for long-range reconnaissance, and with only minor conversion, a formidable fighter-bomber. No. 47 Squadron was to convert to the FB.VI version. Armed with four 20mm cannons under the nose and four 0.303 machine guns in the nose, it could also carry two 500lb bombs in the fuselage and eight under-wing rockets. The Rolls-Royce Merlin engines gave it a maximum speed of 380mph at 13,000 feet and a range of 1,205 miles or 1,705 miles with auxiliary tanks. Unlike the Beaufighter the two-man crew sat in the same cockpit, the pilot in the left-hand seat, slightly forward.

Conversion on to the Mosquito was a rapid affair, as there were no dual trainers available. The technique was similar to that used when converting to the Beaufighter – a couple of demonstration flights with an experienced pilot before moving into the left-hand seat for your own solo. Bob Willis's first solo nearly ended in tragedy when Mosquito HX945 suffered the failure of the constant-speed unit and drive shaft to the starboard engine on take-off, which meant that Willis had to try and gain height on one engine, with a windmilling starboard prop adding to the drag. He managed to get back to the runway and touch down, but now discovered he had no brakes and ground-looped the Mosquito through the airfield boundary and on to the adjacent road, hitting a passing Indian civilian. Fortunately, the aircraft did not catch fire and the crew were able to scramble clear and give first aid to the injured man.

As the squadron prepared for the move to the front line, the aircrew were given lectures on the operational and environmental conditions they were likely to encounter, including escape and evasion techniques, knowing full well that if captured they were likely to receive very rough treatment from the Japanese. Escape and survival kits were issued, which included silk maps on the area, local currency, fishing hook, water purification tablets and other items considered essential. All crews were encouraged to carry their own personal side arm, a Smith and

Wesson 0.38 revolver. Some men retained their revolvers post-war and many have turned up in various police arms amnesties over the years, prompting a few raised eyebrows.

The squadron moved forward to Ranchi, not far from Calcutta, at the beginning of November to start operations, but soon all Mosquitoes were grounded after a series of fatal accidents in the region, which was put down to the climatic conditions and a manufacturing problem with the aircraft's main spar, caused by the type of glue being used. Modifications were made, but for the moment 47 Squadron were to get their Beaufighters back. Some aircrew were not too disappointed by this; compared to the Mosquito the inherent strength of the Beaufighter and its roomier cockpit were preferred. Some were still a bit suspicious of an aeroplane made out of bits of wood. The next few weeks were spent improving skills with cannon and rockets on ground-attack practice before the squadron moved again, this time to Kumbhrigram, about 50 miles west of Imphal and 80 miles north of the border with Burma. Sixteen Beaufighters arrived on 10 January to commence operations, joining 45 and 82 Squadrons, which were both back operating Mosquitoes as part of 908 Wing. The wing was to be a long-range striking force attached to XXXIII Corps, intended to attack and harass the Japanese army retreating down the Chindwin and Irrawaddy valleys towards Mandalay.

Kumbhrigram was an all-weather airfield surrounded by jungle and mountains and with tea plantations on the lower slopes. Living conditions in India were tolerable, but precautions had to be taken to avoid dehydration and the water was heavily chlorinated to cut down on the chances of dysentery. All men had to take their Mepacrine tablets as a precaution against malaria; the preferred way was washed down with a gin and orange.

Being north of Burma, to get to their operational area the aircraft had to fly over mountains rising up to 9,000 feet, and the prospect of trying to get back over these in a possibly damaged aircraft, low on fuel and in poor weather was a concern to many. This was more of an issue for the Beaufighter, which did not have the same aircrew oxygen system as the Mosquito, which limited their safe operation altitude to not much more than the surrounding mountains.

Operations commenced at the end of January 1945 with the first strikes south. Briefing before all sorties was thorough, including Met forecasts, signal codes and up-to-date intelligence on the location of friendly forces, emergency landing grounds and other useful information. Each day a bomb line was identified and crews were forbidden to attack anything on the ground north of the line. Sorties were usually up to five hours' duration, taking the Beaufighters well into enemy territory.

On 21 January a four-aircraft formation was briefed to attack a large factory on the Mandalay waterfront, identified as a Japanese supply dump. The Beaufighters were carrying eight 60lb HE rockets apiece. Take-off was before first light and the formation set out across the Chin Hills before dropping down to ground level for the run to the target, pulling up to 2,000 feet close to the target so it could be identified. Then the aircraft dived down at 10 degrees, having to remain perfectly level, and released the rockets in salvo from about 800 yards at 220 knots, quickly making their escape at low level before any Japanese flak had the chance to open up. Later intelligence reports said that the target had been hit by all thirty-two rockets launched, causing a great deal of damage. Flight Lieutenant Bill Hughes (Beaufighter KW394/B) was on this raid and was the last aircraft to attack, having suffered engine problems that meant he was lagging behind the main formation.

He recalls his concern that 'I would be attacking solo after the hornets nest had been stirred'. But despite his navigator, Flight Lieutenant Al Scott's, warning of flak, most of the danger came from the falling masonry coming down all around them. Satisfied with the result, and conscious that his aeroplane was not 100%, 'All I wanted to do then was get back to base but the CO [Wing Commander Filson-Young] who had other

Squadron transport for the Monsoon, Burma, 1945. *Lowman*

Monsoon floods among the tents, 1945. *Lowman*

ideas took us on a "sector recce" along the Irrawaddy south west of Mandalay prior to returning.'

During a night intruder patrol over Japanese airfields south-east of Mandalay by four Beaufighters on the night of 2 February, Beaufighter /B, flown by Squadron Leader Skinner with his navigator Pilot Officer Laing, failed to return. A 'Mayday' call was picked up by one of the other Beaufighters, but nothing further was heard. The cause of the loss was not determined, but one of the Beaufighters reported seeing a Japanese fighter in the area and it would seem that a Ki-43 of the 64th Sentai might have been responsible.[51] The crew's bodies were never recovered and they are commemorated on the Singapore memorial as having no known grave.

The Japanese air force was not much in evidence, having been badly mauled during the ill-fated operation to invade India a year before, but it could still bite given the chance. During a similar patrol on 8 February two Beaufighters were lost, one (/F, Warrant Officers Ted Daden and Bill Lorrins) was believed shot down by a Japanese fighter reported in the area. The other Beaufighter (KW385/Z, Warrant Officers Ken Thomas and Tommy Bashford), crashed near Imphal, possibly due to bad weather or running out of fuel.

As the Japanese 15th Army pushed further south, the squadron sorties were being carried out at the furthest limit of the Beaufighter's range, and the importance of knowing the location of emergency airstrips should the aircraft run into trouble became paramount. They were to be a lifesaver for a number of crews over the months.

On 22 February A Flight handed over its Beaufighters for Mosquitoes, now that everybody had been assured that the earlier problems had been solved. B Flight was not to get Mosquitoes for a few more weeks and carried on with the Beaufighter into March. For the next couple of months the squadron carried out numerous sorties, long-range strikes against briefed targets and the night and day intruder sorties that have been mentioned above. But there were also 'Rhubarbs', which were seek and destroy missions looking for lines of communication targets such as bridges, river and road traffic and railways. One lesson that was taught was never to fly down river valleys – the Japanese would string cables across the river capable of doing severe, if not fatal, damage to a low-flying aircraft. The tactic was to approach rivers at right angles.

Aeroplanes would also drop leaflets to the local population and 'Pintails', which were Very cartridges that would go off on impact with the ground, confusing the Japanese as to the location of Allied ground forces.

March was to be a very busy month for the squadrons of 908 Wing as the Army pushed forward. During the month the wing would claim the destruction of large quantities of rolling stock and motor and river traffic, with plenty more being damaged – to such an extent that Japanese movement by day and night was badly restricted. Mandalay was reached on 9 March, and further south IV Corps was attacking towards Meiktila, with its strategic airfield and transport links. Close air support to the Army was provided by the Hurricane and Thunderbolt squadrons of 221 Group, while the three Mosquito squadrons assaulted communications, gun positions, supply dumps and oil pipelines behind enemy lines. On the night of the 6/7 March one of the squadron Mosquitoes, flying a 'Rhubarb', caught a convoy of motor transport, which it strafed; one lorry, possibly carrying ammunition, was seen to explode.

The Mosquitoes and Beaufighters were operating using a forward airstrip at Sadaung – about 20 miles north of Mandalay – to refuel, which extended their radius of operations much further south; there were also emergency landing strips cut out of the jungle if needed. During the month the squadron flew 226 sorties without any aircrew losses, although a number of aircraft were damaged by flak. In one incident on 13 March a group of four Beaufighters led by Filson-Young attacked a Japanese HQ at Toungoo with cannon and rockets, where they ran into unexpectedly heavy AA fire. One of the Beaufighters (NE502/H, Flying Officers Hardy and Lidgitt) was hit by flak, losing the starboard engine. The damaged aircraft was escorted back to the forward airstrip at Ywadon. However, on its final approach the port engine also stopped, as Hardy had been forced to run it at full revs to keep airborne. The Beaufighter belly-landed, ending up in the trees at the end of the short runway. Fortunately neither man was hurt. The incident prompted much debate as to the various merits of the Mosquito versus the Beaufighter. The Mosquito crews pointed out that their aircraft had a much better single-engined performance and would easily have made it on one engine. The Beaufighter crews said that was entirely academic as the Mosquito would not have been able to remain flying in the first place because of the damage inflicted by the flak, pointing to the inherent strength of the metal Beaufighter.

The squadron suffered the loss of a Beaufighter and crew (KW315/O, Flight Lieutenants Harold Mackey and Albert Smith) on 10 April, which crashed on take-off when carrying out an air test at Kumbhrigram. It was later discovered that the tail trimmers had been incorrectly set, although whether this was pilot error or a maintenance fault was not established.

On the 14th two Mosquitoes were sent to attack Toungoo, but the aircraft of Squadron Leader Al Scott was hit by AA fire and he was badly wounded. Climbing away from the target he ordered his navigator, Flight Lieutenant Sid Parker, to bail out. Both men managed to parachute from the aircraft, coming down in thick jungle. Scott landed in a tree and died from loss of blood before he could be found. The Mosquito had crashed over 100 miles behind enemy lines, but Parker was picked up by an organisation known as Force 136, which operated escape lines in Japanese-occupied territory, and he was able to make his way to safety. He walked back into the mess at Kumbhrigram three weeks after being shot down.

As the monsoon approached, the pressure on the 15th Army to reach Rangoon grew, and they were quickly moving beyond the

47 Squadron Mosquito, Burma, 1945, with nose art and mission log. *Author's collection*

47 Squadron Mosquito with art on nose and camouflage. *Author's collection*

range of the India-based Mosquitoes and Beaufighters of 908 Wing. The squadrons continued to strike as far south as possible, cutting off the Japanese escape routes and attacking any transport that could be found. Small Japanese units were being isolated from the main army and had to be mopped up by the advancing troops. But the Japanese did not give up easily, which slowed down the advance. During a strike against the railway station at Bamwegu on 22 April a number of fuel and ammunition dumps were set on fire. On the 28th the squadron moved to Kinmagon, about 50 miles south-west of Mandalay and 60 miles north-west of Meiktila, just east of the junction between the Chindwin and Irrawaddy rivers, and 240 miles south of Imphal. Around this time, with the arrival of twelve replacement Mosquitoes, B Flight was able to relinquish its Beaufighters and re-equip with the Mosquito.

Kinmagon had been built by the Japanese as a permanent airfield and had a 2,000-yard runway and dispersed blast pens for the aircraft. Accommodation, however, was of a rather temporary nature, all personnel living under canvas and maintenance being carried out in the open air. In finding a flat enough area of land for the airfield, it was located close to the river, and was liable to flooding. The final attack on Rangoon started on 2 May and it fell quickly. For 47 Squadron the arrival of the monsoon led to difficult operating conditions. The huge thunder clouds were to be avoided at all costs, flying into one was extremely dangerous and the powerful winds and up and down drafts could literally tear a Mosquito apart. The squadron's missions were now more dictated by predicted weather than anything else, and many sorties were either scrubbed or abandoned due to it. The Mosquitoes were now also carrying 500lb bombs for use with the rockets and cannons.

On 8 May the news came that Germany had surrendered and the war in Europe was over. For the men in Burma this was nice to know, but apart from the thought that this could release men and materiel to come out to the Far East to help them, the response was a little muted – they were still the 'Forgotten Army' in their own minds. There remained upwards of 50,000 Japanese solders in Burma and it was a long way to go to reach Singapore. Furthermore, the experience of fighting the Japanese was one of resistance to the end, and with the arrival of the monsoon – which would slow down any advance for months – most of the high command was of the opinion that the war would go into 1946.

A new feature for the attacks was the introduction of a 'cab rank' system, a tactic that had been very successful in Europe. This worked by ground observers in the front line identifying targets for the waiting aircraft that would be circling at between 4,000 and 6,000 feet. Once a suitable target had been identified it would be communicated to the formation leader by R/T, who would then lead the aircraft in a dive attack, releasing the 500lb bombs fitted with 11-second-delay fuses from 1,500 feet, and could be followed up by strafing runs with the cannons.

Wing Commander Filson-Young led an eight-Mosquito formation carrying 500lb bombs against a supply dump and river crossing at Lagunbyo on 15 May. The two groups of four aircraft arrived over the target as planned and Filson-Young peeled off into a dive towards the target. Warrant Officer Bill Powell was the next in line, but as he followed his leader he was shocked to see Filson-Young's aircraft crash and explode in a ball of fire. Both pilot and navigator (Flight Lieutenant Roger Waters) were killed. The loss of Filson-Young was deeply felt by the squadron; he had been a popular and inspiring leader and had flown 232 operational sorties during his wartime career. At this time he was tour expired and should not have been flying, but the temptation of one more sortie was to prove too much.

Flight Lieutenant Etherington took over temporary command, until the arrival of Wing Commander Victor Duclos, DFC, from 45 Squadron who was appointed to replace Filson-Young. Operations continued without pause, although the airfield was liable to become unserviceable due to flooding after heavy storms, which also waterlogged the accommodation lines. After some months of intensive missions a number of crews were either officially tour expired, but continued to fly, or were coming up to that point. The Mosquitoes were also suffering in the hot and wet conditions and on 21 May all the aeroplanes were grounded for inspection following the discovery of a fault in the woodwork of one of the aircraft. Nine aircraft of the sixteen available were declared unserviceable, but operations were more affected by the weather, with the airfield being flooded for much of the rest of the month.

In June, a number of the Canadian and Australian crews were posted home, to be replaced by new airmen arriving from the UK. No. 110 Squadron had also joined 47 Squadron with Mosquitoes in May and 34 and 113 Squadrons flying Thunderbolts at the beginning of June. On 15 June four 47 Squadron and eight 110 Squadron Mosquitoes took part in a victory flypast over Rangoon in appalling weather, but it was back to the real work the following day with an attack on bridges on the Mockri-Martuban, road Flight Lieutenant S. Parker successfully demolishing one of the spans.

The monsoon rains continued throughout the month, but operations were put on whenever the weather allowed, as the squadron continued to harass the retreating Japanese, striking railway lines and bridges as well as anything else that merited the expenditure of two 500lb bombs. On 25 June, during an attack on a bridge near Hpindaw, Mosquito RF716/Q – flown by Warrant Officer Ken Illingworth with Sergeant George Tuck – flew into the ground, killing the crew; whether this was because of ground fire or mechanical failure would never be known. Thankfully, these were to be the squadron's last fatalities of the war.

Wing Commander Duclos led the squadron through July and, despite the many problems with weather and aircraft serviceability, 47 Squadron maintained an impressive operational readiness and efficiency. Duclos sent in a detailed report in answer to a request for details of particularly successful attacks, and he used the example of a raid on the town of Moulmein in July led by Warrant Officer Byatt. Three Mosquitoes, each carrying four 500lb bombs (two in the bomb bay and one under each wing), with 11-second-delay fuses to avoid the chance of aircraft being damaged by the bomb's blast, came in at roof-top level and 280mph. Flak from 20mm guns and small arms was heavy, but fortunately not accurate, and the Mosquitoes were able to add to the chaos with their own cannon, hitting river traffic and suspect AA gun positions. The bomb dropping was accurate and a number of buildings and gun positions were hit. The aircraft all returned safely.

In the Pacific, the Americans had been pushing closer to Japan, facing fierce resistance with every island it gained, but the homeland was taking a huge pounding from B-29 Superfortress bombers based on Saipan, Tinian and Guam. On 6 August the first atomic bomb was dropped on Hiroshima, backed up by firebomb raids on other Japanese cities over the following days. A second atomic bomb was inflicted on Nagasaki on the 9th and the last B-29 raid on Japan was carried out on the 14th, the day before the Japanese surrender. No. 47 Squadron received orders to move to Hmawbi, about 15 miles north of Rangoon, on 8 August, becoming fully established there by the 15th, VJ Day; having carried out its last operational sorties on 12 August.

All squadron members greeted the sudden end of the war with great relief, everybody having been unaware of the existence of atomic bombs. A victory celebration took place in the officers' mess at Hmawbi on the night of the 17th, but it was to be rudely interrupted when approximately eighty Japanese commandos stormed the officers' lines, throwing hand grenades and shooting wildly. Fortunately, nobody was killed, but six officers of 47 Squadron and two from 110 Squadron were slightly wounded, and one Mosquito was written off. Base security was increased. Many Japanese soldiers were unaware of the emperor's order to capitulate, or were unwilling to do so as they felt it would be dishonourable. Slowly the message was filtered out to them by loudspeaker and leaflets dropped from aircraft, and over the next week and months stragglers would come out of the jungle to hand over weapons and surrender.

Chapter 11

PEACE, WHAT PEACE? CONTINUED ACTION

Java, 1946

With the end of the war there was pressure to release men quickly so they could be sent back to the UK and be demobbed, but there was still plenty of work for the squadron to do in Burma. One of the priority tasks was to get to Allied POWs still held in remote jungle camps and awaiting liberation; many of these men were in dire physical condition and required urgent medical attention. Hmawbi soon became an important staging post for the RAF C-47 Dakotas ferrying these men back to India, and nobody from 47 Squadron who was still there would ever forget the sight of these men and could only guess at the deprivations they had suffered and withstood. It was all a far cry from their own experience of the war.

The facilities, what there were, at Hmawbi soon became overwhelmed and so a detachment of six Mosquitoes was sent back up to Meiktila to reduce the congestion, returning in the middle of November. After the intensity of operations in the months before, little flying was done, except for regular practice and air tests. Wing Commander Duclos was posted home at the end of October and the new squadron OC was Wing Commander Melville-Jackson, an experienced Beaufighter and Mosquito pilot who had served in the UK. The squadron was brought back up to strength during September with the arrival of ten new crews and aircraft to replace those airmen who had already been sent home and the somewhat tired Mosquitoes that had weathered the worst of the monsoon.

Much further to the south trouble was brewing on the island of Java. The colony of the Netherlands East Indies, as it was previously known, came within the boundaries of SEAC, but headquarters had little accurate intelligence of the position on the ground. As with many parts of the Far East there was considerable tension between the local population and the colonial powers before the war and the Japanese had fostered this during their time of occupation. The Dutch government in exile had little idea of the political temperature in its colony but was keen to re-establish the pre-war position in Java. (Java is approximately 650 miles long and 100 miles wide and located south of Borneo and Sumatra, and about 700 miles south-east of Singapore.)

To a large extent the US government was anti-colonial and was not going to offer any assistance to the British, French or Dutch to get back their territories in the region. From a British perspective they had no interest in fostering Dutch involvement in Java; their first priority was the repatriation of military POWs and civilian internees, thousands of whom were being held in remote jungle camps. A British RAPWI (Recovery of Allied Prisoners of War and Internees) control team was parachuted into Java soon after the Japanese surrender and was met with a discomforting display of hostility. With Japanese encouragement the Republic of Indonesia was proclaimed three days after their formal surrender and this government did not want the Dutch back.

On 15 September the British teams arrived by ship at Batavia, but reports they received from the first men there was not encouraging and they were faced with a country in political, economic and military turmoil. The Japanese had simply abandoned their weapons or handed them over to the locals.

The size of the British team was too small to achieve anything and therefore it was quickly reinforced with ground troops and 904 Wing, RAF, equipped with Thunderbolts. The strengthened force arrived at Batavia in mid-October and the RAF ground crews quickly established a just-workable airfield at Kemajoran, an abandoned Japanese airfield still covered with wrecked and unserviceable Japanese aircraft. On 21 October, the first of the Thunderbolts from 60 and 81 Squadrons arrived after giving a show of strength over Batavia.

It was soon clear that the Thunderbolts alone would not be sufficient to provide protection to the ground forces and three detachments of Mosquitoes were sent – 84 and 110 Squadron Mosquitoes with bombs and 47 Squadron Mosquitoes with rockets. In addition, to aid the evacualtion of POWs and internees, twenty-four Dakotas of 21 Squadron were dispatched. Other aircraft, including Beaufighters and photo-reconnaissance Spitfires, as well as small numbers of Dutch air force Liberators and Catalinas also arrived, which began to put a huge strain on the airfield resources and infrastructure. While this powerful RAF force was being assembled, the situation on the ground continued to deteriorate. It was obvious that with the forces available, the complete reoccupation of the island was out of the question and the potential for sustaining serious casualties was great and to be avoided. Although part of the plan required the handing back of Java to the Dutch, it was not going to be done at the cost of British lives; the priority was still to get to the POWs and internees. It was therefore decided to restrict occupation to the immediate areas around Batavia in the west, Semarang on the coast near the centre and Soerabaja in the east.

By the time the RAF was fully established at Kemajoran there had been a number of episodes between British troops and local forces as they spread out from Batavia in search of the camps. The Thunderbolts and Mosquitoes were soon flying regular close air support sorties. Even when the ground forces reached the camps they still faced attacks and in a series of incidents, women and children internees were murdered and mutilated before they could be rescued. Low-key but intense armed conflict continued to take place throughout November and air strikes with rockets were carried out by 47 Squadron Mosquitoes on a radio station on the middle of the island on 25 November. The squadron undertook further raids in December and flew reconnaissance and escort sorties to protect internee convoys making their way to the relative safety of Batavia from the centre of the island.

The Dakotas of 21 Squadron did tremendous work in evacuating the civilians, often flying well overloaded and in difficult conditions,

Photo of a Mosquito, FBV1, possibly TE860, and believed to have been taken post-war 1945/46.
via Jack Goodwin

although one event serves to show the vicious nature of this conflict. A 21 Squadron Dakota carrying nineteen Indian troops was forced to make an emergency landing about 5 miles from Kemajoran; the escorting Thunderbolt reported that all the occupants exited the aircraft safely and apparently unhurt. However, when a crash party reached the downed aeroplane, no sign of the crew or passengers could be found. The badly decomposed, dismembered and mutilated bodies of the men were not discovered for some time, and most had had their hands tied behind their backs.

Fighting started to die down towards Christmas as the political position began to stabilise, even if this was not helped by the intransigence of the Dutch and the deep hatred of the Javanese for their previous Dutch masters. The situation was still tense, however, and on 22 December Flight Lieutenant MacLean, DFC, a squadron pilot, was killed after being caught in crossfire during a street fight in Batavia. The new year continued the trend, with no offensive operations being carried out, which was probably just as well as the squadrons were getting very stretched due to the loss of manpower as men were being demobbed.

The monsoon came earlier to this part of the Far East, arriving in February. This contributed to the difficulties at Kemajoran, which had struggled to cope with the intensity of the air traffic, and the runway was starting to fall apart, the rains leaving huge puddles that contributed to a number of aircraft accidents. Further, the very high humidity and monsoon rains began to affect the Mosquitoes, which, with no hangars available, had to be parked in the open. Here there were not the facilities available locally to repair the aircraft and they had to be patched up as best they could; those not repairable were declared non-flyable. Eventually the situation got to the point where 47 Squadron simply handed its last operational Mosquitoes over to 84 Squadron and left for Butterworth in Malaya, where the unit was to be disbanded on 21 March 1946.

But No. 47 Squadron was not to be left on the shelf for long. It was re-formed at Qastina in Palestine on 1 September 1946 by renumbering 644 Squadron, which had been established in 1944 as a transport squadron equipped with Handley Page Halifax aircraft. It had taken part in Special Operations Executive (SOE) missions and supply drops as well as glider towing for D-Day, and Operation Market (the airborne element of the Arnhem assault) in 1944 and Operation Varsity, the Rhine crossing in 1945. It had moved to the Middle East in August 1945 and was now carrying out paratroop dropping as well as a regular mail run to the UK and Met reconnaissance. It was in the charge of Wing Commander W.H. Ingle, who would stay on as 47 Squadron's new OC. The Handley Page Halifax four-engined bomber was a very versatile aircraft and, although it was most used in its original design role, it also carried out anti-submarine work in Coastal Command, and in the transport task now taken on by 47 Squadron. In this capacity the aircraft had their mid-upper turret removed and the interior was fitted out with parachute seats, the paras exiting through a hole (or a hatch in the airborne forces specific A Mk IX version) in the floor just aft of the bomb bay. Stores could also be carried in the fuselage and wing bomb bays. Gliders could be towed using a hook under the tail.

The squadron was to stay in Palestine for only a month, and apart from the change in number it continued with the same aircraft and crews that it inherited from 644 Squadron. On 20 September the unit left for the UK and re-established itself at RAF Fairford in Gloustershire, not far from its current home at RAF Brize Norton, almost exactly 20 years after it had left the UK. It was a squadron that had made a name for itself, in far away places, building a history that this author can only hope he has gone some way to record.

ENDNOTES

1 Quoted in *The Air Defence of Britain 1914 – 1918*, Christopher Cole and E.F. Chessman, published by Putnam (1984).
2 National Archives: AIR 1/1666/204/99/11
3 Ibid.
4 Ibid.
5 C.A. Owers, *Vickers Bullets*, Windsock Datafile No. 154 (2012), Report No. M.97 (National Archives: Air 1/1192/204/5/2599).
6 J.M. Bruce, *The Aeroplanes of the Royal Flying Corps Military Wing*, Putnam (1992).
7 Francis K. Mason, *The British Bomber since 1914*, Putnam (1994).
8 Trevor Henshaw, *The Sky Their Battlefield, II* (2014) Fetubi Books
9 Ibid.
10 No 47 Squadron archives, RAF Brize Norton.
11 National Archives: WO 158/751, General Greenly's Report, January 1919.
12 Henry Albert Jones, *Over the Balkans and South Russia 1917 – 1919*, Greenhills 1987, p. 138.
13 About 20 miles north of Thessaloniki.
14 Raymond Vann, C.O., 'In the Sideshows', *Cross and Cockade*, Vol. 24, No. 1 (1993), p. 31.
15 Jones, *Over the Balkans*, (1987) p. 137.
16 National Archives: AIR 5/1340.
17 Jones, *Over the Balkans*, (1987) p. 138.
18 Philip J.R. Moyes, *Bomber Squadrons of the RAF and their Aircraft* (1964), MacDonald p. 215.
19 Christopher Dobson and John Miller, *The Day We Almost Bombed Moscow* (1986), p. 17.
20 John T. Smith, *Gone to Russia to Fight* (2010), p. 144.
21 Dobson and Miller, *The Day We Almost Bombed Moscow* (1986), p. 18.
22 National Archives: WO 33/971.
23 Raymond Collishaw and R.V. Dodds, *Air Command, a Fighter Pilot's Story*, William Kimber, 1973.
24 Air *1/2375/226/11/17*
25 Jones, *Over the Balkans* (1987), pp. 141 – 42.
26 AIR *1/1959/204/206/28*
27 National Archives: AIR *1/2375/226/11/2*, War Diary South Russia, July 1919 and Smith, *Gone to Russia to Fight.*
28 Mark Grossman, *World Military Leaders: A Biographical Dictionary* (2007), pp. 88 – 89.
29 J.M. Bruce, *The Aeroplanes of the Royal Flying Corps Military Wing*, Putnam (1992), p. 534.
30 AIR *1/1959/204/206/28*
31 Jones, *Over the Balkans*, (1987), p. 156.
32 Jones, *Over the Balkans*, (1987), pp. 155 – 56.
33 National Archives: *1/408/15/323/1*, RAF War diaries and Operational Record Books.
34 C.G. Jefford, *RAF Squadrons Airlife* (1993), p. 40.
35 Jones, H. A., *Over the Balkans and South Russia 1917 – 1919*, (1997), pp. 155 – 156
36 No. 47 Squadron archives: *To War in Russia*, the personal recollections of D. MacKinnon (1984).
37 Ibid.
38 National Archives: WO 33/971 and 47 Squadron war diary.
39 National Archives: WO 33/971.
40 Alexander Boyd, *The Soviet Air Force since 1918* Macdonald and Janes (1997), pp. 2 – 61.

41 Although many who served in south Russia were victims of typhus, interestingly figures show that the largest number of hospital cases were in fact VD-related. Of 736 admitted to hospital from the British military mission, there were 266 cases of VD and 89 cases of Typhus. National Archives: WO 33/971.
42 Mikhail Khvostov, *The Russian Civil War (2): White Armies* Osprey(1997), p. 3.
43 Evan Mawdesley, *The Russian Civil War* Osprey (2007), p. 113.
44 Kenneth R. Whiting, *Soviet Air Power* Westview Press (1985), p. 3.
45 Dimitri von Mohrenschildt, *The Russian Revolution of 1917: Contemporary Accounts* (1971), p. 275.
46 John Bradley, *Allied Intervention in Russia* (1968), p. 175.
47 Robert Service, *A History of Modern Russia* (2009), p. 107.
48 Von Mohrenschildt, *The Russian Revolution of 1917*, p. 275.
49 Abyssinia can also be referred to as Ethiopia; however, in squadron records it is usually called the former and that name is used here.
50 Correspondence with the author, September 1998. 'Digger' Magill stayed with the squadron until the end of the East Africa campaign. Finishing as OC with the rank of squadron leader, DFC, MiD, he retired from the RAF as air vice marshal, CB, CBE, DFC and bar, MiD, FIMgt, in 1970.
51 For a detailed explanation of non-aircrew roles, please see *Observers and Navigators – and other Non-Pilot Aircrew in the RFC, RNAS and RAF* by Wing Commander C.G. Jefford, MBE, BA, RAF Retd, published by Grub Street, 2014
52 Magill correspondence, 1998.
53 Christopher Shores, *Air War For Burma*, Grub Street (2005).

Appendix 1

NO. 47 SQUADRON AIRCRAFT

1916 – 1946

RAF BE2c	**3/16–8/16**
Avro 504	**3/16–9/16**
Armstrong Whitworth FK3	**3/16–7/18**

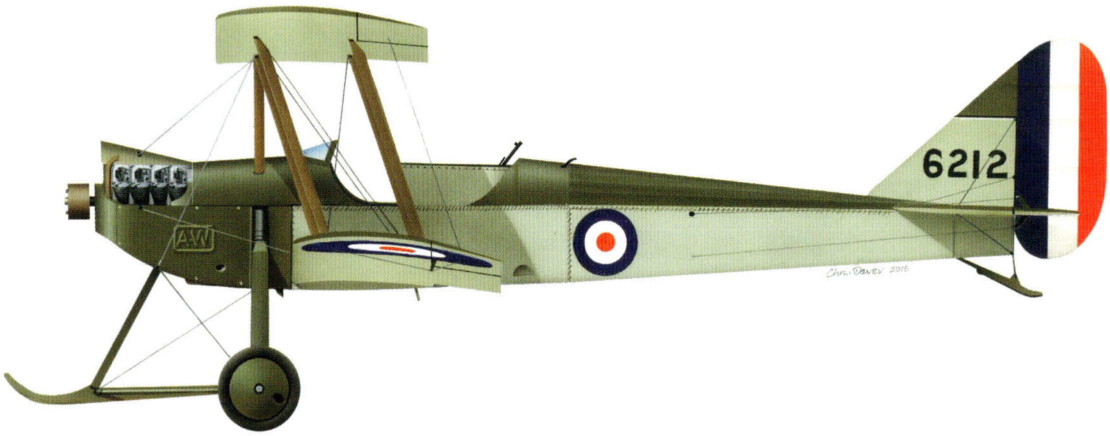

Armstrong Whitworth FK3 'Little Ack' (6212) Salonika 1916-17 fitted with RAF4a engine and in standard colours of clear doped linen lower surfaces and PC10 or PC12 coloured dopes upper surfaces. This colour is very much open to interpretation and ranged from an Olive Drab to Chocolate Brown. This aeroplane is not equipped with a scarf ring for the observer. This aeroplane was lost on the 12th March 1917, shot down over Hudova, the pilot Second Lieutenant D. H. Glasson dying of wounds.

Bristol Scout C/D	**6/16–11/16***
RAF BE12/12a	**10/16–4/18**
Airco DH2	**2/17–3/18**
Vickers FB19	**6/17–4/18**
RAF BE2e	**10/17–4/18**
RAF SE5A	**11/17–4/18**
Bristol M1C	**2/18–5/18**
Armstrong Whitworth FK8	**3/18–1/19**
Airco DH9	**8/18–9/20**

*The squadron certainly had Bristol Scouts in Salonika, but it is not clear when they stopped using them.

De Havilland DH9A **8/19–1/28**

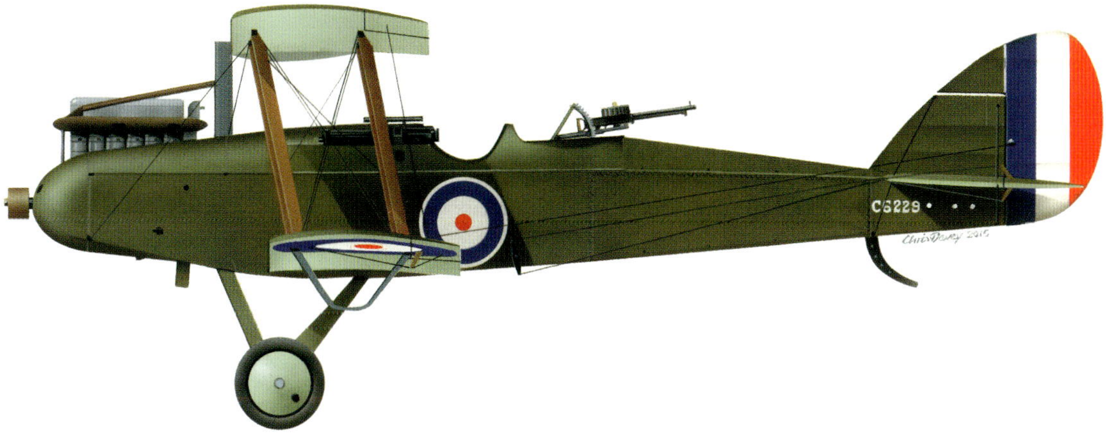

Airco DH9 C6229 delivered to 47 Squadron from 17 Squadron December 1918 and eventually written off on 18th July 1919 whilst serving with 17 Squadron. Aeroplane in standard wartime RFC/RAF colours of PC10/12 on upper surfaces and fuselage with clear doped linen. Aeroplanes in Russia between 1919/20 would also have carried these colours. There is no evidence that DH9s on the squadron carried either individual aeroplane letters or Squadron markings.

Sopwith Camel **9/19–3/20**

Fairey IIIF **12/27–1/33**

Fairey IIIF J9796 delivered to 47 Squadron in 1930 it was relinquished for conversion to a Fairey Gordon and returned to the Squadron in 1934 as JR9796. This aircraft carries a representation of the early squadron badge, the step Pyramid of Djoser with the sun behind it.

Fairey Gordon **1/33–12/39**

Fairey Gordon KR2641/K Originally delivered to 14 Squadron as K2641. Rebuilt as KR2641 and delivered to 47 Squadron. Passenger bounced out of aircraft 24th Jan 1935 and killed. Returned to UK for 207 Squadron December 1936.

Vickers Vincent **7/36–8/40**

Vickers Wellesley **6/39–3/43**

Vickers Wellesley Mk.I L2673 KU-C Ethiopia February 1941. The Wellesley is in standard bomber colours with dark green and dark earth upper surfaces and night black undersides. Most 47 Squadron Wellesleys and some of the Vickers Vincents carried the KU squadron code during the war in East Africa.

Bristol Beaufort I **9/42–6/4**

Bristol Beaufort Mk.I DE111/V Delivered to the Squadron in late 1942 it remained on the Squadron's books until the arrival of Beaufighters in June 1943. By September 1943 it had been transferred to 16 Squadron SAAF. This aircraft has been adapted locally for squadron service, including the removal of the rear turret canopy to give the gunner a better field of observation and fire. ASV aerial are fitted to the nose and leading edge of the wings and sand filters to the engine air intakes. The latter two adaptions had a detrimental affect of aircraft performance. The aircraft is painted in standard desert camouflage of middle stone and dark earth upper surfaces and azure blue underside. It also carried nose art in the shape of a painting of *Popeye*, but this cannot be seen on the profile as it is hidden behind the port engine.

Bristol Beaufighter X	**6/43–10/44**
Bristol Beaufighter X	**11/44–4/45**

Bristol Beaufighter Mk.X TFX JM352/F This aircraft was last seen in combat with Ar.196 during attack on Naussa; crashed into hillside 6th November 1943, killing the crew, Flying Officer L. Rossner and Flight Sergeant Sgt H. K. Levy. Camouflage similar to the previous Beaufort, however all colours faded badly under the desert sun and the effect of low flying over the sea

De Havilland Mosquito FB VI	**10/44–11/44**
De Havilland Mosquito FB VI	**2/45–3/46**

De Havilland Mosquito FBVI HR435/C De Havilland Mosquito FBVI HR435/C Built by Standard Motors and delivered to Far East, served with 47 Squadron until struck off charge in March 1946. Shown in standard late war Far East markings of overall silver with red or black spinners, and blue bands on the wings and tail. Many squadron aircraft also carried nose art and mission marking on the crew door on the starboard side of the front fuselage.

Appendix 2

NO. 47 SQUADRON BASES

1916 – 1946

Base Name	Location	Date
Beverley	Yorkshire, on race course, to west of town on A1079.	1/3/16 – 5/9/16
	Departs for Salonika (5 September 1916).	
Mikra Bay	Near Salonika, on Aegean coast, northern Greece, approx. 50 miles south of border with Bulgaria.	20/9/16 – 27/10/17
Yanesh (Janes)	Approx. 20 miles north of Mikra Bay and 15 miles south of border with Bulgaria.	27/10/17 – 14/12/19
Flights at:		
Mikra Bay	Approx. 20 miles south.	
Kukush	Approx. 5 miles south.	
Snevche	Approx. 10 miles north.	
Hadzi Janus	Adjacent	
Kirec	1/2 mile south-west.	
Hajdarli	Approx. 1 mile south-west.	
Amberkoj	Approx. 15 miles south.	
Kalabac	Approx. 100 miles south-west.	
Detachments at:		
Thasos	On Thasos Island in Aegean, approx. 5 miles off coast and 100 miles east of Yanesh.	
Florina	Just south of border with Macedonia, approx. 70 miles west of Yanesh.	
Moudros	On island of Limnos, 60 miles south of Greek coastand 50 miles west of Gallipoli; approx. 130 miles south-east of Yanesh.	
Gmuldjina	Approx. 120 miles east of Yanesh, between sea and Bulgarian border (10 miles each) and 40 miles west of Turkish border.	
Dedeagatch	On coast approx. 25 miles south-east of Gmuldjina.	
Amberkoj	Approx 15 miles south of Yanesh.	14/2/19 – 24/4/19
	Move to Russia (16 April 1919).	
Novorossiysk	On Black Sea, approx. 170 miles south-east of Sevastopol.	24/4/19 – 4/6/19
Ekaterinodar	40 miles east of Novorossiysk on railway.	4/6/19 – 7/10/19
Flights at:-		
Velikoknyajaskaya	Approx. 160 miles north-east of Ekaterinodar on railway to Tsaritsyn (150 miles north-east), approx. 80 miles south-east of Rostov.	
Zimovniki	50 miles north-east of Velikoknyajaskaya on railway, 30 miles from River Don.	
Kotelnikovo	60 miles north-east of Zimovniki on railway, 80 miles south-west of Tsaritysn.	
Gniloaksaiskaya	35 miles north-east of Kotelnikovo on railway.	

Beketovka	45 miles north-east of Gniloaksaiskaya on railway, 20 miles south of Tsaritsyn.	
Beketovka	20 miles south of Tsaritsyn, approx. 200 miles north-east of Rostov and 360 miles north-east of Novorossiysk.	7/10/19 – 20/10/19
	Disbanded at Beketovka 20/10/19, renamed Nos 11, 12 and 13 Squadrons, Russian 7th Division. Re-formed with renumbering of 206 Squadron (1 February 1920).	
Helwan	Approx 15 miles south of Cairo on Nile.	1/2/20 – 21/10/27
Detachments at:		
Khartoum	On edge of city.	
Khartoum	On edge of city.	21/10/27 – 28/5/40
Detachments at:		
Kapoeta	Approx. 700 miles south of Khartoum near borders with Uganda and Kenya.	
Erkowit	(Carthago) on railway from Port Sudan (50 miles north) to Khartoum (330 miles south-west), 30 miles west of Red Sea, 100 miles north of Eritrea.	28/5/40 –27/11/40
Detachments at:		
Gordon's Tree	Just south of Khartoum in fork of White and Blue Niles.	
Gedaref	On southern railway from Port Sudan (350 miles north), approx. 200 miles south-east of Khartoum and 60 miles from border with Abyssinia.	
Sennar	150 miles south of Khartoum on Blue Nile at railway junction.	
Gordon's Tree	Khartoum	27/11/40 – 24/4/41
Detachments at:		
Sennar		
Kassala	On border with Eritrea, on railway line running south from Port Sudan, 250 miles.	
Agordat	In Eritrea at end of railway line running west from Massawa (90 miles) on Red Sea.	
Asmara	On railway line approx. 35 miles south-west of Massawa, in Eritrea, approx. 50 miles north of Abyssinia.	
Blackdown	On railway line approx. 15 miles east of Gadaref.	
Asmara		24/4/41 – 9/12/41
Massawa		9/12/41 – 22/12/41
	To North Africa (no aircraft).	
Kasfereet	On west bank of Great Bitter Lake (part of Suez Canel), approx. 25 miles south of Ismalia and 20 miles north of Red Sea.	22/12/41 – 25/1/42
Burgh el Arab (LG 28)	On coastal railway approx. 30 miles south-west of Alexandria and 40 miles east of El Alamain.	25/1/42 – 10/2/42
LG 87	South of railway line on Cairo to Alexandria road (approx. 25 miles south of Alex).	10/2/42 – 18/3/42
	Operational echelon established (16 April 1942).	
LG 87	Approx 2 miles south-west of LG 87.	16/4/42 – 1/7/42
Shandur	On Great Bitter Lake, approx. 15 miles north of Red Sea.	1/7/42 – 16/7/42
St Jean	On Mediterranean coast approx. 15 miles north of Haifa in Palestine.	16/7/42 – 10/11/42
LG 227	Approx. 20 miles south of Alexandria.	10/11/42 – 30/11/42
LG 08	Approx. 5 miles south of Mersa Matruh, just north of coastal railway, 150 miles west of Alexandria.	30/11/42 – 4/1/43
LG 07	Approx 20 miles west of Mersa Matruh.	4/1/43 – 3/3/43
	Operational echelon disbanded (3 March 1943).	

	Squadron re-established from elements of 39 and 42 Squadrons (8 September 1942).	
Shandur	On Great Bitter Lake, approx. 15 miles north of Red Sea.	8/9/42 – 29/1/43
Detachment at: Gianaclis	Approx. 25 miles south of Alexandria.	
Gianaclis		29/1/43 – 3/3/43
Detachment at: Al-Berka	Just south of Benghazi, Libya, 200 miles west of Tobruk and 600 miles west of Alexandria.	
Misurata West	Just south of coast, approx. 100 miles east of Tripoli and 350 miles west of Benghazi.	3/3/43 – 22/6/43
Protville II	Approx. 15 miles north-east of Tunis.	22/6/43 – 17/10/43
Sidi Amor	Approx. 10 miles north of Tunis	17/10/43 – 14/11/43
Detachment at: El Adem	Approx. 15 miles south of Tobruk, 850 miles east of Tunis.	
El Adem	(LG 144)	14/11/43 – 25/11/43
Gambut No. 3	(LG 143) Just south of coast, approx. 35 miles east of Tobruk.	25/11/43 – 16/3/44
Amiriya	(LG 29) Approx. 15 miles south-west of Alexandria.	16/3/44 – 25/3/44
	Move to India (25 March 1944)	
Cholavaram	Just north of Madras, southern India.	20/4/44 – 7/10/44
Yelahanka	Just north of Bangalore, approx. 150 miles west of Madras.	7/10/44 – 6/11/44
Ranchi	Approx. 200 miles west of Calcutta, north-east India.	6/11/44 – 11/1/45
Kumbhirgram	Approx. 60 miles west of Imphal, India, 300 miles north-east of Calcutta.	13/1/45 – 28/4/45
Detachment at: Thazi	Approx. 100 miles south of Imphal in Burma and approx. 10 miles west of the Chindwin River.	
Kinmagon	Approx. 50 miles south-west of Mandalay and 60 miles north-west of Meiktila, just east of junction between Chindwin and Irrawaddy rivers, 240 miles south of Imphal.	28/4/45 – 15/8/45
Hmawbi	Approx. 15 miles north of Rangoon, south Burma.	15/8/45 – 15/1/46
Detachments at: Meiktila Kemajoran	Just north of town, approx. 250 miles north of Rangoon. Batavia, on north-west coast of Java.	
Butterworth	On north-east coast of Malaya, approx. 60 miles south of border with Thailand and 180 miles north of Kuala Lumpur.	15/1/46 – 21/3/46
Detachment at: Kemajoran		
	Disbanded at Butterworth (21 March 1946). **Re-formed at Qastina from 644 Squadron (1 September 1946).**	
Qastina	Approx. 25 miles south of Tel Aviv, Palestine.	1/9/46 – 30/9/46
	Returned to UK (30 September 1946).	

Appendix 3

ROLL OF HONOUR

1916–1946

Matthews, Second Lieutenant Henry	15/01/1917
White, Lieutenant Spencer John Meadows	15/01/1917
Black, Major Maurice Adam	11/02/1917
Chalmers, Air Mechanic Second Class A.G., 31384	26/02/1917
Chambers, Air Mechanic Second Class W., 18096	26/02/1917
De-Pomeroy, Corporal C., 17691	26/02/1917
Parkinson, Air Mechanic Second Class W.H., 14417	26/02/1917
Ward, Air Mechanic Second Class Robert, B/32758	26/02/1917
Clutterbuck, Air Mechanic Second Class George, 41410.	27/02/1917
Tansley, Flight Sergeant, Reginald John Cameron, 740. MiD	27/02/1917
Glasson, Second Lieutenant D.H.	12/03/1917
Rawson, Air Mechanic Second Class E.C., 10096	07/04/1917
Watt, Second Lieutenant James	02/05/1917
Brufton, Second Lieutenant Howard Charles	08/07/1917
Lyons, Air Mechanic First Class Albert Frederick, 18286	29/07/1917
Wilkinson, Lieutenant Eric Russell, MC	07/10/1917
Butler, Lieutenant Armar Somerset	16/10/1917
Hunter, Second Lieutenant Patrick Colin	16/10/1917
Montague, Lieutenant Paul Dennis	29/10/1917
Gubbin, Second Lieutenant J.RF.	20/11/1917
Thomas, Lieutenant Frank William MC, CG (F)	05/01/1918
Wilson, Lieutenant Marshall Meredith	29/01/1918
Graham, Lieutenant David Liddell	24/06/1918
Kane, Second Lieutenant Patrick Colin	24/06/1918
Brandt, Lieutenant J.A.	18/09/1918
Gerhardi, Second Lieutenant Harold James	18/09/1918
Arden, Air Mechanic Second Class George, 94590	04/10/1918
Wright, Air Mechanic Third Class Walter John, 44462	26/12/1918
Adams, Captain Allen Percy, DFC. *Mentioned in dispatches*	06/03/1919
Eversden, Captain Robert Ernest	15/08/1919
McLennan, Captain John Lawrance, MC	28/08/1919
Tait, Leading Aircraftman Leonard Henderson, 261765	12/10/1919
Keymar, Captain Basil Graham Homfray , DFC and bar	24/10/1919
Thompson, Lieutenant Douglas Blaxland	24/10/1919
Adams, Aircraftman Second Class Herbert George, 161234	26/10/1919
Freeman, Aircraftman Second Class Frank Oliver, 331013	27/12/1919
Carro, Aircraftman First Class Walter John, 224622	21/01/1920
Walker, Leading Aircraftman, John Wilke, 130334	30/04/1920
Byrne, Observer Officer Brennan Claude Sydney	03/09/1920
Algar, Aircraftman Second Class Albert Charles, 330039	23/06/1921
Lake, Corporal Horace Merilion, 195212	14/08/1921
Potter, Flying Officer Sydney Hugh. *Mentioned in dispatches*	14/08/1921
Slater, Flying Officer H. G.	10/08/1926
Harvey, Aircraftsman First Class T. R.	10/08/1926
Bennett, Flight Lieutenant *(Believed)*	01/03/1929
Turner, Leading Aircraftman *(Believed)*	01/03/1929
Burro, Flight Lieutenant *(Believed)*	01/03/1930
Davey, Leading Aircraftman 'Tarzan' *(Believed)*	01/03/1930
Cleland, Flying Officer Albert Gwillium	22/12/1932
Lovell, Leading Aircraftman Albert Henry	22/12/1932
Searle, Flight Lieutenant	10/04/1934
Wooley, Leading Aircraftman	10/04/1934
Shelley, Sergeant William Robert Theodore 564968.	13/09/1939
Bush, Pilot Officer Colin Graham, 40886	02/07/1940
Davidson, Sergeant Joseph William , 522888	03/07/1940
Nelson, Sergeant Frederick (Freddy) 516778	12/07/1940
Clark, Sergeant John 566218	16/07/1940
Crossland, Leading Aircraftman Walter , 522035	16/07/1940
Style, Sergeant William Charles Harry 521075	16/07/1940
Pope, Sergeant George Robert 746774	11/08/1940
Witty, Pilot Officer Basil Baxter, 44069	12/12/1940
Bainbridge, Pilot Officer Ernest John 78988	07/02/1941
Blofield, Sergeant Edwin Ellis 564554	07/02/1941
Davies, Sergeant John Herbert 563111	07/02/1941
Paine, Sergeant Arthur Harold 749557	07/02/1941
English, Sergeant Stanley William Jack 958277.	16/03/1941
Minn, Sergeant Charles William 975720	16/03/1941
German, Sergeant Douglas Alfred 654446	26/03/1941
Oddy, Sergeant Harold Leslie 530029	01/06/1941
Barbone, Flight Sergeant Dennis George 549793	02/07/1941
Brown, Sergeant Alexander George 564096	02/07/1941
Elsy, Flight Sergeant Samuel Albert 564041	02/07/1941

Illsley, Squadron Leader David Milledge DFC,, 41349	14/11/1941
Bazeley, Flying Officer John Selwyn Standish 89771	27/11/1941
Bull, Sergeant Leon Emile	27/11/1941
Neill, Aircraftman First Class Joseph Herbert, 631004	26/01/1942
Keegan, Sergeant Thomas Bernard, 986282	14/04/1942
Smith, Sergeant Thomas, 996850	14/04/1942
Morse, Warrant Officer Francis William 518560	10/07/1942
Davidson, Flying Officer, Haraldur Johannes, J/6402	26/10/1942
Garriock, Flying Officer Walter, 403733	26/10/1942
Hamilton, Sergeant Roy James, 404689	26/10/1942
Pugh, Sergeant Sydney Ronald Maldwyn 1117286	26/10/1942
Simpson, Flying Officer Robert Wrey, 411228	26/10/1942
Gitsham, Flight Sergeant Stuart Burton, 407929	26/10/1942
Davis, Sergeant Lance George, 407166	26/10/1942
Augustinus, Sergeant Alfred Leslie 401183	18/11/1942
Sprague, Wing Commander Richard Alfonso DFC, 26067	18/11/1942
Ingram, Sergeant Campbell, 1003429	24/11/1942
Boon, Flight Sergeant Dennis Murdock, 776086	10/01/1943
Angus, Sergeant Stephen Sellars 1025313	15/01/1943
Daly, Flying Officer Patrick Gerard 110794	15/01/1943
Hallsworth, Sergeant John 1116215	15/01/1943
Pile, Flying Officer Frederick James 102299	15/01/1943
Barber, Pilot Officer Hubert Knight J/17241	10/04/1943
Blanchard, Sergeant Ernest Stephen 1194928	10/04/1943
Dix, Sergeant Alfred Benjamin 655788	10/04/1943
Drew, Sergeant Alec Benjamin 1169656	10/04/1943
Joy, Flying Officer William Douglas, 132859	23/06/1943
Robertson, Flying Officer Ian Holdsworth, 119052	23/06/1943
Deacon, Sergeant Ronald Horace, 902474	28/06/1943
Taylor, Wing Commander Alistair Murray, DFC, 77612	11/07/1943
Whitlock, Flying Officer Frank, 136711	11/07/1943
Adcock, Pilot Officer Charles Norman , 142561	13/07/1943
Ambrose, Sergeant, William Kenneth, 1128541	03/08/1943
Temple, Flight Sergeant Albert Charles 1344167	03/08/1943
Hastings, Captain James Russell, 102438	02/09/1943
Hill, Flight Sergeant Francis Peter, 1208802	02/09/1943
Cameron, Sergeant Patrick Blair, 1370486	18/09/1943
Dixon, Flying Officer John, 47785	29/10/1943
Terry, Flying Officer George Alec, 132857	29/10/1943
Levy, Flight Sergeant Henry Kenneth 656509	06/11/1943
Rossner, Flying Officer Lewis 131150	06/11/1943
Hayden, Flying Officer John Stephens, 130938	10/11/1943
McMaster, Sergeant	10/11/1943
Freeman, Flight Sergeant George Herbert, 656750	12/11/1943
Greentree, Flying Officer Athol George, 414974	12/11/1943
Clary, Flying Officer Edgar Leroy, J/13088	13/11/1943
Finbow, Flight Sergeant Walter Edwin, 1380965	13/11/1943
Bond, Flying Officer Anthony David, 125666	16/11/1943
Dale, Sergeant Jack, 1516617	16/11/1943
Fletcher, Flying Officer John Bratt, 128593	16/11/1943
Lovell, Flying Officer John Edwin, 136381	16/11/1943
Thwaites, Flying Officer William Walker, 50176	16/11/1943
Gregory, Flying Officer Forrest June, J/20210	26/11/1943
Wood, Flying Officer, Alan George, 136058	26/11/1943
Barrett, Warrant Officer First Class Roger John, R/103983	03/01/1944
Fairfield, Sergeant William Henry 1470735	03/01/1944
Hare, Pilot Officer Herbert, 157317	10/01/1944
Hume, Flying Officer David Balfour, 136846	22/01/1944
Farmer, Flight Sergeant Kenneth Roy, 1215062	13/02/1944
Unwin, Flying Officer Joseph Arthur, 129568	13/02/1944
Macklem, Flying Officer James Douglas J/20592	02/08/1944
Grimshaw, Warrant Officer Leslie, 1002285. MiD.	21/08/1944
Smith, Squadron Leader Albert John J/21249	21/08/1944
Euler, Flying Officer Roy Stanley 132346	05/10/1944
Laing, Pilot Officer Horace Francis, 200528	02/02/1945
Skinner, Squadron Leader Leslie Harold 85652	02/02/1945
Bashford, Warrant Officer Thomas Henry, 1497184. MiD.	08/02/1945
Daden, Warrant Officer Edward Albert, 1335460. MiD	08/02/1945
Lorains, Warrant Officer William, 1451677.	08/02/1945
Thomas, Warrant Officer Kenneth Vernon 1389444	08/02/1945
Mackey, Flight Lieutenant Harold Dee, J/23322	10/04/1945
Smith, Flight Lieutenant Albert, 142345	10/04/1945
Scott, Squadron Leader Alward Elmer, J/5832	14/04/1945
Butler, Flight Lieutenant Norman Grenville, 134152	17/04/1945
Robson, Flight Sergeant Frank, 1672351	17/04/1945
Filson-Young, Wing Commander William D.L. DFC and bar, 39725	15/05/1945
Waters, Flight Lieutenant Roger Claud Vaughan, 142344	15/05/1945
Illingworth, Warrant Officer Kenneth, 1434004	25/06/1945
Tuck, Flight Sergeant George Edward, 1607464	25/06/1945
MacLean, Flight Lieutenant T., DFC, 66023	22/12/1945

A Note from the Author

One thing for the reader to be aware of is the sometimes contradictory sources for the squadron history. The main source is *Over the Balkans and South Russia 1917–19*, being the history of no. 47 squadron RAF, written by H.A. Jones and originally published in 1923. Jones served with the squadron as an observer in the theatre and later contributed to the official history of the RFC and RAF in the First World War; as such he can be considered a fairly reliable witness to events and had access to squadron records post-war. Even so, some of the events detailed in the book are difficult to independently confirm. There are also the various official records kept by the National Archives at Kew (but, frustratingly, some periods covered by the daily summary of work are missing, most importantly 27 October 1916–17 June 1917); a number of the gaps can be made up from the reconnaissance and bombing reports, but these are not without errors. A few contemporary diaries and log books exist, but diaries need to be treated with caution as they can contain shorthand personal to the writer, making it impossible to guess the meaning or relevance of the reference. A very useful diary is that of John Robert Wilson, (http://www.qsl.net/gmofne/diaryt~1.htm), which is available online thanks to the efforts of his relative, Tom Wilson. The diary covers his time with 47 Squadron from mid-January 1917 to the end of March when he was posted to Egypt for pilot training. He flew numerous sorties as an observer and records squadron life. Wilson went on to serve with 70 Squadron on the Western Front and was shot down and killed flying a Camel on 20 October 1917. There are a number of secondary sources and histories of the region and the conflict, but this was very much a sideshow in the First World War and has not and does not get the attention of other fronts. One notable and welcome exception is *Under the Devil's Eye: the British Experience in Macedonia* by Alan Wakefield and Simon Moody. This covers the conflict in general, but has a very useful chapter on the air war and is essential for getting a full understanding of the British involvement in the region.

Clearances

Sources

Correspondence and personal recollections (author and in 47 Sqn Archives.):
AVM Roy Collishaw, AVM G.R. Magill, AVM A MacGregor, Dick Taylor, Doug Bradford, Arthur Claygill, Syd E Townson, David Heden, Roger Hayward, Ray Sturtivant, C. G. Jefford, Pete McDermott, Doug MacKinnon, Rev Lionel Daffurn, Tom Williams, Ron Lowman, Elaine Douglas, Bob Willis, Cliff Sullivan, John Geary, Ron Bramley, David Seymour, Stuart Leslie, August G Blume, H. V. Hard, Frank Salt, Bob Milne, Karl Steinbrecher, Jack Turner, Colin Cooke, Grantly Flook, Harold Fishwick, Tony Crawford, Malcolm MacEwan, H Hodgen, Gerrie Forthergill-Lukes, R F Tregoning, Fabio Maiorino, John Bool, Geoff Powell, Bruce Atkinson, F. A Saunders, Sam Borness, Jack Jarvis, Roy C Nesbit, Stewart Cowan, LAC Isbell.

47 Squadron: Flt Lt Jem Wearing, Flt Lt Gordon Morris, Sgt Rob Hick, Flt Lt Doug Hankin, Wg Cdr G Crawford, Wg Cdr Ian Shields, Wg Cdr Jerry King, Wg Cdr Mike Neville, Wg Cdr Joe Hardstaff, Flt Lt Steve Todd, Flt Lt Catherine Donoghue, Wg Cdr Greg Cook, Wg Cdr Dave Stewart.

Log Books: J. A. Beeney (Dec 17 – Apr 18), Malcolm MacEwan (Feb 18 – Sept19), LAC L.A. Williams (Nov 28 – Sept 30), David Heden (Aug 42 – Oct 43), Cliff Sullivan (Sep 42 – Sep 43), Bruce Atkinson (Nov 42 – Mar 43), Jimmy Gibson (Oct 44 - Feb 46), Bill Hughes (Dec 44 – Jun 45)

University Papers: What Impact did RAF Air Support have on the War in South Russia 1919 – 20? (Rosie Clark, University of East Anglia 2013), The British Intervention In South Russia (Lauri Kopisto, University of Helsinki 2011).

Published Sources: *A History of the Mediterranean Air War 1940-1945* Vol 2, Christopher Shores et al, Grub Street London, 2012; *Aeroplanes of the Royal Flying Corps Military Wing, The* J. M. Bruce, Putnam, 1992; *Air Command A Fighter Pilot's Story*, AVM Raymond Collishaw CB, DSO OBE DSC DFC, William Kimber, 1973; *Air War For Burma*, Christopher Shores, Grub Street London, 2005; *Aircraft of the Russian Civil War*, Vyacheslav Kondrat'ev and Marat Khayrulin, Gauntlet Publications, 2011; *At War With The Bolsheviks*, Robert Jackson, Tom Stacey Ltd, 1972; *Beaufort File, The*, Roger Hayward, Air-Britain, 1990; *Bloody Shambles Vol 2*, Christopher Shores et al, Grub Street London, 1993; *Bomber Squadrons of the RAF and Their Aircraft*, Philip J R Moyes, Macdonald London, 1964; *British Bomber Since 1914, The*, Francis K Mason, Putnam, 1994; *British Fighter Since 1912, The*, Francis K Mason, Putnam, 1992; *British Intelligence in the Second World War*, F. H. Hinsley, HMSO, 1993; *Churchill's Folly Leros and the Aegean*, Anthony Rogers, Cassell, 2003; *Coastal, Support and Special Squadrons of the RAF*, John D. Rawlings, Jane's, 1982; *D.H.4/ D.H.9 File, The*, R. Sturtivant and G. Page, Air-Britain, 1999; *Dust Clouds in the Middle East*, Christopher Shores, Grub Street London, 1996; *Eastward*, Air Chief Marshal Sir David Lee, OHMS, 1984; *Fighters Over The Aegean*, Brian Cull, Fonthill, 2012; *Forgotten Bombers of the Royal Air Force*, Ken Wixey, Arms and Armour Press, 1997; *German Aircraft of the Second World War*, J.R. Smith and Antony L. Kay, Putnam , 1972; *Gone To Russia to Fight - The RAF in South Russia 1918-1920*, John T. Smith, Amberley Publishing, 2010; *K File The Royal Air Force of the 1930s, The*, James J. Halley MBE, Air-Britain, 1995; *Last Train Over Rostov Bridge*, Marion Aten and Arther Ormond, Thin Red Line, 2010; *No Hero Just a Survivor*, G.R.T. (Bob) Willis, Willis Associates, 1999; *Observers and Navigators*, Wing Commander C. G. Jefford, MBE BA RAF Retd., Grub Street London, 2014; *Over the Balkans and South Russia*, H. A. Jones, Edward Arnold, 1923; *RAF Squadrons*, Wing Commander C. G. Jefford MBE BA RAF Retd., Airlife England, 1988; *Red Advance, White Defeat Civil War in South Russia 1919-20*, Peter Kenez, New Academia Publishing, 2008; *Royal Air Force Aircraft J1 - J9999*, Dennis Thompson and Ray Sturtivant, Air-Britain, 1987; *Royal Air Force Bomber Losses in the Middle East and Mediterranean Vol.1 1939-1942*, David Gunby and Pelham Temple, Midland Counties Publications, 2006; *Sky Their Battlefield II, The*, Trevor Henshaw, Fetubi Books, 2014; *Stomping on the Virus Vol 2 Allied intervention in the Russian Civil War*, Perry More; *The Air Defence of Great Britain 1914-1918*, Christopher Cole and E. F. Cheesman, Putnam, 1984; *The Armed Rovers, Beauforts and Beaufighters over the Mediterranean*, Roy C, Nesbit, Airlife England, 1995; *The Day We Almost Bombed Moscow*, Christopher Dobson and John Miller, Hodder and Stoughton, 1986; *Under The Devil's Eye*, Alan Wakefield and Simon Moody, Sutton, 2004; *Vickers Wellesley Warpaint No.86*, Ian White, Warpaint Books; *Voices Without Fear*, Laura Cassidy, 47 Squadron Association, 2015; *War Flying in Macedonia*, Haupt Heydemarck, John Hamilton, 1930; *War in the Air Volume Five, The*, H. A. Jones; *War in the Air Volume Six, The*, H. A. Jones

National Archives, AIR reference

AIR 1 Files in regard to 47 Squadron and Detachment diaries, field returns, nominal rolls, various reports and official communiqués in regard to the Russian campaigns. AIR 23 raid and bombing reports. AIR 27 ORB and Air 29 Squadron reports. WO 158 & 32 reports from Generals.

Journal and Magazine articles

47 Squadron in the Sudan, Vernon Buckman, Flypast; *Arthur Darby and the Air War in Salonika*, Dr Peter Hendford, Cross & Cockade Vol 31 No. 2; *Bush War*, Frank Paget, Flypast, Sept 1991; *Frederick Frank Reilly Minchin CBE, DSO MC*, Lt Colonel RFC 1890 – 1927*, Michael Partridge, Cross & Cockade Vol 41 No. 3; *Guns in the Sand and Snow; the RAF in Southern Russia 1918 – 1920*, Air Comm Phil Wilkinson, RAF Historical Society Journal 60; *In the Sideshows, the flying career of Major F. A. Bates MC AFC DL*, R. Vann, Cross & Cockade Vol 24 No. 1; *Operation Wingate*, Sqn Ldr R. A. Collis DFC and Sqn Ldr F. Bavin-Smith DFM, Aeroplane Monthly Aug - Sept 1993; *Operations to Recover Released Prisoners of War*, Sebastian Fox, RAF Historical Society Journal 56; *Soujourn in a Sideshow*, Peter Chapman Cross & Cockade Vol 44 No. 4; *The RAF in South Russia 1919-1920*, M. W. Rogers, Air Enthusiast no.117; *The Armstrong Whitworth FK3 in Macedonia*, Michael Kelsey, Cross & Cockade Vol 44 No. 3; *Vincent Valedictory*, Philip Middlehurst, Aeroplane Monthly, May 1979; *Wellesleys over the Sudan Pts 1-3*, Grp Capt James Pelly-Fry, Aeroplane Monthly, Mar - May 1984; *Beaufighter Sideshow*, Roy Nesbit, Aeroplane Monthly Aug – Jan 1999

INDEX

Index